AI for Social Sciences

Vicenç Torra

AI for Social Sciences

With an Introduction to Security, Privacy,
Ethics and Society Impacts

Vicenç Torra
Department of Computing Science
Umeå University
Umeå, Sweden

ISBN 978-3-032-07215-3   ISBN 978-3-032-07216-0 (eBook)
https://doi.org/10.1007/978-3-032-07216-0

© The Editor(s) (if applicable) and The Author(s), under exclusive license to Springer Nature Switzerland AG 2026

This work is subject to copyright. All rights are solely and exclusively licensed by the Publisher, whether the whole or part of the material is concerned, specifically the rights of reprinting, reuse of illustrations, recitation, broadcasting, reproduction on microfilms or in any other physical way, and transmission or information storage and retrieval, electronic adaptation, computer software, or by similar or dissimilar methodology now known or hereafter developed.
The use of general descriptive names, registered names, trademarks, service marks, etc. in this publication does not imply, even in the absence of a specific statement, that such names are exempt from the relevant protective laws and regulations and therefore free for general use.
The publisher, the authors and the editors are safe to assume that the advice and information in this book are believed to be true and accurate at the date of publication. Neither the publisher nor the authors or the editors give a warranty, expressed or implied, with respect to the material contained herein or for any errors or omissions that may have been made. The publisher remains neutral with regard to jurisdictional claims in published maps and institutional affiliations.

This Springer imprint is published by the registered company Springer Nature Switzerland AG
The registered company address is: Gewerbestrasse 11, 6330 Cham, Switzerland

If disposing of this product, please recycle the paper.

A l'Agnès i la Nora

Preface

I have been teaching artificial intelligence to different audiences since the early 1990s. Most of my classes were for students in computer science programs, but later, at the Universitat Autònoma de Barcelona, I also gave courses to students in other programs. For example, I gave a course on AI for Aeronautical Management studies. Here at Umeå University, I also had AI students from various backgrounds.

This book is devoted to those that are interested in artificial intelligence but do not have a strong background in mathematics. Nevertheless, I expect the reader to be interested in knowing how artificial intelligence actually works. My goal is to explain how these intelligent systems work internally, which are the main components needed to actually build them, and how they produce the output from the information they collect. So, my explanations include details on how knowledge is represented, reasoning is performed, and learning is implemented. For this, I include examples, as well as a significant number of graphics. Some mathematical expressions appear now and then. In particular, in the chapter devoted to machine learning.

My aim is to provide a broad overview of the field of artificial intelligence, thus one that is not limited to the most successful and noticeable topics related to machine learning and language models. Consequently, I present a variety of topics including knowledge representation and decision support systems. In addition, I include a chapter on security and privacy, a key aspect in current systems, and another in which I discuss some topics related to ethics and society.

The book starts with an introduction where I distinguish digitalization, artificial intelligence, and machine learning. Topics that are often confused. In particular, artificial intelligence is more than just machine learning. Chapter 1 also includes a discussion on what artificial intelligence is.

Then, in Chap. 2, I introduce techniques used for the construction of intelligent systems. Search algorithms are an important family of algorithms that permit to solve different types of problems including scheduling problems and games, but are also used to prove mathematical theorems. I use the game of Sudoku to illustrate how these algorithms work, showing how a Sudoku puzzle is solved by a computer. Then, I present, with examples, some techniques to represent knowledge. I also discuss uncertainty and vagueness. Intelligent systems need to deal with them in real world applications.

Chapter 3 is about decision support systems. In this case, assessment and evaluation of alternatives (as e.g. candidates and products) are based on expert knowledge. I explain how these systems can be built based on the definition of a set of criteria, and the aggregation of the evaluation of individual criteria. Aggregation needs to take into account aspects as mandatory requirements, importance among criteria, and compensation degrees.

Chapter 4 describes machine learning. This is about finding mathematical or computational representations of one (or more) variable(s) in terms of others. This is what we call models. I describe how machine learning models are built, focusing mainly on simple models and then briefly explaining neural networks and deep learning. In addition main concepts associated to machine learning are also defined.

Chapter 5 focuses on security and privacy. In relation to security, I explain concepts as authentication and authorization, but also how cryptography works to ensure that only the intended recipient of an encrypted message reads the message. This is called secure communication. Then, I present examples showing that access control and cryptography may not be enough in some contexts to ensure privacy. The examples motivate the need for privacy-aware solutions. Some of these solutions are described.

Chapter 6 is about applications of machine learning and artificial intelligence in social sciences. I include a discussion focusing on types of applications, and then another one focused on particular science branches.

Chapter 7 discusses a few different topics related to ethics, society, and artificial intelligence. The material includes AI and agency, trustworthy AI, and the relationship between AI and labor (including labor-intensive AI).

Audience and Background

This textbook has been written for readers coming from a social science background, with the aim in mind to introduce the concepts associated to AI in a broad sense (i.e., not limiting to machine learning) in a way that is rigorous but without the level of mathematics and computer science required in AI courses in computer science (and engineering) programs. To make definitions precise, I have included formulas in the text. In particular, in the chapter about machine learning. In this case, illustrations have been added to make (hopefully) the text clear. Nowadays, machine learning is strongly based on mathematical formulation and uses extensively optimization techniques. A lower undergraduate course on mathematics or statistics describing linear regression models would be helpful for reading Chap. 4. While some technical aspects of model building may be challenging (if so, skip then e.g. Sect. 4.3), the general idea of the problem should be clear to most.

I have written books on artificial intelligence, data privacy, and decision modeling for undergraduate and graduate students in computer science, mathematics and engineering. I have also published four popular science books on these topics. In this book I try to use this experience, as well as my expertise on teaching non-engineering students, to write about AI and machine learning in a less technical way.

Umeå, Sweden
April 2025

Vicenç Torra

Acknowledgments The idea to write this book mainly comes from my participation in the project "Appropriate automation: Towards an understanding of robots and AI in the social services from an organizational and user perspective". This is a project (FORTE 2021-01422) supported by the Swedish Research Council for Health, Working Life and Welfare. In addition, this work was partially supported by the Wallenberg AI, Autonomous Systems and Software Program (WASP) funded by the Knut and Alice Wallenberg Foundation.

Since I joined Umeå University, I have been leading the PrivAcy-AWare traNS-parent deCIsions research group. A warm acknowledgment goes to the Ph.D. students and postdocs of my group. During the last months they had to hear in our meetings, "I still have to complete the AI book!" Thank you for the nice environment you created, it also gave sense to be at the office. A few of them are leaving the group this summer after graduation or completing their work, I will miss them all. Last but not least, my children. They very critically read some fragments of previous versions of this text. Thank you so much for your support.

Umeå, Sweden
April 2025

Vicenç Torra

Competing Interests The author has no competing interests to declare that are relevant to the content of this manuscript.

Contents

1	**Introduction**	1
	1.1 From Digitalization to Artificial Intelligence	2
	1.2 Automation, Artificial Intelligence, and Autonomy	9
	1.3 What is AI?	11
	1.4 AI Beyond Machine Learning	13
	1.5 Bibliography	15
2	**Artificial Intelligence and Intelligent Systems**	17
	2.1 Solving Problems in a Generic Way	17
	2.1.1 The Case of Sudoku	18
	2.1.2 From Sudoku to Other Applications	22
	2.1.3 Actually Solving the Problem	26
	2.2 Representing Knowledge	26
	2.2.1 Logic Programming for Representing Knowledge	27
	2.2.2 Logic for Knowledge Representation	30
	2.2.3 Rules for Knowledge Representation	33
	2.2.4 Ignorance, Uncertainty, and Imprecision	34
	2.2.5 Vagueness and Uncertainty	40
	2.2.6 Bayesian Networks and Graphical Models	41
	2.2.7 Fuzzy Sets and Reasoning	43
	2.2.8 Knowledge Graphs and Ontologies	45
	2.3 Multiagent Systems	46
	2.4 Bibliography	46
3	**Decision Support Systems**	47
	3.1 The Main Concepts of a Decision Support System	48
	3.1.1 Alternatives	48
	3.1.2 Variables	49
	3.1.3 Criteria and Their Assessment	50
	3.1.4 Aggregation: Assessment of Alternatives	53

	3.2	Selection of Alternatives: Dominance and Pareto Front	57
	3.3	Aggregation	60
		3.3.1 Importance Among Criteria	61
		3.3.2 Compensation Between Criteria	61
		3.3.3 Mandatory Requirements	64
		3.3.4 Interactions Among Criteria	65
		3.3.5 Summary	66
	3.4	Other Tools for Decision Support Systems	68
	3.5	Bibliography	70
4	**Machine Learning at Work**		**73**
	4.1	An Example of a Data Set	74
	4.2	Different and Competing Types of Data-Driven Models	77
	4.3	How a Data Driven Model Is Built	79
		4.3.1 The Parameters of a Data-Driven Linear Model	82
		4.3.2 Gradient Descent	82
		4.3.3 A Graphical Representation of Linear Models	86
		4.3.4 Neural Networks and Deep Learning	87
		4.3.5 Classification Problems	93
	4.4	Decision Trees	94
		4.4.1 Learning the Tree	96
	4.5	Language Models	98
	4.6	Some Additional Concepts in Machine Learning	99
		4.6.1 Training, Test, and Validation Data Sets	100
		4.6.2 Missing Data	100
		4.6.3 On the Surfaces Defined by Loss Functions	101
		4.6.4 Error, Bias, and Variance	102
		4.6.5 Models, Predictions, and Outliers	105
		4.6.6 Fairness in Machine Learning	107
		4.6.7 Explainability	108
		4.6.8 Correlation and Causation	109
		4.6.9 Models and Privacy	109
	4.7	Machine Learning Beyond Prediction	110
	4.8	Bibliography	111
5	**Security and Privacy**		**113**
	5.1	Security and Data Protection	114
		5.1.1 Authentication	114
		5.1.2 Authorization in Access Control	115
		5.1.3 Secure Communication	116
		5.1.4 How Can We Attack Agnès' Message?	120
		5.1.5 Data Storage and Integrity	121
		5.1.6 Quantum Computers	122

	5.2	Privacy for Databases and Machine Learning	123
		5.2.1 How Can We Provide Privacy Guarantees?	127
		5.2.2 Data Has Different Forms	132
		5.2.3 Synthetic Data	135
	5.3	Security and Privacy by Design	136
	5.4	Bibliography	137
6	**AI Applications in Social Sciences**		**139**
	6.1	From Data to Decisions	139
		6.1.1 Data Extraction	140
		6.1.2 Data Analysis and Visualization	140
		6.1.3 Assessment and Decision Support Systems	141
		6.1.4 Predictions and Recommendations	141
		6.1.5 Gadgets and Accessibility	141
		6.1.6 Workplaces, Work Design, and Workflows	142
		6.1.7 New Challenges	142
	6.2	AI in Social Sciences	143
		6.2.1 AI for Work Management	143
		6.2.2 AI in the Public Administration	144
		6.2.3 AI in Social Services	144
		6.2.4 AI in Criminal Justice	145
		6.2.5 AI in Economics	146
	6.3	Bibliography	147
7	**Ethics, Society and AI**		**149**
	7.1	Is AI Possible in a Machine?	150
	7.2	AI, Autonomy, and Agency	151
	7.3	Trustworthy AI	152
	7.4	AI, Computation, the Cloud, and Energy Consumption	153
	7.5	Labor-Intensive AI	155
	7.6	AI and Labor	156
	7.7	Synthetic Data, Creation, and Art	158
	7.8	The Future of AI Is Not Written	161
	7.9	Bibliography	162
References			**163**
Index			**173**

Chapter 1
Introduction

Abstract Nowadays, the words artificial intelligence (AI) and machine learning (ML) are used everywhere. New software products, tools, and web sites use, or say to use, AI. Some applications are very modest on this AI use. Some do not use AI at all, but just standard computer science methods. Digitalization and automation are other words used in the same contexts. In this chapter we discuss digitalization and introduce artificial intelligence. We establish the main differences between digitalization, automation, machine learning, data-driven models, and artificial intelligence.

> KRAFT
>
> Den ilsnabba tysta kraften sissar långt i hundramila trådar innan den bullras till i skrytsamma städer.
>
> Harry Martinson, Natur, 1934 [105].

Digitalization, Internet and datafication (taking aspects of our life and converting [107] them into data) are changing the way we interact with the world. It has caused the appearance of new technological tools and lies behind some of the technologies that are causing the artificial intelligence–machine learning revolution.

Automation, that mainly started with the industrial revolution, is expanding into new dimensions. On the one hand automatic control systems become more complex and, specially, more autonomous. They do not longer need a continuous human supervision and are programmed to make decisions in case of problems. On the other, automation is not limited to repetitive work but threatens cognitive and knowledge-based works. Artificial intelligence and machine learning are expected by some to produce intelligent systems that can replace costly workers by cheap software with human comparable performance. So, even those jobs that once seemed to be immune to technology are now also threatened. Others think that such replacement will not happen so soon to be a real threat. In any case, these technologies are entering the job environment, and all these technological changes are not only affecting the way we interact with the world, but they are also affecting our work experience.

The poem by Harry Martinson that opens this chapter was written in the early 20th century, and contrasts the silent generation of electricity from water and its roar in a distant bustling city. It is said that artificial intelligence is an invisible technology. It is becoming pervasive, extensively used in all kind of devices and software applications, and in most cases without us knowing it. It roars in our mobile devices when we use social networks, but is usually much more silent. It is often embedded in applications. For example, AI is the one that provides a recommendation when we shop online, and can be the one that selects our CV for interview as well as the one that provides suggestions in the car service.

In this chapter, we will discuss in some detail what we understand as artificial intelligence and machine learning. Before doing so, we will establish the distinction between some of the concepts that appear associated to digitalization and artificial intelligence.

AI comes with a cost. Complex AI systems, as larger language models, need huge computational resources. So, in contrast with Martinson's poem, somewhere in the world a machine is roaring (or working in silence) when the mobile is silent producing text. We will discuss some of these issues related to AI and society, including ecological costs, in Chap. 7.

1.1 From Digitalization to Artificial Intelligence

The increasing adoption of artificial intelligence-based tools is due to the fact that a large part of the daily activity of our society has been moved to the digital sphere. Digitialization is thus, a key concept.

Digitalization is the process of incorporating digital technologies. In its simplest form, this is restricted to the acquisition and use of new software, but it can also correspond to replacing old processes by new ones based on digital tools. Naturally, digitalization is also about converting information into digital form.

Digitalization can have multiple facets, and can be as mild as simply providing digital tools (e.g., integrated online access to all business documents) and as advanced as automated decision tools, and automatic controllers where all information is obtained by digital means.

An example of the former is when social workers need access to databases for providing appropriate assistance to a family. This includes access to a variety of administrative forms, but also to sensitive information about the family: previous assessments by the social services, social assistance interventions, previous financial social assistance, etc. In addition to these simple tools, social services can implement a more advanced automatic system to decide about financial social assistance. Some of these decision makers may be very simple. For example, grant benefits or financial support if the income is below a threshold. Other decisions may be more complex, taking into account information available in the system, as well as some additional one provided by a social worker.

Examples of advanced digitalizations can be found in Industry 4.0, a completely different context. This is about the digitalization associated to the industry. There are industries were smart machines include sensors that provide real-time information of their state. Then, intelligent systems can detect faulty machines or errors in production using machine learning algorithms. In this way, machines are stopped and replaced reducing manufacturing errors. Now, Industry 5.0 is also conceived. It is about the collaboration between machines and humans, and placing the worker in the center of production processes. So, more complex decisions are needed.

Because of all this, the range of tools needed for digitalization is very broad. Artificial intelligence and machine learning, may be used, but they are not necessarily a requirement. Let us first focus on just automation.

Automation is defined by the Collins dictionary [194] as the use of methods for controlling industrial processes automatically often reducing manpower, and by the Merriam-Webster dictionary [197] as the technique of making an apparatus, a process, or a system operate automatically. Automatically, also according to the Merrian-Webster dictionary, means having a self-acting or self-regulating mechanism.

With the digitalization, automation is the result of computer programs that control apparatus, processes, and systems. Historically, automation was developed for machines. For example, a simple automatic control system is the one we find in washing machines. The automatic control system decides the step to apply for your clothes according to the selected cycle: wash, rinse, spin. Then, more sophisticated machines automatically control additional characteristics as e.g. the amount of water or soap taking into account the dirtiness of the clothes (auto-dosing). This is similar in industrial machines. Automatic control permits such machines to operate without human intervention, and adapt the behavior of the machine to their environment.

Another simple example of automation is a room thermostat. It switchs on and off the heating system to achieve a desirable room temperature. A much complex automation system is when we have a smart building heating system with different types of sensors in rooms, corridors and other common areas.

Automation is achieved using mathematical and computational models. That is, simplified descriptions of the environment and the machines (e.g., the heating system). Then, when we develop an automated machine, a model helps us to decide what action to take considering current and previous states of the machine. E.g., the washing machine *decides* that it is time to rinse the clothes if the washing is already completed; and the thermostat *decides* that it is time to warm a bit more the room if the temperature is too cold. Models helps us to choose an action, but also the *intensity* of the action depending on appropriate factors. E.g. how much warm are we going to pump into a classroom if we are in Sweden, the classroom is too cold but full of people, and we have $-20°$ outside? and how much if we are in Catalonia, if we have a similar room, $2°$ outside, but the windows don't isolate the room so well?

The wash-rinse-spin cycle can be seen as a very simple model of a washing machine. No information is included about the weight of the clothes and their dirtiness. Decisions are then limited. In some tasks, more complex models may be desirable. For example, for the thermostat problem, we may use a model that estimates the future temperature of the particular classroom based on current indoor temperature, outdoor temperature, time of the day, occupancy of the classroom, and

> A model is an abstraction, a simplification of the real world. In machine learning and automation models are built to establish relationships between variables or features [143]. There are different types of models as e.g. mathematical and statistical models, logical models, computational models.
>
> An example of a model is the one below. This model establishes a simplified relationship between two numerical variables age and income. So, in short, we can estimate the income for any age. Mathematically, it is expressed as follows
>
> $$\text{income} = -4524.2 + 207.5 * \text{age}$$
>
> where age is expressed in years, and the income is expressed in euros. Our model says that for each additional year a person has, the income increases in 207 euros.
>
> Models are simplifications or approximations. There will be cases were the model is absolutely wrong. In our example, the model will considerably fail for those that have very large incomes (large above the average). It will also clearly fail for any age below 22 because our model will infer that the income is negative, and for 22 years the income is only 40.8 euros. Nevertheless, we expect models to be accurate enough for a given purpose. In this model, for example, we may think that is good enough to estimate the average income for people between 30 and 55.

Fig. 1.1 Definition and example of a model

different amounts of heating. In this way, we can select the optimal amount of heating to provide thermal comfort. This would be energy efficient.

Robotic Process Automation (RPA) is an example of automation for software systems. It allows us to automate the actions we do in a computer to complete a task, and may involve accessing different programs. E.g., copying information from a medical database into a digital form to apply for social service support. The robot will do the same actions the human do, i.e., following a predefined behavior.

Machine learning is a branch or sub-field of artificial intelligence. Its goal is to improve the performance of intelligent systems based on their own experience.

In practice, much of the success of machine learning is in using existing historical databases to build models. There are databases in corporations and administrations containing all kind of information collected and stored. A model is an abstraction, a simplification, of the real world. See Fig. 1.1. Machine learning uses stored data to discover relevant relationships between concepts and variables (e.g., what causes a medicine to work well; when mortgage repayments fail). These relationships can later be used to help decision makers, and to create automated systems that make decisions themselves (e.g., recommend a medicine or grant a mortgage).

Let us go back to the example of the classroom in a Swedish school. Let us consider that the building is a smart building with sensors that communicate information about temperatures (outdoor, and indoor in different rooms and areas), light conditions (e.g., sunny or not), occupancies by people, etc. This is a smart building so, naturally, all this information together with the actual heating operations selected are continuously stored in a database. Then, after two years in operation, the database contains all this historical information, and we can use machine learning to estimate the temperature at the cafeteria at lunch time today, with the current environmental conditions and different heating selections. We can even use this model to *decide* the heating to apply at lunch time, say at 12:00, if we know the expected temperature and solar

1.1 From Digitalization to Artificial Intelligence

Table 1.1 Age and income for 10 people interviewed (fake data, used in another textbook [175])

Interview	Age	Income
i_1	24	1000
i_2	40	6000
i_3	30	2000
i_4	50	2000
i_5	40	3000
i_6	55	10000
i_7	33	2000
i_8	37	2000
i_9	26	1000
i_{10}	42	4000

radiation (e.g., using the information provided by the Swedish Meteorological and Hydrological Institute).

Data-driven models are models that are obtained from data. The model discussed above with 2 historical years data will be a data-driven model. Machine learning and statistics provides methods to build these models from databases. The main difference between machine learning and statistics is on the types of models built. The area of statistical learning has close connections with machine learning, and the two areas are, in fact, becoming closer.

Let us illustrate what model building or model identification means with a simple example. Let us build a data-driven model from data. Although the example is extremely simple, similar considerations would apply in the case of a model on the temperature for the Swedish classroom.

More concretely, our model is about knowing the influce of age into income, or, in other words, how the income changes when age changes. So, first, we need some data. To do so, we interview some people and we ask to each of them their age and income. We obtain the values represented in Table 1.1. We do not discuss here how people is selected for the interviews, whether the selected people are the relevant ones, if some data is missing, over-represented, or biased, and if the data is correct. We just take the values in the table as the *good* ones.

This data can be represented graphically in Fig. 1.2. Each point in the graph represents a respondent. That is, one of the people we have interviewed. We have located the point taking into account the age and the income of this respondent. The age appears in the abscissa or horizontal coordinate (this is often referred as the x axis). The income is in the ordinate or vertical coordinate (this is often referred as the y axis). Naturally, any answer from any respondent would have its representation in the graph based on the actual values for given (age, income). In the figure, the left most point corresponds to individual i_1 with the values (24, 1000). The point in the top-right position is respondent i_6 with 55 years and an income of 10000.

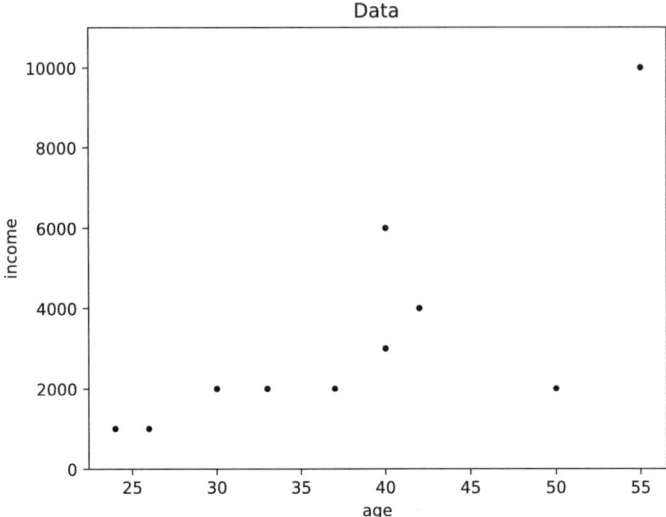

Fig. 1.2 Graphical representation of the data in Table 1.1. In one axis (abscissa, horizontal coordinate and commonly referred to axis x) we represent age and in the other axis (ordinate, vertical coordinate and commonly referred to axis y) we represent salaries. Each dot or point corresponds to a single person

As we have already discussed above, a model permits to establish a relationship between variables (also called features). Here the variables are income and age, and the model is about this relationship between income and age. Machine learning and statistics offer a variety of tools to build models. For a certain type of model (a linear regression model) and using a certain statistical approach (minimizing mean squared error) the relationship we obtain is precisely the one included in Fig. 1.1 that we provide also here:

$$\text{income} = -4524.2 + 207.5 * \text{age}.$$

This model states that the income changes with age, and that the older the people is, the larger their income. Then, the increase in salary when a person gets one year older is 207.5 euros.

We have said that machine learning and statistics offer a variety of models, and a variety of algorithms to build the models. What we really mean with this sentence is that, even with the same data, using other techniques we could find other relationships between the variables. Why? Well, this will be discussed in much more detail in Chap. 4.

Just to illustrate that it is possible to build other models and that in some circumstances it makes sense to consider such alternative ways, we give another example of a model. More precisely, we provide an example of an alternative model between age and income using the same data. Let us first represent graphically the model we have

1.1 From Digitalization to Artificial Intelligence

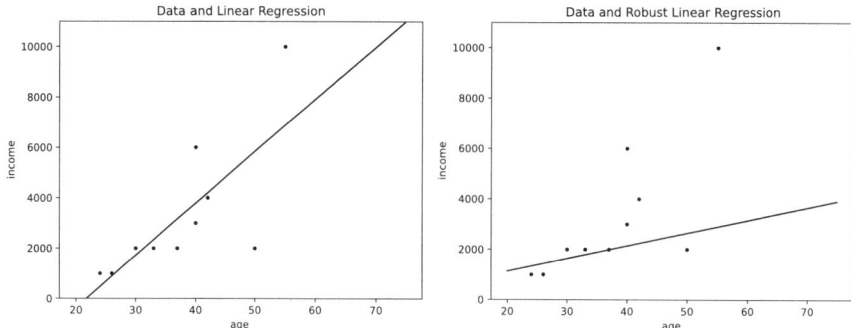

Fig. 1.3 The same data and two different regression models. Each model is represented by a line. Linear regression (left) and robust linear regression (right)

already discussed. We plot this model in Fig. 1.3 (left). The model is represented by the line. For any given age, the line relates the age with the corresponding income. This line represents our equation.

Now, let us build another model from the same data. Why we would do so? Well, because some people we interviewed have more influence than others in the result. If we look in detail to the data, we see that there is someone, respondent i_6, that is 55 years old that has a very much larger income than the others. This can be seen very clearly in the figure. We see in the table that this person earns 10000 euros. This combination of age and income affects significantly the model. In other words, it makes us infer (erroneously) that for most of the people with an additional year they earn much more money than they really earn. In short, they will not earn 207.5 additionally euros every time they have a birthday. So, we would like to "discount" this person with this very high income. In statistics, robust regression models are better to deal with this type of data. A graphical representation of a robust regression model for the same data is given in Fig. 1.3 (right). It corresponds to the model

$$\text{income} = 127.59 + 50.44 * \text{age}.$$

As said, this model reduces the effect of the 55 year old person that earns 10000 euros. So, in this alternative model, an additional year only implies an additional earning of 50.44 euros. Observe the contrast with the previous model where an additional year of age meant a 207.5 euros salary increase. The figure also shows this fact with the differences on the slopes of the curves.

Machine learning is just one of the branches of artificial intelligence. Let us focus on the latter, as not all automated decisions are made using data-driven models and not all intelligent systems are based on machine learning.

Artificial intelligence (AI) is a field of computer science. Its goal is to build, forgive the repetition, artificial intelligence and intelligent systems. There are quite a few definitions of artificial intelligence and we will discuss them briefly in Sect. 1.3.

Here, we are more interested in stressing the difference between machine learning and artificial intelligence than on providing a good definition for the latter. The impact of machine learning is huge, but there are other branches of AI that offer tools that are very useful in real-world applications.

An example is the branch of search and problem solving. Computers play chess and win, and play go and also win. How is that possible? It is not, in general machine learning that provides tools for these problems. It is the branch of search and problem solving that offers techniques to build such software systems and make this success possible. They are built using techniques that are useful for solving a large variety of real-world problems, and not specific to games. This is similar to what happens in mathematics. Within this branch of AI, techniques are proposed and studied in an abstract way so that we can use them later to solve such variety of real-world problems.

For example, let us consider the case of looking for a good schedule for a school, which involves teachers, students, and classrooms. All need to fit in a convenient way so that, for example, a teacher is not in two classrooms at the same time. Naturally, the way to solve this scheduling problem is similar for other institutions: hospitals and railways. From an abstract point of view, finding a good schedule is very similar to finding the solution of a Sudoku, or even to proving a mathematical theorem. In a way, it is like finding a needle in a haystack. The difficulty lies in the size of the haystack and in being able to distinguish the needle from the hay. The good solution that satisfies our requirements is the needle, and all solutions, including bad, very bad, and extremely bad ones, define the haystack.

Another branch of artificial intelligence is knowledge representation. In machine learning when building data-driven systems, scientific knowledge is sometimes ignored or partially overlooked. Useful information and, hopefully, valuable knowledge is extracted from the data. Nevertheless, it is clear that there is already valuable scientific knowledge that may be useful when making decisions. The branch of knowledge representation helps codifying this knowledge so that a computer system can use it when making decisions. For example, we may want to codify existing medical knowledge on the relationship between illnesses and symptoms, and on known contraindications in pharmacology. In physical systems, we may need to represent physical laws, or in mathematics, integration rules or fundamental relations in geometry (e.g., the Pythagorean theorem, and that the three angles in a triangle add 180 in Euclidean geometry).

Not all branches of artificial intelligence are equally successful, or, at least, they are not equally known outside the artificial intelligence domain. Nevertheless, all of them provide tools that are useful in applications. Moreover, some applications combine a collection of techniques. E.g., combine search, knowledge, and machine learning.

To complete the set of terms outlined and discussed in this section, we include below statistics.

Statistics is the science that studies how to collect and analyze data, and draw conclusions from them. To do so, it provides tools and methods, rooted in mathematics, probability, and computation. As happens with artificial intelligence, there is no single definition but several of them, each focusing on different aspects: data analysis, data collection, data interpretation, data presentation, inference, etc. Fienberg [71] provided a discussion and a personal perspective of what statistics is.

1.2 Automation, Artificial Intelligence, and Autonomy

A key concept related to automation and, naturally, artificial intelligence is autonomy. In the context of AI, what is autonomy? and what is automation? If we are automating processes, if automated decisions are made, is the system fully autonomous? partially autonomous? or are, in fact, all final decisions made by a human and all the process is supervised by a human? The more systems are automated, the more this question is of relevance.

Autonomy. There have been several attempts to study and formalize the different levels of autonomy of AI systems. All of them establish autonomy in terms of the collaboration between artificial systems and humans. A useful discussion on the levels of autonomy can be found for autonomous cars. In this area, the concept of autonomy becomes crucial, as software is becoming more and more complex and increasingly dealing with tasks to support and replace humans, and, as it is well known, there has been a clear industrial push towards driver-less or self-driving cars.

The Society of Automotive Engineers (SAE) proposed [141] a taxonomy of levels of driving automation. More precisely, a taxonomy for "automation systems that perform part or all of the dynamic driving task (DDT) on a sustained basis". As the preliminaries of the document state clearly, one of the purposes of the document is to clarify the role of the human *driver*. Driver in italics, as, of course, in a fully autonomous vehicle this human *driver* has no role at all.

The proposal provides 6 levels, and these levels are "intentionally discrete and mutually exclusive". We list them below. Using the same terminology as the report, we use the term user to denote the human that, if the system is not autonomous, is the driver.

- Level 0: No driving automation. The automation systems, if any, do not perform on a sustained basis and the user is the driver at all times.
- Level 1: Driver Assistance. The automation systems can do part of the driving tasks but always under the control of the user, who is the driver. The automation system can control accelerating and braking functions (i.e., longitudinal vehicle motion), and also steering (i.e., lateral vehicle motion), but not both at the same time. For example, level 1 automation systems can keep speed and distance from the vehicle in front. Lane keeping systems also belong to Level 1.
- Level 2: Partial Driving Automation. The user is still the driver in control of the automation systems. Nevertheless, the automation system can control both longitudinal and lateral vehicle motion at the same time. A parking assistance feature can park the car under the supervision of the user. The user can exit the vehicle during the execution of the automated parking feature, but is in control of

> **Human-in-the-loop.** This refers to AI systems in which the human is involved in their operation. There are human interactions with the system, and the human can control it. This applies to semi-automated decision process.
>
> **Human-out-of-the-loop.** This refers to AI systems that are fully automated, and, therefore, the human does not take part in the operation process.
>
> **Human-on-the-loop.** This mainly refers to systems that are fully automated, but the human is monitoring it and can stop if necessary.

Fig. 1.4 Human interactions with AI systems

the process. E.g. holding a button pressed while the car is self-parking and, thus, can stop the vehicle in case of need.
- Level 3: Conditional Driving Automation. The user is no longer in control, but it is expected that the user is responsive when needed. For example, a traffic jam feature fully controls the vehicle on a fully-access-controlled highway in dense traffic conditions. Nevertheless, the control is back to the user when the conditions change. So, in a way, there are tasks that are fully automated, but when the conditions or requirements change (i.e., the traffic is no longer dense or the car leaves the highway), the control is transferred to the user. There are already cars that provide level 3 automated driving.
- Level 4: High Driving Automation. Under certain conditions the user is no longer required to intervene. This is the case, for example, of a fleet of vehicles in a closed campus, or of a low speed car in designated areas. If a system failure occurs, the automation system transitions to a minimal risk condition. The requirement that the system is able to reach this minimal risk condition without any user supervision or help is the main difference between level 3 and 4. So, any human in the car is just a passenger. Passengers can also force the car to transition to a minimal risk condition.
- Level 5: Full Driving Automation. The system can operate "under all road conditions in which a conventional vehicle can be reasonably operated by a typically skilled human driver" [141]. So, there are no longer "conditions", as in level 4, for the system to work.

These levels can be compared with the three levels of AI outlined by Rao [135]. They refer to AI systems in business, but, as can be seen below, there is a strong correlation with the 6 levels presented above in the car industry. In addition, in Fig. 1.4 we describe the concepts of Human-in-the-loop, human-on-the-loop, and human-out-of-the-loop that relate to the interaction between operators and systems.

- Assisted AI systems. In this case, the artificial system is implementing tasks that are already performed in a company. They are performed faster and better. Decisions are left for humans. Most current AI systems belong to this category. Examples include robotics in the industry (e.g., automotive industry where robots are used

to build cars) and software robots for clerical tasks (as e.g., scanning CVs for shortlisting candidates).
- Augmented AI systems. In this case, the artificial system permits to do tasks that cannot be performed without them. The use of natural language processing systems for some tasks is an example (e.g., summarizing large quantities of documents or classifying them). Resources to build these systems are beyond the possibilities of most companies, but they can be nowadays incorporated into decision processes. Systems are under the supervision of humans. Humans "should be open to those alternatives, but also skeptical" [135].
- Autonomous AI systems. Systems operate acting on their own and without human intervention.

These definitions for autonomy must be qualified. Machines can be autonomous in isolation, but they may require facilitation work. That is, work that is done by humans so that the computer systems and robots can work properly. The example provided by Soma et al. [158] illustrates what facilitation means. A robot vacuum cleaner cannot work in a messy environment, and therefore the environment needs to be prepared before its operation. More particularly, the robot needs pre-, peri-, and post-facilitation work [158, 159]. That is, work that is done before, during, and after the robot autonomous activity. While some facilitation is also needed if we hire a cleaning service, the performance of the robot is completely at stake if this is not done. In contrast, if "you have forgotten to tidy a room or forgotten to pick items up from the floor, the housekeeper is able to do this work for you or downright refuse work under such conditions" [158]. Also, consider a self-driving car refueling and paying at a fully automated gas station, and compare [147] this with human drivers at a station staffed by attendants. The latter can be also compared with the futuristic station depicted in the film Back to the Future II.

1.3 What is AI?

In a previous section we have left the definition of artificial intelligence for further discussion. This is because there is no agreement on what it is, and there are different points of view on the ultimate goals of artificial intelligence. Not only that, there has also been discussion on the name itself, and some prefer to use terms as computational intelligence [89] (CI), and advanced informatics [144] (AI) to move away from the term and its connotations. Different definitions focus on different aspects, but there are some points in common. Let us try to clarify this issue here.

I like to start the discussion with a quote by H. A. Simon from his seminal paper [156] (p. 96) written in 1995: "The moment of the truth is a running program". This is to make clear the view of AI as a field of computer science, and, as such, the ultimate objective is to build programs. The discussion then moves into the goals of these programs. In other words, we may discuss on what we want to achieve with the programs, and what should these programs do.

Russell and Norvig provide in their book [140], which has become, probably, the most widely used AI textbook in university courses, an account of existing definitions classified into two dimensions. One is about how these programs are built. That is, about the internalities of the program. The other focuses on the goal of the program itself? What do we want to achieve, independently of the means we use to achieve it? I.e., independently of the internalities of the program. So, the two dimensions are

- how the program is built, and
- what the goal of this program is.

Using these two dimensions, Russell and Norvig [140] distinguish four types of AI related systems.

- Acting humanly. This corresponds to computer systems that try to mimic human behavior. The Turing test (the imitation game as called in Turing's original work [180]) is the paradigm of this type of systems. In brief, a system passes the Turing test if it is not possible to distinguish the answers provided by the system by those provided by a human.
- Thinking humanly. While the Turing test focuses on the behavior, trying to make it as similar as possible to humans, how this behavior is achieved is of no relevance. I.e., nothing matters about how the decisions provided by the system are actually implemented. In contrast, there are systems that are built with the goal of producing the same type of reasoning that humans do. Cognitive models [183] follow this research direction. The reasoning process itself is more relevant than the acting process.
- Thinking rationally. When we consider the internal process that produces behavior in AI systems, the alternative to use human cognition as the model to follow is to consider an abstract ideal model of what rational thinking means. In what respects to reasoning, logic is one of the most well regarded model. For example, we can make decisions based on logical inference. Nevertheless, this is not the only type of models considered. In decision making, rational preferences and rational decisions are often defined and used.
- Acting rationally. The focus is on the behavior of the systems, but the measurement of a system success is not based on human behavior but on an abstract model of rational behavior. The rationale of this approach is that humans make mistakes, and, thus, the goal is not to copy human behavior but to produce more effective systems.

Russell and Norvig [140] seem to stress the last definition. Nevertheless, each type of AI system may focus on one or the other of the approaches. In some occasions we only require an AI system to proceed as fast as possible to the best solution, and we do not care about how this solution is achieved. In other cases, we need to understand how a system made a decision, that the system explains it to us, and it would be nice that the reasoning process itself is as similar as possible to how we make conclusions ourselves. Also, rational and logical inferences may be a must for some applications. Moreover, AI systems are implemented and used by people. Therefore, they should

1.4 AI Beyond Machine Learning

> 'AI system' means a machine-based system designed to operate with varying levels of autonomy, that may exhibit adaptiveness after deployment and that, for explicit or implicit objectives, infers, from the input it receives, how to generate outputs such as predictions, content, recommendations, or decisions that can influence physical or virtual environments;

Fig. 1.5 Article 3. Artificial Intelligence Act. European Parliament legislative resolution of 13 March 2024

be seen as a socio-technical system. In this respect, the technical component needs to be put into context so that it is valid and useful for people (see Sect. 7.3).

In addition to these academic discussions, we currently have the definitions that appear in a legal context. They are found in regulations and recommendations for the construction and deployment of AI systems, written and approved in the last years. For example, we have the definition in the AI Act approved by the European Parliament in 2024. We provide it in Fig. 1.5. It can be seen that it includes the concept of autonomy that we have already discussed above, and otherwise it focuses on the actions that the systems can do. Nothing is said in how these systems reason.

Note that in this section we have completely ignored the question of whether AI is even possible. Properly speaking, we have ignored whether it is possible to build a program that displays intelligence. The field of AI mainly takes this for granted. We discuss this issue in more detail in Chap. 7 (Sect. 7.1).

Exercise 1.1 John Searle introduced in a paper in 1980 [149] the Chinese room argument. It is about the impossibility of a program to have understanding. Discuss this argument.

Exercise 1.2 Some distinguish between Strong AI (or artificial general intelligence, AGI) and Weak or Narrow AI. Discuss these definitions.

1.4 AI Beyond Machine Learning

We have already underlined that artificial intelligence is not only machine learning and we have briefly presented some of the other branches. We provide in Fig. 1.6 a graphical representation of these main branches. Let us review them here.

We have mentioned above the branches of problem solving and search. They provide algorithms for playing games as chess and go, as well as for games where there is some uncertainty because e.g. we play with dices, or because cards are shuffled. Software products for solving scheduling problems, and configuration problems have also been created based on search algorithms.

Then, knowledge representation helps to incorporate knowledge into AI systems. Logic (or logics as there is not a single one) is one of the ways. If an AI system needs to reason, uncertainty is often a key component. If we play a card game, we probably cannot know with certainty the card that the next player is going to lay down. If a self-driving car is crossing the street, there are expectations on what is

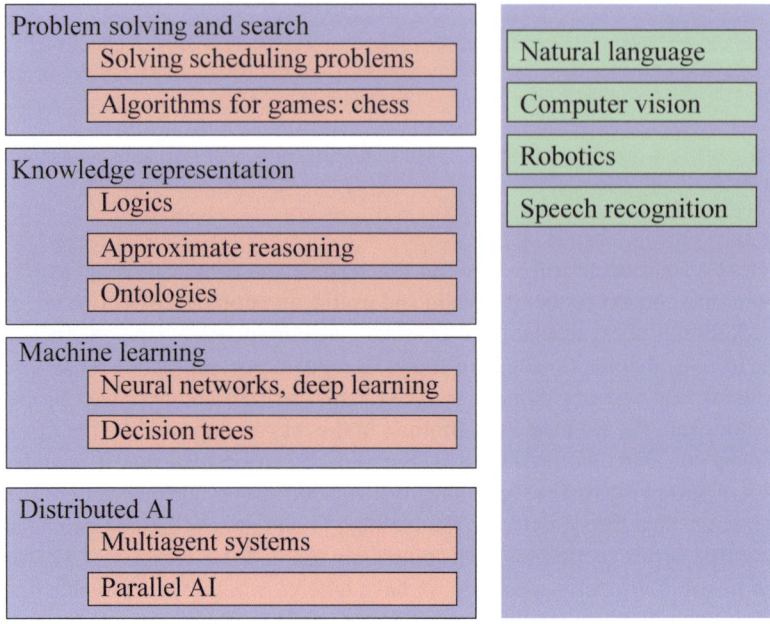

Fig. 1.6 Main branches of artificial intelligence, and some of the tools and techniques that they have developed, and main areas strongly connected with it

possible to happen, based on previous stored knowledge and on what it is observed now. But there is uncertainty. Not all that can happen will actually happen. Also, even if we plan and execute some actions, the outcome of these actions may not be what we planned. E.g., we order a robot to follow a path, giving precise instructions on the moves. Nevertheless, after following them, errors on the sensors and on the actuators of the robot make the robot to be in a different position. The robot may not be even certain of where is located. The same applies to other contexts. E.g., in text and machine translation we have uncertainty in the actual meaning of a word, or on the word that is the best for filling a blank in a sentence. Approximate reasoning and reasoning under uncertainty provide tools to deal with uncertainty. For example, we can use probabilities and probability theory. This is the most well known and used approach. Nevertheless, other tools exist as well. Fuzzy set theory is one example. We can structure the knowledge of the AI system with an ontology. There are graphical tools to visualize the ontologies, so, ways to visualize the knowledge that we have incorporated in a system.

Finally, distributed AI is about exploiting computational power of multiple processors and computers. Some methods are built for just computing faster. This would be the case of using a supercomputer to play faster and better in chess, considering more moves, evaluating more boards, etc. Other methods try to do things a bit different. During COVID-19, some models of disease spread were based on social simulations [48] (simulation of the behavior of individuals). Multiagent systems [153, 190] allow for this type of computations.

There are some areas that have strong connections with AI, because their own goals are closely related to the goals of AI, and because AI techniques are needed to implement the solutions. These areas have fostered the development of new AI techniques due to this close relationship. These areas, which are listed in Fig. 1.6, include natural language processing (see e.g. machine translation and conversational systems), computer vision (see e.g. image processing and understanding), robotics (with both sensing and actuation, reasoning about the environment, and planning robot actions), and speech recognition.

1.5 Bibliography

Russell and Norvig [140] is a comprehensive book on Artificial Intelligence. Vernon [183] focus on cognitive systems. Multiagent systems and their fundamentals are well described in Wooldridge's book [190]. The imitation game (the Turing test) appears in Turing's paper [180].

Chapter 2
Artificial Intelligence and Intelligent Systems

Abstract Dissimilar problems are solved in AI using similar techniques. What characteristics are in common between building a schedule and solving a Sudoku? In this chapter we describe how problems are solved using search mechanisms. Another key element in AI systems is knowledge, and knowledge representation. We discuss logics and uncertainty as key elements of embedding knowledge in an intelligent system. Concepts as vagueness, fuzzy sets, and knowledge graphs are also mentioned.

> Me falten paraules per explicar què significa per jo.
> me falten paraules ...
> es diccionaris són plens de paraules gratis i certes.
> paraules d'amor senzilles i tendres.
>
> Antònia Font, Me sobren paraules, from Lamparetes, 2011 [5].

Problem solving and reasoning are key components of complex AI systems. In this chapter we will illustrate how problems are typically solved by intelligent systems. We will use the Sudoku as an example of a problem to be solved, and then show that similar techniques can be used for other types of problems. Then, we focus on reasoning. Some AI systems need to incorporate knowledge on their application domain. E.g., what are the illnesses and medicines under consideration?, which medicine is good for what illness?, which are the side effects? We will present logics as a way to do reasoning. We will also discuss how to deal with uncertainty, imprecision and vagueness when building AI systems.

2.1 Solving Problems in a Generic Way

What have in common problems like preparing a schedule, planning the stops in a trip, solving a Sudoku, and proving a mathematical theorem? If we make an abstraction (i.e., remove unnecessary details), all these problems can be seen in a similar way, and, then, they can be solved also in a similar way.

© The Author(s), under exclusive license to Springer Nature Switzerland AG 2026
V. Torra, *AI for Social Sciences*,
https://doi.org/10.1007/978-3-032-07216-0_2

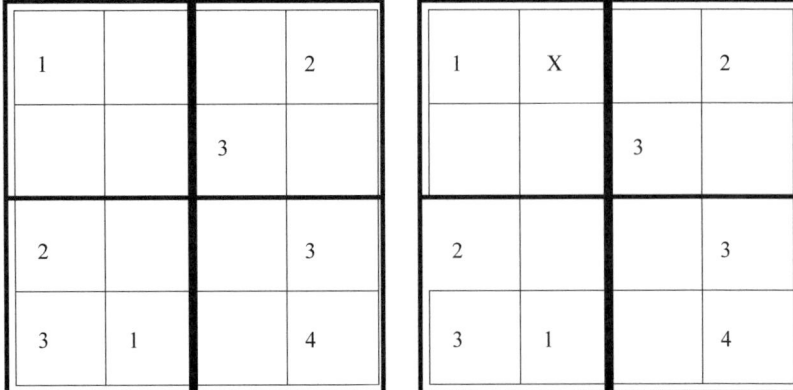

Fig. 2.1 Sudoku of size 4 × 4 (left) and the same Sudoku with a mark in the cell that we will consider first (right)

2.1.1 The Case of Sudoku

Maybe the simplest way is to think about the Sudoku. We will use a simpler, with less cells and less values to fill, than the regular Sudoku so that it is more manegeable for our illustration purposes. We have the Sudoku in Fig. 2.1 (left), so, there are four columns, four rows, four boxes, and each empty cell is going to be filled with a number that is one of the following ones: 1, 2, 3, and 4. The instructions are

- (i) no number can be repeated in a row;
- (ii) no number can be repeated in a column;
- (iii) no number can be repeated in one of the four boxes of size 2 × 2.

Note that a box corresponds to each of the four squares with bold margins.

How can we solve this problem with a computer? We need to find a number for each cell. We know which are the possibilities. Each cell can only be 1, 2, 3 or 4. So, a way is to consider one possibility for each cell, and see if the option works. If it does not work, then we try another one. Of course, as there are several empty cells, once we decide for an alternative (i.e., we decide a number) for a cell, we may not be able to know if such alternative (i.e., number) is really suitable. To get such conclusive information on a particular alternative (number), we will need to consider further cells. Nevertheless, if it is a good alternative (number) we will know at due time. In general, when there is a solution to the Sudoku, if we consider all possible options, we will be able to find it.

To make things simple, we will set the cells in order of *appearance* in the Sudoku (from top to bottom and from left to right. So, the first one to be considered and filled will be the cell marked with an X in the Sudoku in Fig. 2.1 (right). Then, we will consider the cell on its right, then the ones in the second row and so on.

2.1 Solving Problems in a Generic Way

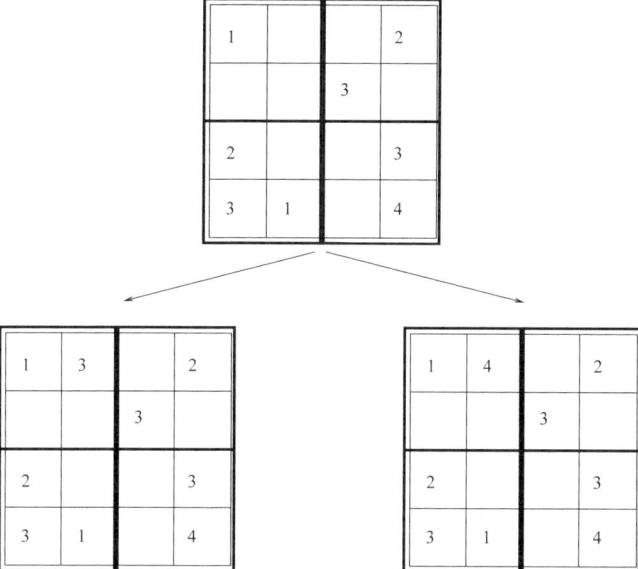

Fig. 2.2 Sudoku of size 4 × 4 when we fill the first cell with 3 and with 4

Let us look to the problem again, considering its key elements focusing on how the Sudoku is going to be solved. These key elements we use for the Sudoku are the same used to solve other problems as well.

- **States**. We have the Sudoku puzzle that corresponds to the 4 × 4 cells. Some of these cells are already filled, some are not. Using the jargon in AI we call each of the possible Sudoku puzzles a state. So, the Sudoku puzzle in Fig. 2.1 (left) is a state. If we fill a position with a number, then it is another state. Each of the puzzles in Fig. 2.2 is a state.
- **Action**. We can act on the Sudoku puzzle filling it. In the most simple case, we can fill a cell with a number. Using the jargon in AI, in the context of solving a Sudoku, with *action* we refer to setting a cell to a number. As we have said, to make things simple, we will act on the cells in order of *appearance* (from top to bottom and from left to right, starting with the one marked with an X in Fig. 2.1 (right)). So, as the order of cells is fix, we have, in general, four possible actions: setting the cell to 1, 2, 3 or 4.
- **Action effects**. If we apply an action on the Sudoku, we need to know which is the resulting state. Actions modify states. This is very simple in the Sudoku, the action is just filling the cell with the corresponding number. In a more abstract way, we need to know the effects of any action, and this can be complicated and require some computations.
- **Goal**. We need a way to know that our goal is achieved. In the case of Sudoku, the goal is to have all cells filled and that numbers are compatible. I.e., numbers can neither be repeated in a row, in a column, nor in a box.

Exercise 2.1 Identify states, actions, action effects, and goal in a scheduling problem.

Exercise 2.2 Identify states, actions, action effects, and goal in the problem of planning a trip from Barcelona to Paris. Discuss the difference when we only consider using a car and highways, and when we also consider planes and trains.

Then, to solve a problem is to start with an initial state and find a sequence of actions so that we reach a goal state. Note that in our problem what is important is to reach the goal state and we do not care so much on the sequence of actions. In other problems, the sequence of actions may be of relevance (e.g., when building a plan to move from a city to another one).

Let us now try to solve the problem. We will proceed as we have explained above, and we will represent graphically what we are doing. So, we take the Sudoku puzzle (initial state) and we fill the first cell (Fig. 2.1 (right)) considering our four actions (filling 1, 2, 3 or 4). Nevertheless, some actions are not possible here! As we need to have a number that is not in the row, nor in the column, nor in the box, only two actions are possible. We can set the cell only to 3 or 4. Note that we do not further think on what may happen later. We just focus on what happens now when we try to set the values. So, for the Sudoku puzzle, there are two actions (fill with 3 and fill with 4) that are possible and each will lead to a different Sudoku puzzle. Let us draw these puzzles in Fig. 2.2. We have on the top the original Sudoku puzzle and then the two new ones we have built in the second layer of Sudoku puzzle.

Then, we can proceed in a similar way with the resulting Sudoku puzzles. We have two to consider. The one on the left with the cell filled with a 3, and the one in the right with the cell filled with a 4. We consider for each of them the next cell to be filled (the only one left in the first row of the Sudoku puzzle). In the puzzle on the left there is only one action possible. We can only set the cell to 4. The other three values already appear in the first row of the puzzle. Figure 2.3 represents this only possible Sudoku below the one we have built filling the first cell. Then, we consider the other case. I.e., the Sudoku on the right filled with number 4. If we look with care, we see that we cannot fill the cell with any number. According to the first row, only 3 is possible, however this is already in the column (and the box). So, 3 is not possible. We should discard this Sudoku. In Fig. 2.3 we have used a black box to illustrate that no other option is possible here.

In the puzzle we added a 3, we would now proceed with the next empty cell. Again there is a single option. I.e., to fill it with 4. The same happens later with the next empty cell. It should be a 4. Then, we complete the first box with a 2. If we repeat the process, we will have only one option to complete the second box. The same happens with the remaining cells. Only one option each time. In this way, we can solve the Sudoku and we obtain the solution in Fig. 2.4 (left).

Exercise 2.3 Complete Fig. 2.3 with the next puzzles until the Sudoku is complete.

Figure 2.4 (right) is another Sudoku that has the same solution but is more difficult to solve. To solve it, we can proceed in the same way. Start with the first cell, consider the options, then proceed with the second cell, and so on. Figure 2.5 represents the

2.1 Solving Problems in a Generic Way

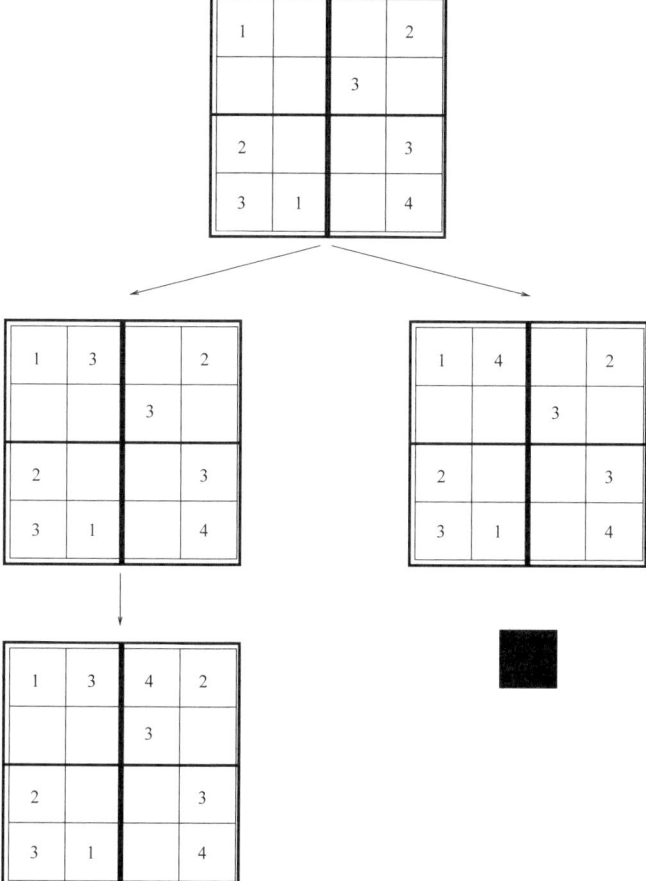

Fig. 2.3 Sudoku of size 4 × 4 when we fill the first cell with 3 and with 4, and the second cell with the only possible number (a 4)

first three consecutive decisions to fill. In the first cell, three actions are possible (filling the cell with 2, 3, and 4). Then, we can proceed dealing with the second level. Only in the case of having filled the first cell with 3 we have two options (filling the second cell with 2 or 4), in the other cases we have only one option. Nevertheless, three of the new Sudokus are impossible to complete. There are no actions possible to fill the third cell. These puzzles are marked with black boxes. The only possible Sudoku leads to a single new possible Sudoku (filling the last cell of the first row with a 2). We proceed from this last Sudoku. The three next cells can only be filled with a single number (only one action is possible). Nevertheless, if we keep repeating the process until we reach the end we see that later in the process we have alternative options again. The full computation is provided in Fig. 2.6.

1	3	4	2
4	2	3	1
2	4	1	3
3	1	2	4

1			
		3	
2			
			4

Fig. 2.4 Solution for the Sudoku of size 4 × 4 (left) and a more difficult problem for the 4 × 4 Sudoku (right)

The structure in this Fig. 2.6 is called a search tree. Solutions are in the bottom of the figure, and the initial state is on top. A path from the initial state to a solution on the bottom of the tree describes how we have built this solution (in our case, filling one cell at each step). The height of the tree corresponds to the length of the longest path. In our case, all paths to solutions have the same length, but this is not necessarily the case in all problems.

2.1.2 From Sudoku to Other Applications

The approach we have used to solve the Sudoku is the same used for solving other problems. For example, if we need to build a schedule for a school we need to fill time slots with courses (i.e., course names), teachers, and students (or groups of students). Naturally, courses need to be assigned to classrooms and laboratories. Then, we have some constraints to be taken into account. Neither students nor teachers can be in multiple places at the same time; students and teachers need to have an appropriate number of spare hours; etc. We would solve the scheduling problems in a similar way. We need to assign values (i.e., professors to classrooms and groups) so that the constraints hold. We consider the options, and we go ahead with new assignments until we have a valid schedule or we see that it is impossible to complete. Alternative options will be considered to find a valid solution. A graphical representation of the possible assignments will be similar to the figures we have built with the Sudoku.

In the case of Sudoku we have not considered costs. All *actions* had the same cost and all solutions are equally valid. This is not necessarily always the case. We may have solutions that are better than others. E.g., booking a classroom may have a cost, and we need to book cheaper (e.g., smaller) classrooms, if possible, or teachers may have different costs associated (e.g., they may have different salaries). If we are

2.1 Solving Problems in a Generic Way

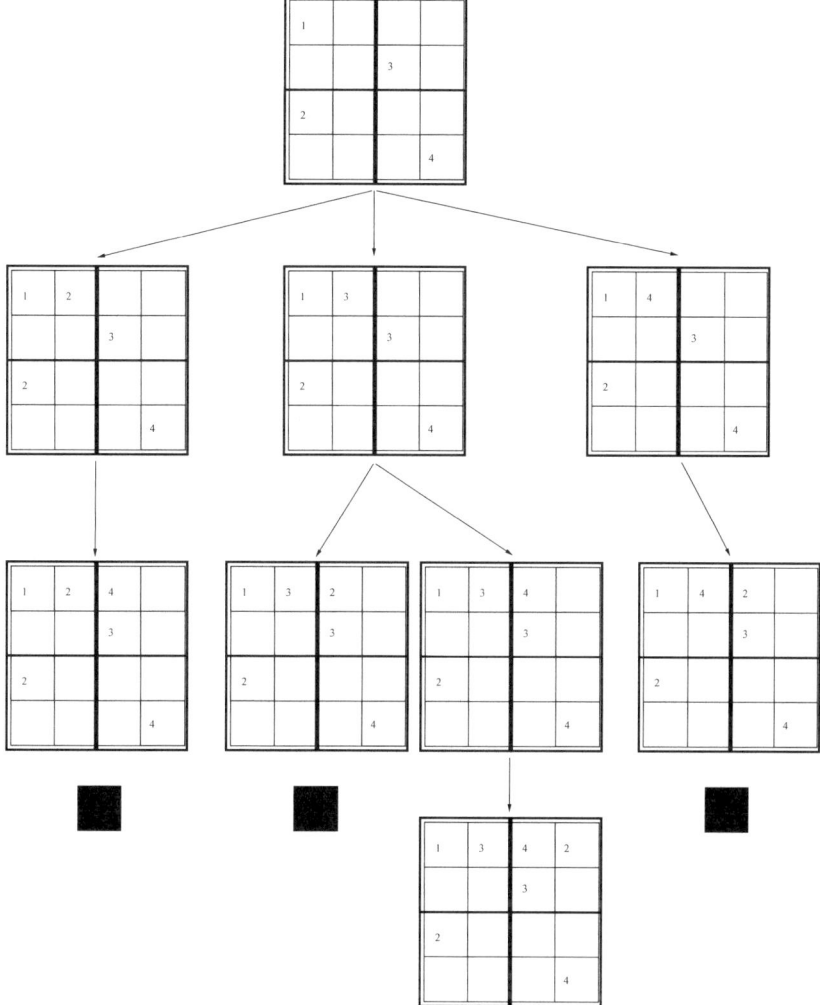

Fig. 2.5 Initial steps to solve the 4 × 4 Sudoku of Fig. 2.4 (right)

planning a trip, some options may be cheaper than others (e.g., traveling by plane and car have different costs). Costs may have also different flavors. It is money or time what is relevant? A good schedule may mean with less spare hours, and a good trip to Rome may require (or not) to plan the largest time in Rome, instead of a five days trip and one night in Rome. Then, the optimal option needs to be defined and found accordingly.

When costs are considered, each state in the figure will have associated a cost that will depend on the actions applied (i.e., how we have reached the state from the initial state). Then, an optimal solution is typically one that reaches the goal and

Fig. 2.6 Complete computation to solve the 4 × 4 Sudoku of Fig. 2.4 (right)

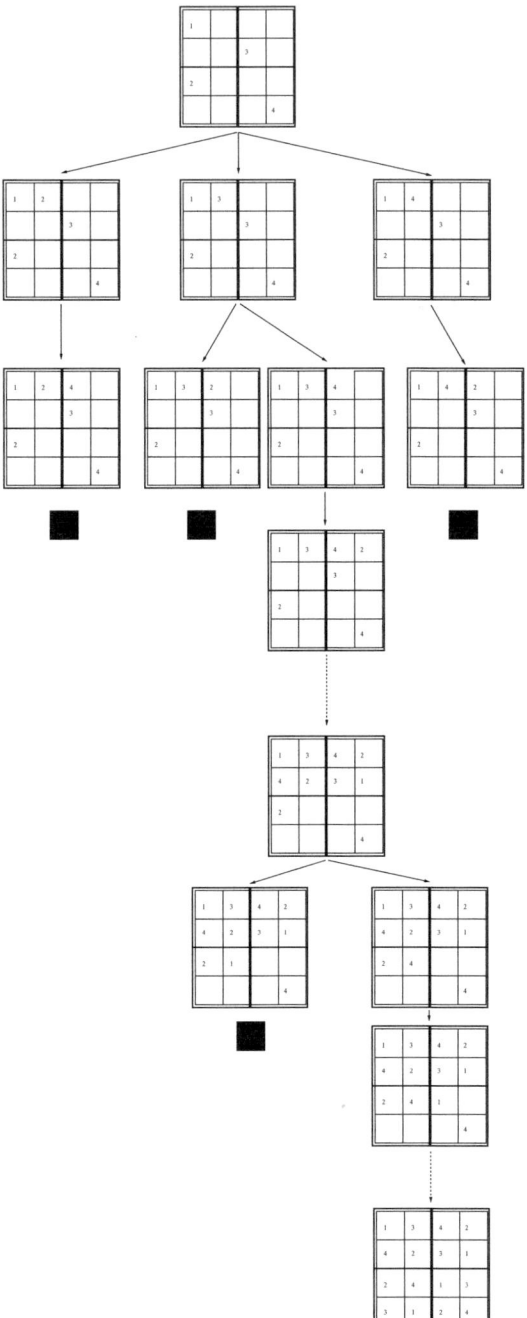

2.1 Solving Problems in a Generic Way

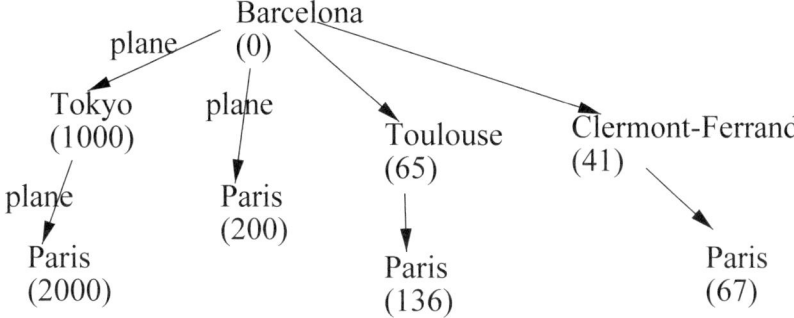

Fig. 2.7 From Barcelona to Paris. Searching a solution using car and plane. Edges using car are not labeled, only the trips using planes. Within brackets the cost to reach a city

minimizes cost. E.g., when traveling from Barcelona to Paris, we select an option with minimal economical cost among all possible solutions that reach Paris. Graphically, this means to select a path from the initial state (top) to a goal state (on the bottom of the figure) where this goal state has the minimal cost. Figure 2.7 illustrates this search. In the figure only a few options are considered. As before, in the case of the Sudoku, each edge corresponds to an action. In the figure, actions are the use of a car or of a plane. Note that only the case of planes are explicitly mentioned in the figure, unlabeled edges correspond to trips by car. Then, each node (or town) is annotated with the cost of reaching it (in euros). It is important to note that a city can appear multiple times (as is the case of Paris) if we can reach the place in different ways. Each appearance can have associated a different cost, as the cost depends on the trip. This is the case of Paris. The optimal solution (according to the figure) is 67 euros.

Planning is another problem that can be solved using the same approach. For example, planning an intervention. There are actions/options to consider, and constraints. The order in which actions/options are taken are also important. Some options may be incompatible, other preferable to do together. Costs, in whatever sense, may be of relevance.

In the Sudoku, constraints are hard. We cannot fill a cell with 2 if 2 is already in the same row. In the scheduling problem, some constraints are also hard. We cannot sit more students in a classroom than the number of seats. Nevertheless, some constraints are not hard. E.g., maybe we may have some classes at 14:00 while it is recommended to finish at 13:00. *Soft constraints* or *preferences on constraints* can be incorporated into the requirements of the system.

It is not the purpose of this book to discuss about gaming, but it is relevant to mention that playing games as chess, go, or even backgammon (which requires rolling a dice) is done by computers in a similar way. Boards need to be represented (e.g., chessboards are represented as we did with the Sudoku puzzle), there are actions to apply (e.g., legal moves in chess) which transform states (e.g., boards), and a goal to achieve (e.g., a board in which whites win). A structure similar to the one in Fig. 2.6 would be built. In the case of backgammon, each player rolls two dice in each turn. This means that, in general, as we do not know what the dice will show, we will consider all options in the graph.

Then, in order to make a decision, we need to take into account that there are two (or more) players, and while the software program has the goal of winning, the other (human) player has a conflicting goal (i.e., all players want to win). This is coded in the evaluation of boards. At each decision step evaluation of moves takes into account who is doing the move. Say, that we have scores for each player in chess. Then, decisions for whites optimize white scores, and decisions for black optimize black scores. The same with the uncertainty associated to the dice. I.e., if we have an extremely good board, but the chance of getting it is very low, we may prefer another move that give a less optimal result but with more chances.

Exercise 2.4 Investigate how the minimax algorithm works for games with two players.

2.1.3 Actually Solving the Problem

In actual problems the number of options are too many and the size of the associated graph (as the one in Fig. 2.6) would be too big to build. For example, if instead of the 4×4 Sudoku we have the 9×9 Sudoku with e.g. 11 filled positions, the height of the figure would be $9 \times 9 - 11 = 70$ puzzles as we need to fill 70 cells to complete the puzzle. Then, as any cell has multiple options (between 0 and 9) we would have an immense figure. Similarly, if instead of Sudoku we consider chess, with an average of 100 moves (50 each player), the height of the figure is 100, and the total number of boards, if we consider all possibilities as above, is estimated around $10^{46.5}$. In the game of go, the number of positions is still larger. It is estimated as 10^{170} (for a 19×19 board).

Within AI, the area of search studies how to build programs that are able to obtain an optimal solution, or a good enough solution, for these problems without needing to actually build this whole structure and not even looking to all states. Some algorithms try to focus on paths that are promising by means of the so called *heuristics*. They look to a state (e.g., a puzzle board) and decide if it seems worth to proceed going down in the structure. So, the states are evaluated using these heuristics, which allows to rank the states and disregard those that seem bad. Heuristics help on this process.

When the problem is too difficult to solve, a valid solution may be just good enough even if it is not the optimal one.

2.2 Representing Knowledge

AI systems require knowledge to be embedded in software to make decisions, and to help machine learning algorithms to produce good models. This knowledge is the

2.2 Representing Knowledge

one that experts and specialists use to make decisions and assess cases. Then, this means we need a way to codify this knowledge in the computer, so that it can be later exploited by the AI system.

Knowledge can appear in different forms. In fact, in a way, it was already present in the 4×4 Sudoku we have solved before. In our solution, the knowledge was somehow implicit. We have described what we need to solve the problem: the states, actions that permit to change states, and the goal. For some problems a hardwired description of the problem is enough for solving it. We can nevertheless describe what is a solution of a 4×4 Sudoku in an explicit, and computational way. We will do this now.

2.2.1 Logic Programming for Representing Knowledge

We will use logic programming for representing what a solution of the 4×4 Sudoku is. In particular, we provide a solution in the logic programming language Prolog to solve this problem in Fig. 2.8. The program explains when a solution is valid. The notation in the figure may seem cumbersome but we will try to explain it here.

The first line establishes the game of the Sudoku and gives names to the cells. Then, with the symbol :- we explain when the assignments of numbers to cells provide a valid solution.

```
solve([A11,A12,A21,A22,B11,B12,B21,B22,C11,C12,C21,C22,D11,D12,D21,D22]):-
    options(A11),options(A12),options(A21),options(A22),
    options(B11),options(B12),options(B21),options(B22),
    options(C11),options(C12),options(C21),options(C22),
    options(D11),options(D12),options(D21),options(D22),
    different(A11,A12,A21,A22),
    different(B11,B12,B21,B22),
    different(C11,C12,C21,C22),
    different(D11,D12,D21,D22),
    different(A11,A21,C11,C21),
    different(A12,A22,C12,C22),
    different(B11,B21,D11,D21),
    different(B12,B22,D12,D22),
    different(A11,A12,B11,B12),
    different(A21,A22,B21,B22),
    different(C11,C12,D11,D12),
    different(C21,C22,D21,D22).
different(O1,O2,O3,O4):-O1\==O2,O1\==O3,O1\==O4,O2\==O3,O2\==O4,O3\==O4.
options(O):-O=1.
options(O):-O=2.
options(O):-O=3.
options(O):-O=4.
```

Fig. 2.8 Program in the programming language Prolog to solve a 4×4 Sudoku. With the program above, we can solve the Sudoku in Fig. 2.4 (right) as follows: solve([1,A12,A21,A22,B11, B12,3,B22,2,C12,C21,C22,D11,D12,D21,4])

Fig. 2.9 Names of the cells for the Sudoku of size 4 × 4

A11	A12	B11	B12
A21	A22	B21	B22
C11	C12	D11	D12
C21	C22	D21	D22

More precisely, we name the cells in the Sudoku by A11, A12, .., D22. For the cell names, we refer the reader to Fig. 2.9. The first letter refers to one of the squares, and then the numbers are the relative position in the square. E.g., B21 refers to the second row, first column in block B. Then, after the symbol :- we explain the conditions or constraints that apply to have a correct assignment. Say, a solution with A11 = 1, A12 = 1, C11 = 1 is not valid because there are repetitions of value 1 in rows and columns. We need to formally define when a solution is indeed valid. Let us look to this.

It is clear by now that we only solve the Sudoku (i.e., we have assigned numbers to the cells correctly) if each of the cells is assigned to one of the possible options, and then we have that the four values in each block, row, and column are different. This is what is said in the first lines of the program. E.g., when we write

```
options(A11)
```

we are requiring A11 to be one of the four possible options. We come back to this later; and when we write

```
different(B11,B12,B21,B22)
```

we explicitly say that the four values for the block B need to be different. Naturally, we need to explicitly write all these requirements as well as, otherwise the computer will miss them and will provide us with a wrong solution. So, there are 12 of these requirements (4 for the 4 rows, 4 for the 4 columns, and 4 for the four blocks). Here we have required the values to take one of the options and the four values to be different, nevertheless we have not really explained which are the options, and what it means to be different.

2.2 Representing Knowledge

We start formalizing what it means that four values are "different". Different means here that all four assignments need to be different to each other. This is established in the line:

```
different(O1, O2, O3, O4) :- O1\== O2, O1\== O3, O1\== O4,
                             O2\== O3, O2\== O4, O3\== O4.
```

The definition is a bit long, because to ensure that all values are really different we need to consider all pairs and require the values to be pairwise different. There are six of such pairs!

Finally, we have four lines in our program where we define which are the possible options for each cell. As we know, there are four values possible: 1, 2, 3, and 4. Each of these four last lines of the program states a different alternative.

Once this program in Prolog is provided to the appropriate software, we can ask it to solve our original problem (Fig. 2.1 (left)). To do so we can write

```
solve([1, A12, A21, A22, B11, 2, 3, B22, 2, C12, 3, 1, D11, 3, D21, 4]).
```

and we would get the appropriate values that solve the problem. As this is a program that solves all the 4 × 4 Sudokus, we can also solve other problems, as for example

```
solve([1, A12, A21, A22, B11, 2, 3, B22, 2, C12, C21, C22, D11, D12, D21, 4]).
```

and, even ask to solve problems that have no solution,

```
solve([1, A12, A21, A22, B11, 1, 3, B22, 2, C12, C21, C22, D11, D12, D21, 4]).
```

which of course will not be solved but we will be informed that there is no way to assign any value so that the puzzle is solved.

Exercise 2.5 Discuss how our search (as described e.g. in Fig. 2.6) will show that a puzzle has no solution.

The program to solve this 4 × 4 Sudoku is short. We could proceed in a similar way to solve the 9 × 9 Sudoku. It would be just a longer definition: there will be more cells to consider, more possible values for the cells, more values that need to be different, and more blocks, rows, and columns that need all values in them to be different.

Problems as the ones discussed above (scheduling problems) can be programmed using logic programming languages easily. We need to describe well which are the options, and which are the constraints. Then, the language tries to find a solution that satisfies the constraints in a way similar to what appears in Fig. 2.6. Typical algorithms for solving problems in logic programming go back and forth through a structure similar to the one in the figure, unfolding the structure according to the actions, reaching dead ends and backtracking (returning) to previous decisions and reconsidering them and unfolding the structure in another direction. As we have stated above the area of search algorithms studies which are good ways to solve this type of problems.

2.2.2 Logic for Knowledge Representation

As we have said, the program we have presented above is written in Prolog. Prolog is a programming language based on logic, and, in fact, what we have written in the program are logical formulas. Prolog only allows a very strict set of them: Horn clauses. They are clauses, i.e. type of logical formulas, similar to rules in which given some conditions we infer that a predicate is true. E.g., something like,

```
if it rains, the road is wet.
```

For example, in our example above (program in Fig. 2.8) we stated that if O1 is different than O2, and O1 is different than O3, ... then the four values O1, O2, O3, and O4 are different. That was an example of Horn clause. Formulas that are not Horn clauses cannot be written in Prolog. An example is:

```
it is sunny or the road is wet, but not both.
```

In *logic*, we can write this.

Well, while we have used the term *logic* in singular, there are multiple types of formal systems in logics. Each formal system allows to represent some knowledge and not others, and allow some inferences and not others. In a formal system, there is a formal language that explains what is a valid expression (i.e., the syntax of the valid formulas). This is similar to mathematics where we know that something like

$$2/*3*/+*54.21.22223323.$$

is not a valid expression or like $(3 + 2i) * (2 + 5i)$ which is not a valid expression for natural numbers but it is valid for complex numbers. Then, in logics we have a deductive system that describes how we can infer or deduce new formulas from the ones we already have. For example, if we know that it rains now, from the rule above we infer that the road is wet now. In an AI application, we need to select the appropriate logic so that we can express what we need to express, and we are able to infer what we need to infer. Moreover, we need to have a good balance between expressivity and computational complexity in the inference process.

In addition to how the knowledge can be represented, a key aspect is how inference is done. Here, inference refers to how we can deduce new information from the one we have codified in our system. As we have said, if we have the rule above about the rain, and we also know that now it rains. Can our system infer that now the road is

2.2 Representing Knowledge

> The formula
>
> > if it rains, the road is wet.
>
> is written as if it had a direction (i.e., from the rain to our conclusion: a wet road), nevertheless, from a logical perspective, there is no. Note that we can equally conclude that as the road is not wet, it does not rain. The two types of inferences correspond, in logic, to *modus ponens* and *modus tollens*. This is the advantage of representing knowledge in this abstract and generic form. We can use it in different ways.

Fig. 2.10 Inference and reasoning

wet? If, instead, we know the rule and also that the road is not wet, can our system infer that it does not rain. Logic provides ways to make inferences (see Fig. 2.10).

Let us see some examples of alternative logics. First, let us consider propositional logic that allows us to represent the expression

> it is sunny or the road is wet, but not both

as follows

$$(\text{sunny} \lor \text{road\_wet}) \land \neg (\text{sunny} \land \text{road\_wet}).$$

Here, $\lor$ represents a disjunction (i.e., "or"), $\land$ a conjunction (i.e., "and"), and $\neg$ represents negation (i.e., "not"). So, the formula means that it may happen "sunny or wet" but also that it is impossible to have "sunny and wet" both at the same time.

Propositional logic has a big advantage against other logics. It is decidable. That is, when we have a set of formulas we know to be true, and we ask whether another formula follows from them, it is always possible to know if it follows or not. For example, let us assume that the following is always true: "if I have a headache, I don't go to work", then

- if we also know that "I have a headache", then, we can conclude that "I don't go to work". This later fact follows from the other two formulas; consider instead that, on the contrary,
- we know that "I don't go to work". In this case, we may consider if it is true that "I have a headache". This fact does not follow from our knowledge. The two other formulas don't imply this one. We can formally (logically) prove that this is not a valid inference. In reality, this does not follow because I may be absent from work because of other reasons e.g. I am on holidays (or because I didn't feel like going). So, this formula can be either true or false, and, thus, in short, it is not *necessarily* true.

Nevertheless, propositional logic has also drawbacks. It is complicated, or impossible, to state and infer properties about objects. Let us consider a classical example. The following type of knowledge can not be properly expressed: If someone is a man, then this someone is mortal; Socrates is a man. From this knowledge we can infer (i.e., this logically follows from the previous knowledge), that "Socrates is mortal". In contrast, first-order logic can be used to represent this type of knowledge. To do so, we use x to represent the *someone*, and $\forall x$ to represent that for all *someones* this applies. To represent the inference, we use $\vdash$ to represent that a formula follows from some others. All together, we write:

$\forall x \, (\text{man}(x) \to \text{mortal}(x))$
man(Socrates)
$\vdash$ mortal(Socrates)

Unfortunately, first-order logic is not decidable. That is, in general, given some knowledge (a set of formulas) we cannot always infer if another follows or not. Also, from a computational point of view, some inferences (if even possible) are costly. So, a way to make computations feasible is to use a logic that is a kind of between propositional logic and first-order logic.

Prolog, with its Horn clauses, is one way to have this mid term solution. Horn clauses are a subset of all possible formulas usually permitted in propositional logic. The example above about Socrates is a set of Horn clauses, and Fig. 2.11 includes the corresponding Prolog program. We describe in Fig. 2.12 the use of variables and constants in Prolog.

An example of first-order logic clause that is neither propositional logic nor a Horn class, is the following:

$$\forall x \, (\text{rich}(x) \lor \text{poor}(x)) \land \neg (\text{rich}(x) \land \text{poor}(x))$$

Here, we say that everybody is rich or poor, but not both (i.e., it is not true to have rich and poor).

Description logic is another type of logic very much used for knowledge representation in intelligent systems. In terms of expressivity is also between propositional logic and first-order logic. Its main advantage is that it is (in general) decidable.

Figure 2.13 represents the expressiveness of the different types of logics we have discussed so far, including the programming language Prolog. A box A inside a box B means that B can express more than A. We see that First-order logic (FOL) includes description logic and the restriction of FOL to Horn clauses. These two logics are both more expressive than propositional calculus, but different. Prolog includes some particularities to help the programmer to control the execution of the program, which makes it differ from first-order logics.

In both propositional logic and in first-order logic, the truth of a formula does not change with time. Nevertheless, there are contexts in which we need to represent

```
mortal(X):-man(X).
man(socrates).
```

Fig. 2.11 Prolog program for the example of all men is mortal. The query `mortal(socrates)` will answer positively that Socrates is mortal

2.2 Representing Knowledge

> You may have noticed that in the Prolog program we write Socrates without a capital letter. In Prolog we do not explicitly use ∀ and when we use a capital letter the language understands that we are referring to a variable usually quantified with a ∀. In contrast, when we use a non capital letter, the language understands that we are referring to a constant or to a particular object or person. So, we need to use socrates instead of Socrates, to mean that we are referring to someone in particular. If we were using Socrates, anyone would be him!

Fig. 2.12 Variables and constants in Prolog

time, and then the truth of a formula will change with time. We may be at the office now, but later we are not there, we are at home. Similarly, the washing machine is now on, and, say, it is in the rinse cycle. Then, it is spinning and no longer rinsing. Temporal logic permits us to represent time, and reason about time. We are able to express that some facts need to be true in some periods of time, and infer what can come next if we know that something takes place now.

2.2.3 Rules for Knowledge Representation

Rules have been used for long in AI to express knowledge. They are used to build expert systems. To define the rules, we need a process of modeling or knowledge acquisition. Field experts can help in this process, or, if there is appropriate data, we can build data-driven rule-based systems.

Rules are related to the implications in logic. Nevertheless, implications in logic are assumed to always hold. That is, we absolutely know that when the condition or antecedent (left side) is true, the conclusion (right side) is also surely true. Also, in a logical implication, although the formula is written as if it had a direction, we can use it in different ways. We have discussed this above with an example. On the contrary, rules may have a direction. So, they are then only applicable from the condition to the conclusion. In addition, they are not necessarily always completely true. For example, we may know that in *most of the cases* when we observe a symptom, it is because the patient has a certain illness. Nevertheless, this may not always be the case. Rules allow us to express this type of uncertainty. Then, rules are combined in the inference process. Namely, we are able to chain rules to model complex decisions. Also, as due to uncertainty, conclusions are not necessarily true given the conditions, we may consider combining several evidences to increase the support of a given conclusion. I.e., if there are multiple symptoms of the same illness, our conclusion about the illness is much more supported. We finish this section with actual examples of rules.

Lin et al. [102] describe a system for lower back pain diagnosis. It is a rule based system with 140 rules. The system can lead to 14 different diagnosis outcomes including, for example, *Gynecological*, *Hip joint-related pain*, and *Neuropathy of a peripheral nerve*. To make a decision, the system may need information about the

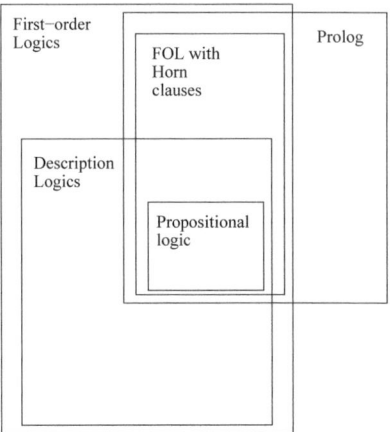

Fig. 2.13 Relationship between logics in terms of their expressiveness. A similar figure is provided by Grosof et al. [80]

patient as e.g. gender and age, number of pain episodes the patient has experienced before. They provide an actual example of a rule:

If observation shows patient age is between 30 and 40, then recommend diagnosis "Chronic Disc Degenerative" with a certainty level of "likely"

Corny et al. [38] describe another system to identify prescriptions with a high risk of medication error. The system combines machine learning with a set of rules related to medications. These rules are to raise alerts for the prescriptions. They provide the following example of an alert rule:

A prescription order of a concentration >4 g/L of potassium chloride was considered as inappropriate

Systems based on rules are called expert systems. Also, we can use the term knowledge-based system. In this latter case, other types of knowledge may be used as well.

2.2.4 Ignorance, Uncertainty, and Imprecision

When we build an AI system for decision making, dealing with uncertainty is crucial. Uncertainty is associated to what we observe in the world, and also to the knowledge we have about the world. Absolute certainty is not always the case. Therefore, the same applies to AI systems. For example, when we need to represent that we are not fully sure that a symptom is associated to an illness. We have seen a rule with this type of uncertainty above. We may also need to represent that we are not completely sure about some of the information we have registered into the system. Also, if we ask or

2.2 Representing Knowledge

interview people (e.g., in the urgency room or for knowledge elicitation) some words are not precise. E.g., the parent says "the child was warm", and also "I think she had a fever this morning". Then, we need to reason taking into account this uncertainty. The area of AI that deals with uncertainty is known as approximate reasoning and reasoning under uncertainty.

Uncertainty is sometimes used as a generic term related to lack of knowledge, but it is also used with a more specific meaning. There are related terms of relevance. They are

- Ignorance.
- Uncertainty.
- Risk.
- Imprecision.
- Vagueness.

We will describe each of them below.

Ignorance

Do an AI system know that something is not known? When we state some facts in logic, and some logical expressions, we are able to make inferences about the facts. There are however facts that we cannot infer. We cannot know whether they are true or false. We simply don't know. There are different ways to tackle ignorance.

In some logical systems we assume that all that needs to be known is known (what is explicitly stated or can be infered from the knowledge we have), and, thus, what is not known is false. This is known as the closed-world assumption. Prolog uses this approach. For example, if we ask to our program if Parmenides (another philosopher) was mortal, the answer will be no. This is so because there is no information that Parmenides was a man (nor that he was mortal). Similarly, if we add woman(hypatia) to our Prolog program and we ask if Hypatia was mortal, we will also get no. In this case, it is because we have restricted the property of being mortal to men, and we cannot chain woman to mortal. To make our Prolog program to work as expected for this questions, we need to add the following lines to what we already have:
   mortal(X):-woman(X).
   man(parmenides).
   woman(hypathia).
The first one means that all *x* that are women are mortal. The second and third that Parmenides is a man, and that Hypathia is a woman.
So, in Prolog, it is important to represent all required knowledge so that the inferences are correct and that we can answer what we need to. In the context of databases, the closed world assumption is also commonly used, and we take for granted that the database is complete. E.g., we would assume that all our customers are in the database, and, thus, if someone is not there is not a customer. Description logics does not use this assumption.

Fig. 2.14 Closed world assumption (CWA)

In some AI systems the closed world assumption applies (see Fig. 2.14). It mainly means that those facts that cannot be inferred as true are taken as false.

Uncertainty

In AI and knowledge representation, it is said that the current state of the world is often uncertain. This is understood as not being able to assess with certainty all the properties that are needed to reason and make decisions.

For example, the exact position of an object can not be known with certainty. Similarly, the cause of a symptom is not fully known. In this type of situations, uncertainty is modeled in terms of probabilities. We may not know where an object exactly is, but we know with high probability that is in front of us, at exactly 30 cm, and that the probability of being somewhere else fades away with the distance. For example, the probability of finding it at 40 cm is zero. Similarly, we may have uncertainty on any type of knowledge we represent in the system. For example, on the relationship between illnesses and symptoms, and we can represent using probabilities.

It is not only our knowledge that is prone to uncertainty. Actions also. When an action is performed, we may not be fully knowledgeable on its effects. We may expect an effect, but there may be a large number of possible outcomes for this action. For example, giving a medicine to a patient may not always cause the desired effect. Similarly, our order to a robot to advance one meter does not always mean that the robot will be exactly one meter away from the current position. The effects of actions, actions in the actual physical world or in a virtual world, are prone to errors and uncertainty.

Probability measures are well defined mathematical objects, defined by a set of axioms. That is, conditions that need to hold for any probability measure. We provide them in Fig. 2.15. We use the typical example of rolling a dice to illustrate probabilities. If the dice is a standard fair one, we have that there are 6 possible outcomes $\Omega = \{1, 2, 3, 4, 5, 6\}$. Then, we can consider the probability of any set of outcomes, and the probability of getting any number is the same 1/6. So, $P(\{1\}) = 1/6$ means the probability of having a 1 equals to 1/6. Then, the probability that the outcome is an even number is 3/6. This probability is expressed as $P(A)$ and, thus, $P(A) = 3/6$ where A is the set $\{2, 4, 6\}$. This fact, that is well known because there

---

Let Ω be a (discrete) reference set. Then, a probability measure P on Ω is a set function (i.e., $P(A)$ is the probability for any subset A of Ω) into [0,1] that satisfies the following axioms:

1. $P(\emptyset) = 0$ (boundary condition)
2. $P(\Omega) = 1$ (boundary condition)
3. $P(A \cup B) = P(A) + P(B)$ if $A \cap B = \emptyset$ (additivity axiom)

Fig. 2.15 Probability measures. Axioms

2.2 Representing Knowledge

are half of the outcomes that are even numbers, is formally deduced using the third axiom in Fig. 2.15 because

$$P(\{2, 4, 6\}) = P(\{2\}) + P(\{4\}) + P(\{6\}) = 1/6 + 1/6 + 1/6 = 3/6.$$

Graphical models and Bayesian networks are useful tools to model and reason under uncertainty. We discuss Bayesian networks in Sect. 2.2.6 and include an example with probabilities.

Risk

Decision theory studies how to model agents (e.g., people or software agents) making optimal decisions. It differentiates on their knowledge about the outcomes. A decision under certainty corresponds to the situation in which the outcome of an action is completely known. In this case, preferences and analyses of the outcomes permit us to select the optimal action.

Then, it considers decisions under uncertainty and risk. Decisions under risk and uncertainty apply to the case when actions have several possible outcomes, and we are not certain about which will be the actual one in the current circumstances. Decision under risk corresponds to the case in which for each action the set of possible outcomes are known, and also the probability of each outcome is known. Decision under uncertainty is when the probability is not known.

In artificial intelligence, the term uncertainty is used for both types of scenarios. In some applications, if probabilities are not available but a probabilistic model is meaningful, we can elicit them from experts or learn them from data.

Imprecision

We face imprecision when our knowledge does not allow us to distinguish among several alternatives, all being equally possible. A typical example is the following: *the temperature in Barcelona is between 20 and 22.*

Then, it may be perfectly possible that the temperature is 20, but also that it is 21.

Imprecision is common and then inference can lead to possible but not necessarily true conclusions. This is the case in our example. If we ask if the temperature in Barcelona is 19, we can conclude: no, it is not 19. Nevertheless, if we ask if the temperature in Barcelona is 21, we don't know for sure. We can only answer maybe, or likely. In any case, it is possible, but not necessarily true.

Vagueness

In knowledge representation, we understand vagueness in connection with borderline cases, as it is also understood in philosophy (see e.g. the discussion by

> "Truth is generally understood as the conformity between a statement and the actual state of facts to which it supposedly refers. Here, however, a degree of truth is rather a measure of agreement between the representation of the meaning of a statement and the representation of *what is actually known* about reality. This view is supported by Zadeh (1981, [192]), who defines procedures for the computation of meaning. What is known of reality is supposedly stored in a database B, in the form of statements. What can be said of the truth of a statement of a query statement S depends upon our state of knowledge (the information in B), and derives from a matching procedure between the meaning of S and of the contents of B. According to the respective precision of S and the information in B, the truth of S is asserted, refuted, but may also be only partially known (pervaded with uncertainty), or may be a matter of degree (S is vague)."

Fig. 2.16 Truth, conformity, and agreement, by Dubois and Prade [51] (p. 288)

Sorensen [160]). We consider a concept vague if there are cases that are disputable when we assess someone or something. These disputable cases are the borderline ones.

A common example of a vague concept or predicate is "tall". Let us consider that we all agree that, when talking about people, those that are higher than 1.80 are tall. Nevertheless, then, what about those people that are 1.78, 1.75, or even 1.70. People with these heights would be the borderline cases. Can we state that they are also tall? A way of looking to this is that we can neither say that they are "completely" tall neither that "tall" does not apply at all.

From a logic point of view, we can consider that "tall" is a predicate that can be true and false (as usual), but that can also take partial truth. That is, we may have a truth value in between total truth and total falsity. Alternatively, that for those that are 1.78 neither true nor false (completely) apply. A discussion of the interpretation of truth in this sense is provided by Dubois and Prade [51] (see Fig. 2.16).

Fuzzy logic provides tools for vague and imprecise concepts. Mathematically, fuzzy logic extends standard Boolean logics. We have briefly mentioned propositional logic and first-order logic. In both of them, as well as in their extensions as temporal logic and modal logic, predicates are either true or false. When we make inferences it may happen that we do not know when a predicate holds or not, so, if it is true or not. Nevertheless, even if we do not know which case applies, we do not have any other option.

This is known as the rule of the excluded middle. For any predicate p, it says that either p is true, or $\neg p$ holds (i.e., that the negation of p is true or, equivalently, that p is false). In logic terms:

$$p \vee \neg p.$$

In order to explain fuzzy logic, let us rewrite or interpret "true" as 1, and "false" as 0. Then, the truth of each standard predicate can only be 0 or 1. Nothing else

2.2 Representing Knowledge

is possible. When we lack knowledge we may not know if the truth of a particular predicate (e.g., the sun shines just now over the Kepler crater on the moon) is 0 or 1, but nothing else is even possible, and with appropriate knowledge we would be able to know.

Fuzzy logic is based on the fact that the truth of predicates are not necessarily 0 and 1, but anything else between 0 and 1 is also possible. In words, is like that we say: it is quite true that Ariadna is tall, while it is quite false that Berta is tall. For the first, we assign a value 0.8 to "Ariadna is tall" and for the second 0.2 to "Berta is tall". We can also say that 32 C is hot, but only temperatures above 35C are "fully" hot and, then, that it is clearly false that 25 C is hot. To model this we assign 0.9 to "32 C is hot", 1.0 to "35 C is hot" but 0.0 to "25 C is hot".

Then, in fuzzy logic the principle of the excluded middle does not longer hold. It is not (fully) true that either p or $\neg p$. Note that in the example above, 32 C is neither fully hot neither 32 C is neither fully falsely hot.

Vagueness is modeled in fuzzy logic by means of fuzzy sets and membership functions. From a mathematical point of view, they are generalizations of standard sets and characteristic functions. Note that in mathematics, elements can either belong or not belong to a set. For example, we have the set of possible outcomes in a dice. That is {1, 2, 3, 4, 5, 6} and then 1 belongs to the set, and 10 does not. We can also define "even numbers", "odd numbers". Let us consider a vague concept and define both a usual set and then a fuzzy set to see the difference. In the standard case, we can define the concept "values close to zero" in terms of all numbers between −1 and 1. That is, we define the set "values close to zero" as the interval [−1, 1]. Then, similar to the case of the outcomes of a dice, we can check for any value if it is in the set. For example, 0.8 is close to zero, −0.6 is also close to zero, but neither 1.4 nor 20.4 are in the set. They are not close to zero. We represent this interval in Fig. 2.17 (left). We have all possible values in the x-axis (the abscissa) and in the y-axis (the ordinate) we have one for those elements in the set and zero for the ones that are not in the set.

Fuzzy logic allows to represent vagueness softening the limits of the interval. So, we can have a smooth transition between the elements that belong to the set (i.e., with a value 1 in the figure) and the elements that do not belong to the set (i.e., with a value 0 in the figure). This is done using membership functions in which the membership of an element to a set is any value in the interval 0 and 1. So, we can say that the value 1.1 is still almost in the set "values close to zero" assigning a value of membership that is not zero. Figure 2.17 (right) represents the fuzzy version of

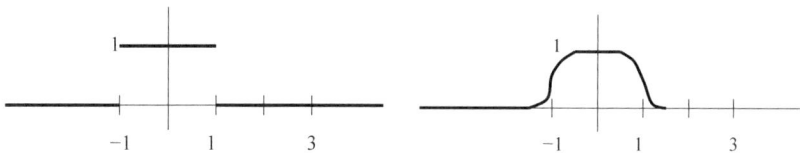

Fig. 2.17 Characteristic function of the interval [−1, 1] to represent close zero (left) and the membership function of close zero (right)

"values close to zero". In this case, we have considered that all values between −0.5 and 0.5 are "fully" "close to zero" and, thus, the membership function returns in this case one. Then, any number smaller than −1.5 and any number larger than 1.5 is definitely not "close to zero" so the membership function returns zero for any of these numbers. For those numbers between 0.5 and 1.5 we have values between 0 and 1, which mean that we have partial membership. Same applies to those numbers between −1.5 and −0.5.

Comparing the crisp and the fuzzy intervals (Fig, 2.17 (left) and (right)) we can observe that we have changed the crisp limits for fuzzy ones. In this way we can represent the borderline cases, and, thus, vagueness. We can represent the concept "tall" in the same way.

In our example, we define near to zero as between [−1, 1]. Of course, this definition depends on the application. If we are talking about minutes waiting for a main course in a restaurant we may consider that 5 min is still close to zero. In general, the process of defining membership functions corresponds to concept modeling. Models, and membership functions, are context and application dependent.

2.2.5 *Vagueness and Uncertainty*

Vagueness and uncertainty are two different types of knowledge, and to underline their difference we provide the following example taken from Bezdek [18].

Let us consider the set of all liquids, and consider the concept "potable liquids" where potable is understood as "suitable for drinking". Then, we may show the difference between fuzziness (and vagueness) and probability as follows. Consider you are in the desert and there are two bottles A and B. A is marked with membership 0.91 of being potable, and B is marked with probability 0.91 of being potable. Which one are you going to drink?

In the case of probability, potable is a Boolean concept. So, in short, it is only about being potable or not. So, say, poisonous. In the way that probability is usually understood, of 100 trials (or, of 100 bottles), 91 would be fine and bottles would have good water, but 9 can be deadly.

In the case of fuzziness, the concept "potable" is vague. We may have bottles with perfect drinkable water and even bottles with a poisonous liquid, nevertheless we may consider the whole spectrum between potable and poisonous. Then, a value of 0.91 would mean that the bottle is "fairly similar" to perfectly potable water.

So, someone aware of fuzzy set and fuzzy logic will probably take bottle A, although it may be swamp water.[1]

In the same way, if we have a membership of 0.8 of being near to a place, e.g., the Eiffel Tower, it means that we are quite near to it, and, for sure, we are in Paris. In contrast, a probability of 0.8 of being near to a place means also that we have a

---

[1] Marty McFly in the film "Back to the Future III" is offered such type of water by his great-great-grandmother Maggie McFly.

2.2 Representing Knowledge

probability of 0.2 of being really far away. We can be in Barcelona or Tokyo, for example.

2.2.6 Bayesian Networks and Graphical Models

In probability theory, the Bayes' rule permits to update the probabilities given some observations. For example, if we have rolled a dice and we know nothing (but we know that the dice is fair), we know that the probability of any outcome is 1/6. If we learn that the outcome is even, then we know that the probability of the outcome being 2, 4, and 6 is 1/3. The Bayes rule provides a way to compute these probabilities from the original ones and the probability of being even (which is 1/2).

Similarly, learning about a variable can affect our knowledge on another one. Say, following our example above about the rain and the wet road, that learning about the variable "rains", affects our knowledge on the "road" conditions. Say, that if it rains the probability of being wet is 0.9 and if it does not rain the probability of being wet is 0.2 (there are other causes of being wet as a cleaning road water truck).

Graphical models are a way to represent the interactions between variables. These models are built considering first the variables of interest, and then we add arrows between those variables that influence each other. We provide an example in Fig. 2.18 of a graphical model associated to three variables. They are "Rain", "Power outage" and "Solar panel". Here we understand "solar panel" as whether we are using electricity produced by our solar panels at home or from the power grid, and "power outage" as whether there is a power blackout that hinders us from using external electricity at home.

These variables are not independent. If there is a power outage, the probability of using solar panels at home will be higher. Also, rain (or absence of rain, so, sun) may also have some influence on us using the solar panels. In fact, rain can also have some influence on the power outage. These relationships are also represented in the

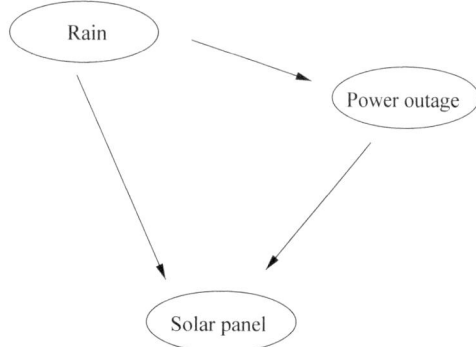

Fig. 2.18 Graphical model associated to rain, power outage, and the use of solar panels

graph. In particular, the graph includes arrows showing how variables influence each other.

In Bayesian networks, this graphical structure needs to satisfy some properties. For example, paths built from arrows cannot form cycles (i.e., if we start in a variable and transit to other variables following arrows, we should not be able to go back to a variable we have already visited). We can observe that this is the case of the graph in Fig. 2.18. From "Rain" we can transit to "Solar panel" via a direct arrow, or going through "Power outage" (using a path with two arrows). Nevertheless, there is no way to go back to any previously visited variable.

This graphical structure needs to be complemented with probabilities to define the Bayesian network. For each variable, we have a table with probabilities with all the cases related to the arrows that reach the variable. This means that for our example we need three sets of probabilities, one for "Rain", one for "Power outage", and one for "Solar panel". Each table includes the probabilities taking into account the variables that influence the variable.

Let us start for the probabilities for "Rain". This variable has no arrow that points to it. So, we need just to state the probability of having rain. Let us assume that we live in a rainy city and that the probability of having a rainy day is 0.7. So, we have "Rain" is true (T) with probability 0.7, and that is false (F) with probability 0.3. Then, we need to provide the probabilities for the variable "Power outage". As we have an arrow that states that it depends on whether it rains or not, we need to have conditional probabilities according to our knowledge on the rain. Let us say that if it rains, we have a power outage 30% of the days, and so 70% of times not. If it does not rain, we have a power outage 0.10% of the days. So, if it does not rain, the power is working almost always (with a probability of 0.999). This defines all the necessary probabilities for "Power outage". They are included in Fig. 2.19. Finally, we need to establish the probabilities about using the solar panels. Our graph establishes that this depends on whether it rains or not, and whether we have a power outage or not. Each of these two situations may happen or not. So, there are four cases. That is,

- If it rains and there is a power outage, then we use solar panels 50% of the times

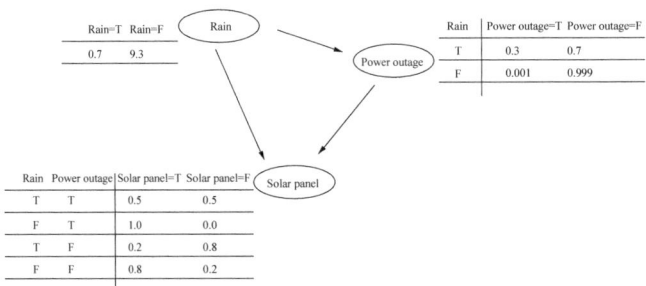

Fig. 2.19 Bayesian network associated to rain, power outage, and the use of solar panels. We represent the graph as well as the conditional probabilities

2.2 Representing Knowledge

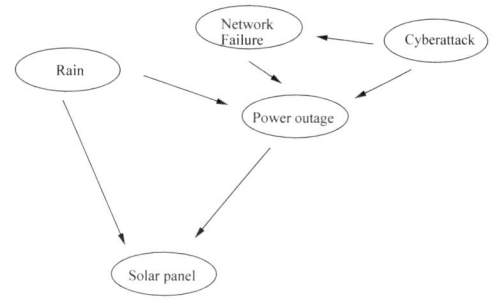

Fig. 2.20 Graphical model with five variables related to the use of solar panels in our home. Variables: "Rain", "Cyberattack", "Network failure", "Power outage", and "Solar panel"

- If it does not rain and there is a power outage, then we use solar panels 100% of the times
- If it rains and there is no power outage, then we use solar panels 20% of the times
- If it does not rain and there is no power outage, then we use solar panels 80% of the times

Naturally, this information permits us to know when we do not use solar panels. E.g., if it does not rain and there is no power outage, then we will not use the solar panels 20% of the times.

All these values can be translated into probabilities and added into the graph. We will have then the graph in Fig. 2.19.

This graphical model is very simple, with only three nodes associated to three variables. In real problems, more complex models can be built. To illustrate a slightly more complex model, we expand this very simple graph with two additional variables in Fig. 2.20.

From the point of view of inference, a Bayesian network permits us to infer the probability of observing a particular state of a variable giving some information about the other ones. For example, the probability of a power outage if we know that we are using solar panels. In order to build these models in practice, there are algorithms to extract both the structure and the probabilities from data.

2.2.7 Fuzzy Sets and Reasoning

Fuzzy sets can be used for reasoning. We can use them to define concepts and use these concepts in rules. We have seen above the rule provided by Lin et al. [102] in a lower back pain diagnosis system. Let us remind it.

If observation shows patient age is between 30 and 40, then recommend diagnosis "Chronic Disc Degenerative" with a certainty level of "likely"

We can revise the rule and take advantage of fuzzy sets theory to represent the age of the patient with a vague concept. E.g., define *between 30 and 40* as a fuzzy

Table 2.1 Truth table for conjunction (and, ∧) and disjunction (or, ∨)

a	b	$a \wedge b$	$a \vee b$
T	T	T	T
T	F	F	T
F	T	F	T
F	F	F	F

concept so that the rule also applies to some borderline cases. E.g., apply the rule even in the case that the patient age is 29 or 41. When the system computes the conclusion, it needs to take into account how much the patient age is *between 30 and 40*, allowing partial membership for those of 29 and 41. That is, for a given patient we will compute the truth value of the concept.

When rules include fuzzy concepts, we need to combine truth values. In the case of classical Boolean logic, this corresponds to truth tables. The truth table for conjunction and disjunction appears in Table 2.1. Let us consider that we have a rule in our intelligent system that states the following.

If the patient is young and the patient is sad then we give a sticker

We start assuming that there is no fuzziness in the rule. We can see that in this rule, we have a conjunction (and) in the antecedent (left side) and only when the antecedent applies, we will do what is on the right: give a sticker. Then, if a 5 years old girl reaches the hospital crying, we will apply the rule and give her a sticker. From a logical point of view, what we are doing is to check two conditions of the antecedent of the rule *patient is young* and *patient is sad*. That is, we are applying an operator "and" denoted by ∧ to combine two truth values. When both are true (we use T in Table 2.1 to represent true) then it is also true the statement *patient is young* **and** *patient is sad*. This is shown in the table in the first row and, mathematically, is:

$$T \wedge T = T.$$

However, if the girl is not crying and arrives happy, then we would not give her a sticker. In this case the antecedent does not apply, as we evaluate it as false. This corresponds to the calculation:

$$T \wedge F = F.$$

We could have the same rule but with a disjunction (i.e., *If patient is young* **or** *patient is sad*), then, we would be giving stickers even to old people if they are unhappy. In such cases the computation would be $F \vee T = T$.

If we consider that the rule uses fuzzy concepts, the statement *patient is young* will have associated a numerical truth value that can be 0.8 (e.g., the patient is a 12 year old boy). Then, we need to make clear what it means **and** and **or**. Mathematically, they are functions that need to combine values. E.g., 0.8 for the 12 year old boy, and 0.7 because he is not crying but not happy neither. Therefore, we need to compute

$0.8 \wedge 0.7$.

In the literature of fuzzy sets and fuzzy logic, these functions to model conjunction (**and**) are known as t-norms. For disjunction (**or**), there are other functions that are known as t-conorms. Then, we can write a rule as this one
If the patient is young and the patient is sad then we give a sticker

where *young* and *sad* are fuzzy concepts and we can assess if the rule applies (and how much the rule applies) using membership functions and the fuzzy conjunction t-norm.

2.2.8 Knowledge Graphs and Ontologies

In Fig. 2.20 we have provided a graph with several variables and how they affect each other. It was for our example of a Bayesian network. Knowledge graphs represents entities and their relationships and have a similar form. They define ontologies. Nevertheless, we may have different type of entities and different type of relationships.

For example, we can represent that there are different types of cyber-attacks as e.g. phishing attacks, ransomware, password attacks, and denial-of-service (DoS) attacks. So, we can represent that "ransomware is a type of cyber-attack". Similarly, we can state that the solar panel is a type of electrical device. Adding this into the graph above, we will have two type of relations, the one we already had about what affects what, and the one "type of". Nevertheless, others can be defined as well depending on the type of application we are building (e.g., "capital of", "part of", "type of"). For example, in the example above, we could state that solar panels are a "type of" electrical device, but also that they "arranged in" arrays or systems, that they "produce" direct current, etc.

Knowledge graphs (or subsets of knowledge graphs) can be represented graphically, but they are usually represented in a machine-readable form so that they can be easily incorporated in intelligent systems to allow reasoning. There are multiple examples of knowledge graphs. For example, and linked with the example above, there are knowledge graphs for cybersecurity (see the review by Sikos [154]).

Ontology is a broader concept that knowledge graph. In knowledge representation, it refers to a formal representation of knowledge. So, of course, knowledge graphs are examples of ontologies. Nevertheless, machine readable dictionaries are also often considered as such. This is the case of wordNet, although it is not formal enough and has some semantic inconsistencies.

2.3 Multiagent Systems

In AI, multiagent systems [153, 190] are implemented as a set of software agents that all together to solve a problem. Each of them is an AI-based software that has some level of autonomy, has its own information or knowledge, makes its own decisions, and can even learn from the environment. They also communicate with each other in a pre-established way. For example, in games, they can be used to control the behavior of characters. That is, each agent governs a character, and, thus, different characters may have different behaviors. Agents receive some information about their surroundings (in an appropriate form) and make decisions about where to move, what to collect, and whom to attack. They have also been used in character animation in films. Their AI-capabilities can be used to have more realistic behaviors, and, in the case of games, to adapt their behavior to the one of the human players.

Some agents may be reactive and have limited reasoning capabilities. That is, they simply react to their inputs. This will be the case of a game character that always approaches the player, whatever the circumstance. This agent may only need to know the direction in which the player is, and approach to it.

More sophisticated agents may need reasoning capabilities and use knowledge representation formalisms to store what they know about the environment. E.g., they can store a map of the places they have visited. In addition, they may need to plan their tasks to reach their objectives. Planning consists of building a sequence of actions to achieve a goal. For this, search mechanisms are usually needed. We have discussed this issue in Sect. 2.1. Currently, there are agents built using large language models (LLMs). The term agentic AI is often used in this context.

In a multiagent system, agents may have different capabilities (i.e., use different types of knowledge and learning), and, thus, the system can be rather heterogeneous.

Another application area of multiagent systems is social simulations. In this case each agent can model a person, or a group of people. Then, the behavior of a society can be studied by means of executing the agents. Different policies can be implemented in the system and their effects on the society simulated.

2.4 Bibliography

Search algorithms appear in most AI textbooks. E.g., in Russell and Norvig [140]. This book also includes chapters for logic in knowledge representation, and graphical models.

Fuzzy sets and systems are very well described in the book by Klir and Yuan [94]. Uncertainty and risk, and its role in decision, is explained very nicely by Gilboa [73]. Wooldridge wrote an introduction [190] to multiagent systems.

Chapter 3
Decision Support Systems

Abstract This chapter describes how to provide assessment of alternatives in a knowledge-based approach. That is, we describe decision-support systems. We explain the main characteristics and components of these systems that are based on knowledge elicited from experts and policy makers. The chapter includes examples showing how decision support systems can be used in prioritising and ranking as e.g., ranking patients for interventions.

> Un dia, sortint de l'òpera—mai no havia sentit uns cantants tan meravellosos—jo li vaig dir que ens quedéssim a París, o que ens en anéssim a Londres o a qualsevol altra banda.
> Maria Antònia Oliver, Joana E., 1992 [118].

Assessment, evaluation, and triage of different alternatives is a task that can often be automated. The field of decision making, and more concretely, multicriteria decision making, multiatribute decision making, and multiobjective decision making, provides tools for alternative evaluation and selection. Decision support systems is a term that can be used for these types of automated systems.

These systems allow us to assess, classify, and rank alternatives (people, products, objects, or cities as in the quotation) taking into account a set of predefined criteria. For example, we can use them for shortlisting candidates for interviews, for job scoring, for assessing people's needs for assistance in social welfare programs, and for people's triage for a medical treatment. Examples of triage in medicine include vaccination priorities, mental health telephone triage, and managing acute psychiatric crises [79].

These type of systems can be built from expertise. That is, they are based on knowledge from field experts. To build such systems, we need one or more experts that can provide us with the critical knowledge about assessing alternatives, and then we need to represent this knowledge in our system. Then, we are able to automatize the evaluation of cases or alternatives. In this chapter, we will explain the main components of such systems. The alternative, when such knowledge is not available but there is historical data, is to use these data to build our system. This corresponds to data-driven models using machine learning, and this is discussed later in Chap. 4.

So, let us discuss how such a system is built.

3.1 The Main Concepts of a Decision Support System

A system to assess and evaluate a set of alternatives following a decision making approach is based on the following main components.

- Alternatives. This is the set of objects that we need to assess. The nature of these objects is problem dependent, and can be the candidates for a position, drugs to be administrated to a patient, machinery to be employed for a task, and patients that need to be sorted for a transplant. Moreover, the set of alternatives can be finite and *manageable* (e.g., some candidates for a position), a very large one (e.g., the set of apartments on rent in New York), or even infinite (e.g., possible prices and quantities of produced products).
- Variables. Alternatives are to be assessed or evaluated in terms of a set of properties, factors, or attributes that we consider the relevant ones for their assessment. For example, in hospital admissions, for screening, the temperature of the patient may be relevant.
- Criteria. Each of these properties need to be properly stated and evaluated. Selection of the basic and relevant criteria is important for any decision making process. For example, considering again hospital admissions, we need to consider (and, thus, define) fever, which will be based on the variable temperature.
- Assessment of criteria. In order to assess the alternatives, we need first to assess each of the criteria independently. It is usual to use for this a scale (for example, a value between 0 and 1). Then, we have for each pair (alternative, criteria) a value in the scale. In this way, for particular people reaching the hospital, we can assess if they have fever or not. Say, 1 if the patient has fever, and 0 if not.
- Aggregation. Partial assessments are then combined into an overall assessment (for each alternative). This process provides the evaluation for each alternative, and, if needed permits their ranking or selection.

We will discuss these components in more detail now.

3.1.1 Alternatives

As we have stated above, alternatives are the objects we need to assess. They can be almost anything. They can be people to be evaluated or assessed, machinery, software products, apartments, protocols, medical treatments, travel options, etc.

In these examples, alternatives are actual objects. That is, objects that exist, and that we want to assess. Nevertheless, alternatives can be associated to possible decisions, and we may need to build them if required, and only if their assessment is good. Consider that we plan to launch a *new* product: a package of a new type of cornflakes. Then, some characteristics of this product are the weight of the package, and its price. We can also consider the color of the package. Then, possible alternatives are of the form *(weight, color, price)*, with *(1000g, blue, 300 euros)* and

3.1 The Main Concepts of a Decision Support System   49

(242g, yellow, 1 euro) two examples of alternatives. Given any set of colors, we can construct possible alternatives with arbitrary weights and prices. Systems that need to be configured, as e.g., a car or a type of machine with multiple options, fall also in this case.

We have pointed out that we may have a small or manageable set of alternatives, a large set, and even an infinite one. For a large set, just take the available flats in Barcelona. Decision making solutions can be usually applied to large sets of solutions without major difficulties when the criteria and the corresponding evaluations are easy to compute. When an alternative is defined by different components (as in the case of the cornflakes package), and one of the components is infinite (as, in theory, the price can be whatever number) the number of alternatives is arbitrarily large.

In these examples, we have considered several alternatives, but it is also possible to have a single one: a single candidate for a position, or a possible donor for a transplant. Even in this case, we may need to evaluate the alternative, and if the evaluation is not good enough reject it in the decision process.

3.1.2 Variables

As we have explained above, variables and criteria are the building blocks to assess the alternatives. Variables are the set of properties or factors that the experts consider relevant for the proper assessment of the alternatives. Each of these factors need to be explicitly stated. Then, we build the criteria that help us to establish the range of values that are relevant for selecting an alternative. Then, for a given alternative, the actual value of the variable is assessed according to the criteria.

Let us consider the case of buying a flat. Size, in square meters, is relevant. So, we need to add this variable in our set of relevant variables. This is to establish the group of relevant flats with respect to this variable. For example, a criteria is to select only those flats between 80 and 100 m^2.

The set of variables naturally depend on the problem, and on the evaluation system we need to implement.

For example, both the suitability of a patient for a treatment and the suitability of a person for a position depend on multiple variables. Some variables may be common to both problems, and some not. The academic degree of someone is relevant for being selected for a position but it is not for a medical treatment, while age can be relevant, in some cases, for both.

A proper selection of variables and criteria is essential for the system to work well. Variables need to provide a good overview of e.g. the state of the patient, and the capabilities of the candidate. Therefore, we need variables and criteria that provide complementary information.

While complementary variables are necessary, it is also usual to have variables that provide similar or related information. Although they can be kind of redundant variables, they are necessary because they help to complete the picture.

Fig. 3.1 Portion of the attribute tree for COVID-19 vaccination priority evaluation by Dujmović and Tomasevich [54]

```
1 COVID-19_Vaccination_priority
  11 Role and responsibility priority factors
    (...)
  12 Personal COVID-19 risk factors
    121 Age and medical conditions
      1211 Age risk factors
        (...)
      1212 Personal medical conditions
        12121 Current health conditions
        12122 Patient medical history
        12123 Race and ethnicity risk factors
    122 Professional risk factors
    (...)
```

In complex evaluation problems, the number of variables is typically large. If so, it is necessary to structure them in a convenient way, both for helping in their identification as to ease the computation of the assessment. We can proceed first identifying the key factors for the assessment, then, each factor is decomposed into simpler ones. This process is repeated until we are able to directly assess the factor directly from the alternative. That is, until we have the basic variables to define the criteria.

Dujmović [52, 53] proposed Logic Scoring of Preference (LSP) as a decision method in which the relevant variables are structured in a hierarchical structure (the attribute tree). As an example, we can consider the system, described by Dujmović and Tomasevich [54], for vaccination priority evaluation for COVID-19. They consider 21 input variables (attributes) which include some variables related to health (age criterion, current health conditions, patient medical history), but also some related to work (the person is a medical personnel directly exposed to COVID-19, an essential active police personnel), and to living (degree of urbanity, density of population). A portion of the attribute tree is found in Fig. 3.1. The authors define the vaccination priority in terms of three main factors: role, personal, and social factors. These factors are further decomposed to be able to assess them. The figure includes part of the decomposition of personal risk factors (12) up to the variables that can be directly assessed with the information from the candidate. In this case, one of the variables is current health conditions. Another one is patient medical history.

3.1.3 Criteria and Their Assessment

As we have explained in the previous section, the proper evaluation of alternatives (e.g., candidates) needs to be based on the characteristics or variables we have selected, and the criteria we have defined, which are associated to the goal of our decision making system.

Let us consider the triage problem in the emergency department as discussed by Wireklint [188]. The author lists a few variables to identify unstable patients. They include temperature, pulse, breathing frequency, and degree of consciousness. Let

3.1 The Main Concepts of a Decision Support System

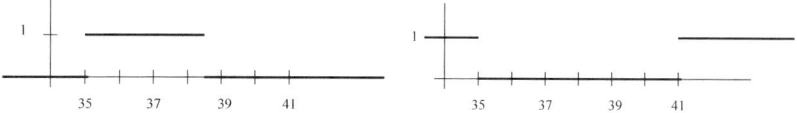

Fig. 3.2 Stable patients have a temperature on the range 35 and 38.5 °C (left) and unstable patients on the range 35 and 41 °C (right). Representation of the mathematical function for these criteria

us consider the simple case of temperature. It is stated that unstable patients have a temperature either larger than 41 °C degree or smaller than 35 °C, in contrast, an stable patient has a temperature between 35 and 38.5 °C. Then, when a patient arrives, we would check the temperature and use its ranges (i.e., criteria) to assign them into the classes of unstable and stable patients. Similarly, a stable patient is expected to have a pulse between 50 and 110.

Within a decision support system the criteria help the assessment. Formally, criteria are mathematical functions that establish for a given value associated to a variable a degree of satisfaction (how much the criteria are satisfied). For example, take patient's temperature and use the function to check if the patient is stable or unstable. The same for other variables as pulse.

These functions can be represented graphically. Figure 3.2 (left) represents appropriate range of temperatures for the stable patients. Here a value of 1 means that the criteria is satisfied. Then, if we have checked the temperature of a patient, and it is, say, 37, the assessment establishes that this temperature is stable. In the figure, we can read that all those that have a value in the interval [35, 38.5] will be assigned a value of 1. This is the case for 37. All the other temperatures lower than 35 and larger than 38.5 will be assigned a value of zero. Note that a value of one means fully agreement with the concept "stable temperature". Similarly, in Fig. 3.2 (right) we represent the temperatures which are unstable. In this case, any temperature smaller than 35 or larger than 41 will be considered as unstable, and the graph produces a value of 1. So, in this case, a value of one means fully agreement with the concept of "unstable temperature".

We would have analogous graphics and functions for the pulse, establishing which are stable pulses and which are not.

In a more abstract way, for each of the criteria we have a range of possible values that satisfy them (i.e., stable temperature, range 35–38.5). Some values are optimal (i.e., 35–38.5), and some are absolutely unacceptable (i.e., outside the range). Nevertheless, for some applications we have also ranges that are partially acceptable, or values that are increasingly acceptable/unacceptable.

Consider the case of buying a flat. We have decided that we want one that is between 80 and 100 m^2. Then, the range 80–100 is the range of optimal values. Nevertheless, we are not so strict to consider 101 m^2 as an absolutely unacceptable flat, or even 100.5 m^2 unacceptable. The same applies to 79.5 m^2. So, we may consider a smooth transition between acceptable and unacceptable flat sizes. Figure 3.3 (left) represents our preference for flats according to size. Note that the figure is not symmetrical, and that the decreasing part is larger on the right than on the left. This is

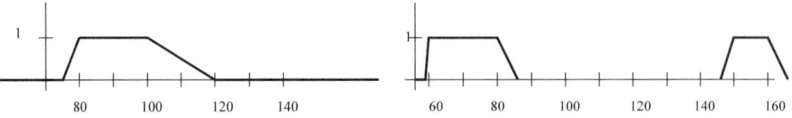

Fig. 3.3 Graphical representation of our preferences for flat size. Fuzzy interval between 80 and 100 (left) and either a small flat or a flat with our atelier (right)

because from our point of view it is somehow acceptable to have a flat up to 120 m^2 but less than 75 is absolutely unacceptable. That is, we are more flexible on larger sizes than on smaller sizes (i.e., larger than 100 m^2 than smaller than 80 m^2).

The functions we have used here to represent the criteria and represented in Figs. 3.2 and 3.3 are known as utility functions in decision theory and as fuzzy membership functions in the area of fuzzy sets and systems.

The three functions displayed so far show a variety of functions. We have seen in Fig. 3.2 (left and right) classical sets of values, and in Fig. 3.3 (left) what is called a fuzzy interval. It is a fuzzy interval because we have that the limits of the interval are blurred allowing us to represent some flexibility on these limits.

It is very important to highlight that the shape of the function associated to a criteria is absolutely arbitrary as solely depends on the type of problem we need to solve. For example, let us consider that we may want either a small flat (say, between 60 and 80 m^2) or a big one (larger than 150 m^2) because we are artists and we want to have our atelier in our residence (so, we need space) or have it somewhere else (so, a small flat is then good), but a large flat where our working space does not fit is absolutely useless. Then, we may have a function as the one in Fig. 3.3 (right).

Recall that we have already seen fuzzy sets and membership functions in Sect. 2.2.4. They were used to represent vagueness.

Exercise 3.1 What kind of function is a utility function? Indicate which of the following options is true:

- (a) A utility function needs to be always increasing. E.g., when the price is larger, the utility is larger.
- (b) A utility function needs to be always decreasing. E.g., the lower the price, the better.
- (c) A utility function needs to be first increasing and then decreasing. E.g., there is an optimal price we want to pay, and then the utility is maximum when we are precisely paying this price, and then the more different is the price, the worse.
- (d) A utility function can be defined according to (a), (b), or (c), but also using any other shape.
- (e) All the other alternatives are false.

3.1 The Main Concepts of a Decision Support System

3.1.4 Aggregation: Assessment of Alternatives

Once the set of variables and criteria are properly stated, we can report for each candidate the corresponding values. In a way, this means to fill a form for a candidate where we have a value for each pair (candidate, criteria).

For example, for the flat assessment problem, we take each of the flats we are considering and we fill fields such as size, construction age, etc. Similarly, for the patient triage problem, we fill the fields for each patient as temperature, pulse, etc.

In a very simple problem, the evaluation is based on very strong requirements. For example, we want the house to be between 80 and $100 \, \text{m}^2$, 3 rooms, and a chimney. If some of these criteria do not hold, the flat is unsuitable. In practice, the number of criteria is large, none of the alternatives fully satisfies all the criteria, and assessment needs to take into account trade-offs, and logical constraints between the criteria. For example, if the price is really good we may buy a larger flat than the one we initially planned to, or if the location is really good we may buy a more expensive flat. Nevertheless, we will not select a flat that we can definitely not pay.

Table 3.1 provides the evaluation for five flats in terms of the three criteria mentioned above. See the three columns criteria with the evaluation in [0, 1] of the three criteria: size, 3-rooms, and chimney. The flats considered are as follows:

- The first flat has size $90 \, \text{m}^2$, but only one room and has no chimney.
- The second one is, in fact, a very large house, with 6 rooms, but with a chimney.
- The third flat is a bit larger than $100 \, \text{m}^2$, with 3 rooms, and no chimney
- The fourth is too large, but has 3 rooms, and also a chimney.
- The fifth is a bit larger than $100 \, \text{m}^2$ (and a bit larger than the third flat), but has 3 rooms, and also a chimney.

To obtain the overall assessment of each flat we need to aggregate partial assessments. That is, we need to combine the assessments of each criteria and obtain an aggregated value. There are lots of ways to do this. Three simple ways are the following ones. We discuss them explaining what they mean in practice (a kind of semantics), and the result we obtain. We use them to illustrate that there are different options for aggregating assessments and we will use them later to explain important concepts related to aggregation and aggregation selection.

Table 3.1 Evaluation of some flats according to the three criteria: size between 80 and 100, 3 rooms, and chimney. Aggregation of the criteria using minimum, maximum, and average

	Criteria			Assessments		
	Size	3-rooms	Chimney	Minimum	Maximum	Average
Flat-1	1	0.2	0	0	1	0.4
Flat-2	0	0	1	0	1	0.333
Flat-3	0.8	1	0	0	1	0.6
Flat-4	0.2	1	1	0.2	1	0.733
Flat-5	0.7	1	1	0.7	1	0.9

- Take the minimum of all assessments. This is, we compare all the three values and take the one that is the worst. In short, this procedure means that we require all criteria to be satisfied, and from a logic perspective minimum can be considered a conjunctive operator. That is, we want a flat with appropriate size **and** 3 rooms **and** chimney. Note that a single zero in one criteria makes the alternative not eligible. Observe that this is the case of flat-3. As there is no chimney even with all other assessments good, its overall evaluation is zero (see column minimum in Table 3.1). In general, one criteria strongly failing our expectations makes the alternative not eligible. In contrast, we are able to distinguish and select really good alternatives, if they are listed there. Observe that flat-5 is highly rated, and clearly distinguished from the others, as the worse criteria (the size) has an assessment of 0.7. All other flats have overall assessments less or equal than 0.2.
- Take the maximum of all assessment. This is, we compare all the three values and take the largest one. In this case, a single criteria being very good leads to the alternative being well assessed. Observe the case of the large house (flat-2), just having a chimney provides a perfect evaluation of the house (overall assessment equal to 1). This is probably not acceptable in our type of problem. Nevertheless, it can be convenient in other ones. Consider screening of patients, using this approach, if a single criteria (e.g., temperature) is assessed as unstable, then, the patient will be assessed as unstable. From a logic perspective, maximum is considered a disjunctive operator. That is, we want our flat to have given appropriate size **or** 3 rooms **or** a chimney. In the case of screening, someone is unstable if temperature is unstable **or** pulse is unstable **or** breathing frequency is unstable.
- Take the average of all assessments. This is, compute the arithmetic mean of the numbers and provide this average as the overall assessment. In this way, we are allowing some trade-off between the criteria: one criteria with a large value will compensate another one with a low value. From a logic perspective, this is a kind of neutral method, between conjunction and disjunction.

There are lots of alternative ways to combine the assessments of the criteria. We will discuss this with more detail in the next section.

In the previous example we have considered a single aggregation for all considered criteria, or a flat aggregation. That is, we have taken all three values and e.g. taken their average. In a more complex problem with a large number of variables and criteria, we will not aggregate all criteria at once, but we will compute partial results and combine them in appropriate ways. Let us keep the same example, but we consider now that price is also a criteria when assessing the flats. Then, it is reasonable to consider on the one hand all the properties of the flats with respect to our preferences (as we have done above) and on the other hand consider their prices and our satisfaction with them. Figure 3.4 represents the variables and factors of this example. Then, formally, we do a two step aggregation process. The first one is the one represented in Table 3.1 which corresponds, say, to quality and that combines size, 3-rooms and chimney. Then, we combine this quality assessment with our assessments of the price.

Note that Dujmović [52] objects on the combination of the evaluation of the alternative (suitability) and the price (cost) in the attribute tree, and both elements are

Fig. 3.4 Attribute tree for apartment assessment

```
1 Apartment assessment
 11 Price
 12 Quality
  121 Size
  122 3-rooms
  123 Chimney
```

only considered together in a cost-suitability (suitability-affordability) analysis. See Fig. 1.1.1 in his book [53]. Nevertheless, if the two scales are comparable, the values can be combined using an aggregation function. Otherwise, if the two evaluations are in incommensurable scales (i.e., scales that cannot be easily converted from one to the other), then we should avoid the aggregation. In practice, we would list the flats according to their quality assessment, or provide a 2D graph as the ones we see later in Fig. 3.6 with the most relevant and interesting flats.

Let us consider some prices to complete the example. Say that prices of flat-1, flat-3, and flat-5 are kind of acceptable for us, and we evaluate their prices as 0.8. Then, the house (flat-2) is really expensive and we cannot afford it, and the same happens with flat-4 because in addition of being large, it has been renovated recently, and the price is too high. We assess both prices with a 0.

Then, to have the final assessment of each flat including the price, we need to combine both assessments: flat quality and price. As price is an essential criteria, and we cannot allow for any trade-off between price and the apartment quality, we need a conjunctive aggregation: we need both quality and price. So, we take the minimum to combine the two assessments. The combination results are as follows. Note that for the flat quality assessment, among the three options discussed above, we use here the average.

- flat-1. Flat quality: 0.4; price assessment: 0.8
  Overall assessment: min(0.4,0.8) = 0.4
- flat-2. Flat quality: 0.333; price assessment: 0.0
  Overall assessment: min(0.333,0) = 0
- flat-3. Flat quality: 0.6; price assessment: 0.8
  Overall assessment: min(0.6,0.8) = 0.6
- flat-4. Flat quality: 0.733; price assessment: 0.0
  Overall assessment: min(0.7333,0) = 0
- flat-5. Flat quality: 0.9; price assessment: 0.8
  Overall assessment: min(0.9,0.8) = 0.8

These computations show that flat-4 was the second best rated flat when only quality was of concern, but considering price the flat is absolutely ineligible. Flat-2 was also removed from the list due to its price, but it had already a low quality assessment. Among the remaining ones, flat-5 keeps its leading position.

The system discussed above on COVID-19 vaccination is another example where partial aggregation also takes a role. The structure of variables and factors (the attribute tree) displayed in Fig. 3.1 describes which variables are assessed and how

Table 3.2 Assessment of candidates according to the variables for the COVID-19 vaccination priority evaluation [54]

	11	1211	12121	12122	12123	1212	121	12	...	1
	ℂ	ℂ	Assessment			ℂ	ℂ	ℂ		ℂ
$cand_1$	x	x	0.4	0.8	0.0	ℂ(0.4,0.8,0)	x	x		x
$cand_2$	x	x	0.8	0.8	0.0	ℂ(0.8,0.8,0)	x	x		x
$cand_3$	x	x	0.6	0.7	0.0	ℂ(0.6,0.7,0)	x	x		x
$cand_4$	x	x	0.6	0.5	0.2	ℂ(0.6,0.5,0.2)	x	x		x

criteria are going to be combined, building meaningful partial results. Table 3.2 illustrates how this computation is going to be done. In the table we have the assessment of 4 candidates for three of the variables (e.g., 12121 refers to Current health conditions in Fig. 3.1). We have that candidate $cand_1$ has a bad medical history but current conditions have improved. In contrast, candidate $cand_2$ has a medical history that is also bad and currently is neither well. The assessment associated to these three variables (columns 12121, 12122, 12123) will be aggregated to obtain a combined value for Personal medical conditions (column 1212). That is, for the first candidate, we aggregate the values 0.4, 0.8 and 0. We denote in the table the combined result by ℂ(0.4,0.8,0). Similarly, for candidate $cand_2$ we will compute ℂ(0.8,0.8,0), based on the three assessments 0.8, 0.8, and 0.0.

Note that the table is not complete. The complete table would include all other variables and factors. For example, one of the variables missing is: 112 medical personnel directly exposed to COVID-19, and the assessment of this variable would be also in the table. Values associated to factors will be computed from other factors or variables.

For example, we compute the values associated to 1211 age risk factors (which will be obtained as a combination of the associated variables), and later proceed to compute 121 Age and medical conditions. From the outcome associated to factors 121 and 122 we will compute the value associated to 12 Personal COVID-19 risk factors. Finally, combining the values associated to factors 11, 12, and 13 we have the final assessment of each candidate.

To actually implement this we need to select a way to aggregate the values. That is, how to combine them, or, mathematically, which function ℂ we are going to use at each step. Note that at different points of our computation we can use different functions, as it was the case in the example of the flats. Before, we have used the average to combine the criteria about the flat quality (allowing for some trade-offs), and minimum to combine price and quality (so, being strict on both price and quality). In our current example, the personal health conditions may be disjunctive (i.e., priority in one of the three variables about medical conditions, implies priority for the patient), but other factors may require another type of aggregation function.

We discuss in more detail aggregation functions in the next sections.

3.2 Selection of Alternatives: Dominance and Pareto Front

Assessment of alternatives is often associated to alternative selection. In this case, we want to select the ones that have a better assessment. Here, with better, we understand a larger value in the assessment. When we have more than one criteria, some concepts are useful for a good selection of alternatives.

Let us consider a simple case with two criteria. Say, for example, price and quality, each evaluated in the range [0, 1]. Then, the best alternative would be, of course, the one that has a price assessment of one, and a quality assessment of also 1. Unfortunately it is difficult that we find such optimal alternative in reality. Moreover, we would expect that price and quality are contradictory from the point of view of our needs. That is, when the price is better for us, we expect that the quality of the product is, in general, worse. In contrast, the products of better quality, are expected to have a worse price (i.e., higher price).

Let us consider a set of 13 products. We have already assessed them in terms of their quality and their price. We have therefore for each of the 13 product, two values in [0, 1] that correspond to how much they suit our requirements, and how much we are happy with their price. The assessment of the two criteria for each 13 products are given in Table 3.3.

We have also plotted the assessments of these products. They are in Fig. 3.5. Each point represents a different product. The position of each point depends on the degree of satisfaction for quality (x-axis, or abscissa) and the degree of satisfaction for price (y-axis, or ordinate). As we have stated above, the best product would be the one for which both quality and price assessments have a value of 1. So, it would be an object

Table 3.3 Table with 13 products and their criteria assessment in terms of quality and price. Aggregation of the two criteria using: minimum, maximum, average (columns min: minimum, max: maximum, am: arithmetic mean)

Product	Quality	Price	Min	Max	am
p_1	0	0.8	0	0.8	0.4
p_2	0.1	0.75	0.1	0.75	0.425
p_3	0.2	0.6	0.2	0.6	0.4
p_4	0.4	0.55	0.4	0.55	0.475
p_5	0.5	0.5	0.5	0.5	0.5
p_6	0.6	0.2	0.2	0.6	0.4
p_7	0.8	0	0	0.8	0.4
p_8	0.1	0.5	0.1	0.5	0.3
p_9	0.3	0.4	0.3	0.4	0.35
p_{10}	0.5	0.1	0.1	0.5	0.3
p_{11}	0.2	0.3	0.2	0.3	0.25
p_{12}	0.15	0.5	0.15	0.5	0.325
p_{13}	0.05	0.6	0.05	0.6	0.325

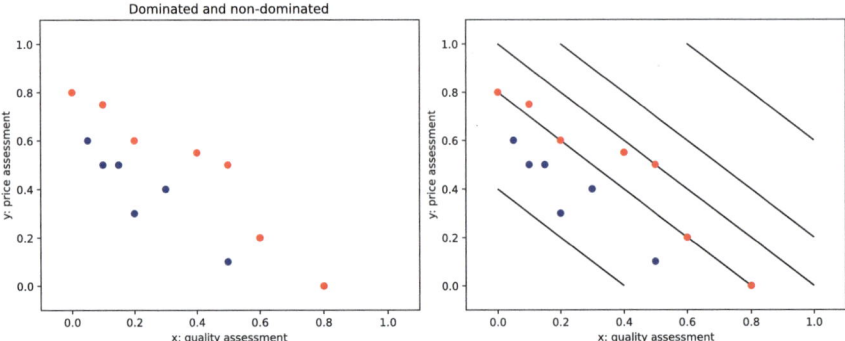

Fig. 3.5 Graphical representation of the criteria assessment of the 13 products (left). Each point represents a product, and in the abscissa (or x-axis) we represent satisfaction of quality, and the ordinate (or y-axis) we represent satisfaction of price. Level curves associated to the average, or arithmetic mean (right)

situated in the high right position of the graph. On the contrary, the worst product would be the one for which both quality and price assessments are zero. This product would be located in the lower left part of the graph.

The graph also allows us to illustrate products that are clearly better than other products. That is, if a product is better in both price and quality than another product, it would be placed in a higher and more to the right position. From the point of view of alternative selection, those products that are known to be worse in both price and quality than another product are of no interest. They are irrelevant. A decision making process would discard them. In Fig. 3.5 we have plotted in blue those irrelevant products, and in red those products that are worth considering by the decision maker.

Dominance is the mathematical concept that formalizes this idea. We say that a product b dominates a product a when for all criteria, the assessment of b is always better than the assessment of a. So, in our case, this corresponds to the following:

b dominates a when
price-assessment$(a) \leq$ price-assessment(b), and
quality-assessment$(a) \leq$ quality-assessment(b).

In a selection process, we are only interested in non-dominated alternatives. That is, the set of alternatives for which there is no other alternative that dominate them. This set of alternatives is known as the Pareto front, the Pareto set, the Pareto frontier, or non dominance set. This set of alternatives are precisely the ones plotted in red in Fig. 3.5. So, the blue ones are the dominated alternatives and the red ones the Pareto front. In the table, for convenience, the products in the Pareto front are the first ones (products p_1–p_7) and the remaining ones are dominated alternatives (products p_8–p_{13}).

Aggregation is a way to select an alternative from the Pareto front. Aggregation functions, as the arithmetic mean, the minimum, or the maximum, are mathe-

3.2 Selection of Alternatives: Dominance and Pareto Front

matical functions that when they combine larger values produce larger results (this mathematical property is called monotonicity). This means that dominated alternatives will be always worse than non-dominated ones. For example, for any aggregation function we will have that product $p_{13} = [0.05, 0.6]$ will be always worse than $p_2 = [0.1, 0.75]$. For example, if we aggregate the two criteria using the minimum we have for p_{13} the value of 0.05, and for p_2 the value 0.1; if we use the maximum we have $p_{13} = 0.6$ and $p_2 = 0.75$; and if we use the average we have $p_{13} = 0.325$ and $p_2 = 0.425$. In Table 3.3 we provide the aggregated values for all the products using the minimum, the maximum and the average.

If we look to the table in detail we will see that the best rated product is always in the Pareto front. This holds for all three aggregation functions: minimum, maximum and average. We also see that the best rated product is different for the three cases. In the case of the minimum we have that the best product is p_5 which has an evaluation of 0.5. In the case of the maximum we have two products with a value of 0.8. They are p_1 and p_7. In the case of the average, it is again p_5.

So, aggregation functions allow us to distinguish the alternatives that are preferable than the others. They will assess among the best alternatives some in the Pareto front. Note that, as in the case of maximum, we may have several with the same assessment. In this case, at least one will be in the Pareto front.

The difference between aggregation functions is which of the alternatives will be rated as the best. Different aggregation functions will produce different orders of the ones in the Pareto front, as illustrated in Table 3.3.

Aggregation combines the different criteria in a single value. This makes that different alternatives are equal after aggregation. Note for example that the average makes indistinguishable a product $p_{101} = [0, 1]$ with another one $p_{110} = [1, 0]$ and $p_5 = [0.5, 0.5]$. All three of them will produce the same overall assessment equal to 0.5. We illustrate in Fig. 3.5 (right) products that would produce the same average with a connected line. Each line in the figure corresponds to a different value, being the one crossing the center of the figure the one leading to 0.5. That is, the one associated to the products p_{110}, p_{101} and p_5 (note that only p_5 is in the figure). These lines are called level curves. In the figure, we have five level curves associated to the outputs 0.2, 0.4, 0.5, 0.6, and 0.8. It can be seen that the one associated to output 0.4 crosses the products p_1, p_3, p_6, and p_7.

Changing the aggregation function implies a modification of the curves, and the alternatives distinguished as the best. In any case, recall that we would prefer the elements that are nearer to the top right position of the figure. To make this idea clearer, we provide in Fig. 3.6 the level curves associated to the minimum (left) and the maximum (right). The same level curves with outputs 0.2, 0.4, 0.5, 0.6, and 0.8 are provided. We can see clearly that in the case of minimum the best product is the one associated to 0.5 (i.e., product p_5) and that in the case of maximum we have two products with output 0.8 (which correspond to products p_1 and p_7). The figures show that we always select as the best a product that is in the Pareto front (a red product) and that the regions change when the aggregation changes.

Exercise 3.2 Answer the following questions:

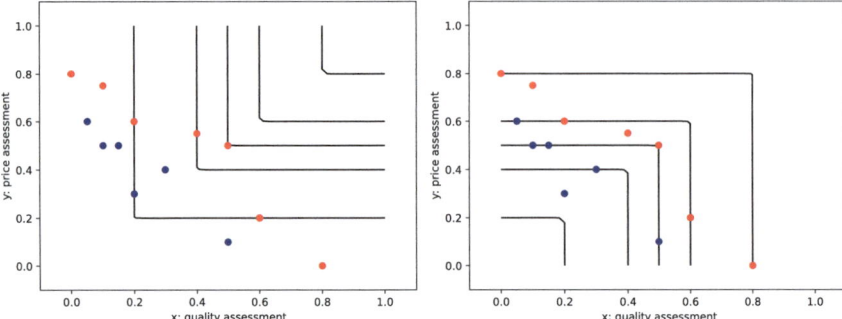

Fig. 3.6 Products to be selected according to price and quality, and level curves associated to two aggregation function: the minimum (left) and the maximum (right)

- 1. What is the relationship between contradictory criteria and dominance?
- 2. What is the relationship between Pareto front and dominance?
- 3. What is the relationship between Pareto front and aggregation?

Exercise 3.3 What is the relationship between the Pareto front and the monotonicity condition for aggregation functions?

Exercise 3.4 We want to buy a laptop. We have preferences on brands and processors, and, of course, prices. So, only one criteria is numerical. Is still applicable the concept of Pareto front when criteria are not numerical? Is it applicable in this problem? Why?

3.3 Aggregation

There are different ways to combine partial assessments. We have seen three examples above that are quite representative of the alternative options we have. One was the average, that aggregates the values in a way that we have some trade-off between the different criteria. Then, the minimum that can be understood as conjunction of criteria, from a logical point of view. Finally, the maximum that can be understood as disjunction of criteria, from a logical point of view. We have also seen that these different ways of combining the assessments correspond to different orders for the alternatives in the Pareto front.

In this section we discuss the main differences on aggregation functions that are relevant in decision making, for both assessment and selection. Differences are associated to the following properties.

- Importance among criteria.
- Compensation between criteria.
- Mandatory criteria.
- Interactions among criteria.

3.3 Aggregation

We will discuss each of them in the next sections.

3.3.1 Importance Among Criteria

> To have or not to have a chimney, that is the question.

In any decision making process involving different criteria we find that not all of them are equally relevant. Consider for example security versus comfort when we are planning to buy a car, or size vs. location when we are planning to buy an apartment. Some aggregation functions permit to weight different criteria differently.

The weighted mean is an example of such aggregation functions. Given n criteria we need to assign a weight to each of them corresponding to their relative importance. Weights typically add to one. For example, let us consider that security is twice as important as comfort. Therefore, we assign a weight of 2/3 to security and 1/3 to comfort (if only these two criteria are of relevance and considered in the aggregation). Naturally, the weighted mean when all criteria have the same weight corresponds to the average (i.e., the arithmetic mean). I.e., when all weights are $1/n$.

Including weights cause changes in the ordering of the alternatives. As we have discussed, a preferred one will be still a non-dominated alternative and, therefore, a member of the Pareto front. Nevertheless, we may have a larger assessment for one that is not the one we had for the arithmetic mean. Note that in the arithmetic mean, products p_{110}, p_{101}, and p_5 had the same assessment (equal to 0.5), but this will not be the case if the two criteria weight differently. Depending on which is preferred we will select p_{110} or p_{101}. The effects of the weights can be displayed in the level curves. Figure 3.7 show the level curves of different weighted means. One case (left, top) corresponds to giving to variable quality (abscissa, x) a weight of 0.3 and to variable price (ordinate, y) a weight of 0.7. The second one (right, top) corresponds to giving the variable quality a weight of 0.4 and to variable price a weight of 0.6. Then, we consider weights for quality equal to 0.7 and price equal to 0.3 (left, bottom) and quality equal to 0.6 and price to 0.4 (right, bottom). It can be seen that the level curves have different slopes, and that these slopes are also different to the slope of the arithmetic mean shown in Fig. 3.5 (right). Recall that the arithmetic mean for two criteria corresponds to weights equal to 0.5. The figures also show which would be the best ranked product for each of the four pairs of weights.

3.3.2 Compensation Between Criteria

> I am happy enough with this flat.

Compensation appears when badly rated criteria do not matter when other ones are satisfied. Say, that one extremely good criteria makes us to decide to buy a car. In

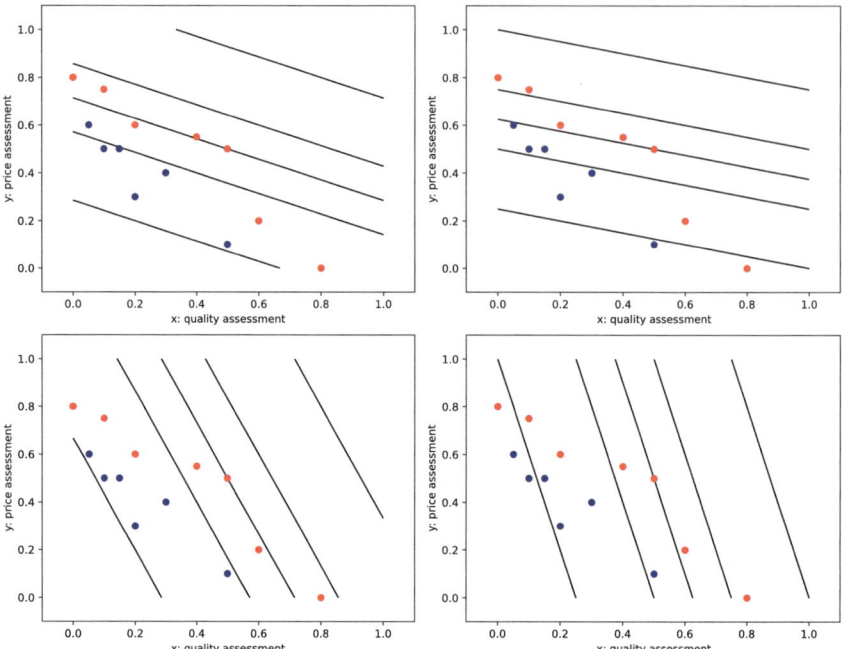

Fig. 3.7 Graphical representation of the level curves for the weighted mean with the weights quality: 0.3 and price: 0.7 (left, top), quality: 0.4 and price: 0.6 (right, top), quality: 0.7 and price: 0.3 (left, bottom), and quality: 0.6 and price: 0.4 (right, bottom)

another decision making process, two criteria being satisfied are enough for selecting a flat. On the contrary, we may have no compensation at all when we require all the criteria fully satisfied.

The degree of compensation is associated to the degree of conjunction and disjunction of the criteria. When we require **all** the criteria to hold, then, we mean that we want e.g. price **and** quality to be both good. So, we speak of a high conjunction level or andness degree. When we only need **any** of the criteria to hold, to select an alternative, then, an alternative with e.g. good price **or** good quality can be selected. So, we speak of a high disjunction level or orness level.

We have already seen in Sect. 3.1.4 the use of maximum and minimum in aggregation. Maximum is a model for disjunction (or) and minimum is a model for conjunction (and). Then, orness is mathematically defined as the similarity to the maximum, and andness is defined as the similarity to the minimum. Moreover, andness and orness are defined so that

$$orness = 1 - andness.$$

Then, of course, minimum has orness equal to one, and orness equal to zero. In contrast, maximum has andness equal to zero, and orness equal to one. The arithmetic mean has an andness and orness equal to 0.5. The weighted mean has also and andness

3.3 Aggregation

and orness level equal to 0.5. This is so because both allow for some compensation but not as much as the maximum.

Besides of these three examples already seen, there are other aggregation and means with other andness degrees. In fact, if we select an arbitrary andness degree between 0 and 1 we can find an appropriate aggregation function with such degree. This is called andness-directedness. Examples of aggregation functions with other compensation degrees are given below.

- Geometric mean. This function defined for two criteria as $GM(a,b) = \sqrt{a \cdot b}$ is more conjunctive than the arithmetic mean. So, its andness degree is larger and its orness degree is smaller. There is also the weighted version (with weights w_1 and w_2) of the geometric mean: $GM(a,b) = a^{w_1} \cdot b^{w_2}$. Its andness is equal to 2/3.
- Harmonic mean. This function is still more conjunctive than the geometric mean. Its andness is equal to $ln(16) - 2 = 0.77$.
- Power mean. This function depends on a parameter (we use r below) that can be used to set the required level of andness. Its weighted version with weights w_1 and w_2 corresponds to
$$WPM(a,b) = (w_1 a^r + w_2 b^r)^{1/r}.$$

Here WPM stands for weighted power mean. By setting the parameter r appropriately, we can tune the andness to be any number we desire between zero and one. This means that this is an andness-directed aggregation function. Note that for $r = 1$, this is just the arithmetic mean and, thus, orness = andness = 0.5. For $r = -\infty$ it tends to the minimum (i.e., andness=1) and for $r = \infty$ it tends to the maximum (i.e., andness=0).

- Ordered Weighted Aggregation operator (OWA). This function first orders the values and then applies a weighted mean to them. Formally, it is defined as a linear combination of order statistics. This is another example of a function that we can use for andness-directedness. For any andness level we can find proper parameters so that the function has the selected andness. In the case of simply two inputs, this function corresponds to the following.

$$OWA_\alpha(x_1, x_2) = \alpha min(x_1, x_2) + (1 - \alpha) max(x_1, x_2).$$

In this definition, α is the andness level.

We illustrate in Fig. 3.8 the level curves of the geometric mean, and the OWA operator with andness equal to 0.3. It can be observed that the level curves have different shapes in the two graphics as the geometric mean has an andness of 2/3 so larger than 0.5, and the OWA has an andness smaller than 0.5. Compare with the level curves of the arithmetic mean (andness equal to 0.5) which we have seen in Fig. 3.5 (right).

Dujmović [53] (see Chap. 15) classifies compensation level in five basic ranges. They are built based on the verbalization of how many criteria need to be fulfilled in our decision making problem.

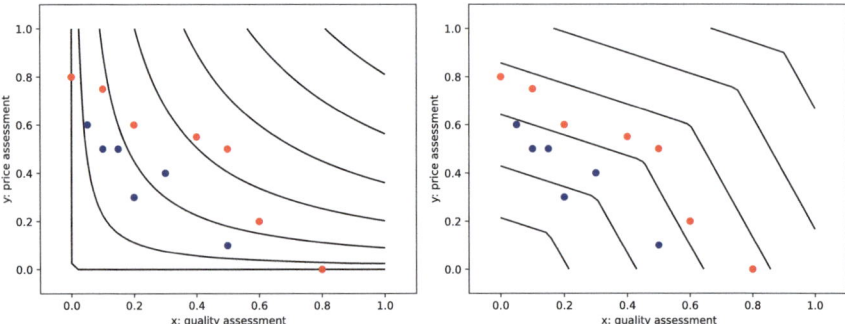

Fig. 3.8 Graphical representation of the level curves for the geometric mean (left) and for the OWA with andness level equal to 0.3 (right)

- Must have all. This is a hard conjunctive function, with $\alpha \geq 0.75$.
- Nice to have most. This is a soft conjunctive function, with α between 0.5 and 0.75
- Nice to have. This corresponds to a soft neutral function, with $\alpha = 0.5$, as in the case of average.
- Nice to have some. This corresponds to a soft disjunctive function, with α between 0.25 and 0.5
- Enough to have any. This corresponds to a hard disjunctive function, with α smaller than 0.25.

For example, the case of a patient that is classified as unstable solely based on a single criteria being unstable corresponds to a hard disjunctive function.

3.3.3 Mandatory Requirements

I cannot afford this flat.
I love this garden with this cherry tree. I buy this flat.

In a way independent of the level of andness and orness, we may have criteria that are mandatory, and, thus, they need to hold whenever we have an assessment equal to zero. That is, if a mandatory criteria has a zero degree, even in the case of all the other criteria having high assessments, we cannot evaluate that alternative as good. We can model this situation with appropriate aggregation functions. In mathematics, such functions are said to have annihilators. Properly speaking, these functions have the annihilator zero. When the value is zero, the output of the function is zero.

In fact, we have already seen examples of such functions. The minimum, the geometric mean, and the harmonic mean behave in this way. Any zero in one single input produces a zero in the output, independently of any other input. E.g, minimum between zero and one is zero, the same for the geometric mean and the harmonic mean. Note also that even in the case of having 10 criteria, and having 9 of them evaluated as 1, a single criteria with 0 produces an output equal to zero.

Mandatory requirements and annihilators are fundamental in decision making. Observe that price is an example of a mandatory requirement. If we cannot pay the product, it does not matter how good are all the other qualities, we will not be able to have a good rating of the product because we cannot afford it.

The same applies for those cases in which one of the criteria is assessed to one, and then we expect the output to be one. In this case we need an aggregation function that has the property of annihilator one. So, any input value equal to one produces an output equal to one independently of the other values. We have this behavior if we are using the maximum, as we have already seen above.

Mandatory requirements and compensation are often related. When there are mandatory requirements, we usually have low compensation degree. Similarly, if we have a very low compensation degree (e.g. an andness larger than 0.75) the criteria are usually mandatory and we have zero as annihilator. In the previous section, with the term hard conjunctive function we mean a function that has very low compensation ($\alpha > 0.75$) and has annihilator zero. In contrast, with the term hard disjunctive function we mean a function that has very large compensation ($\alpha < 0.25$) and has annihilator one.

For a technical discussion on annihilators in relation to aggregation see e.g., Mas et al. [106, 161].

3.3.4 Interactions Among Criteria

> It's always the same: the closer you are to the train station, the better the shops and restaurants.

In an ideal world, when we build a decision support system, we would select a minimum number of independent variables and criteria. E.g., age and eye color, or age and fever. That is, each of them accounting for a different aspect of the alternatives. Then, we aggregate all these criteria taking into account their importance weights and our requirement on the compensation degree between them.

In practical problems, criteria are not independent. E.g., income salary, size of the flat, and type of car, or age and weight. We have aspects that are evaluated at the same time by several of the criteria. Then, if we do not take this fact into account we may be over representing these aspects that appear somehow implicit in several criteria.

There are several ways of avoiding or trying to minimize this fact.

- Criteria based on multiple variables. In the examples above we have defined criteria that depend on a single variable. Recall the case of unstable for fever, and the same for pulse. We can do the same using multiple variables. E.g., we can define the criteria overweight that uses age and weight, or even age, height, and weight.

- Selection of weights. A proper selection of weights can help minimizing the interactions and avoiding over representation of some characteristics. This is the case, for example, when we are using a weighted mean. We can take special care on defining its weights for correlated variables. Consider the case of a criteria based on a medical analysis to assess a characteristic and assume we use a weight of 0.4. Then, if instead of one analysis we have two, but both of them assess the same characteristic, we will use a weight equal to 0.2 for each. Analogously, if there are four analyses, each will have a weight of 0.1. We are just splitting the same weight for as many analysis or criteria we have to evaluate the same characteristic of the patient.
- Grouping of variables. Partial aggregation of similar criteria help reducing the effect of interactions between attributes. For example, in the attribute tree associated to COVID-19 represented in Fig. 3.1 we have that two very much related variables Current health conditions (12121) and Patient medical history (12123) and they are grouped together with Race and ethnicity factors (12123) to build the variable (and criteria) Personal medical conditions (1212). This criteria is then combined with Age risk factors (1211) and so on. In our previous example, we could also combine first the criteria associated to the two (or four) analysis, and then use its aggregated value at another decision level.
- Aggregation functions. There are aggregation functions that allow us to accommodate criteria that are not independent. This is the case of fuzzy integrals (as e.g. Choquet and Sugeno integrals). In a way, they are similar to weighted means but with special types of weights so that the interactions can be properly represented and dealt with.

3.3.5 Summary

We conclude this section listing the necessary properties of aggregation functions in the context of building decision support systems. We also explain how such system would be built in ideal conditions.

Necessary Properties of Aggregation Functions

Aggregation functions play a fundamental role in decision support systems. We have discussed how they are used. Following a previous work of ours [55–57] we summarize here their main properties, which have already appeared above.

- P1. Semantic identity. Aggregation in decision support systems is used for combining criteria which are built from variables. Therefore, each input has a well defined semantic (meaning) and, therefore, the aggregation process that the aggregation function performs needs to be seen as a logic process. That is, a logic expression that is being evaluated.

3.3 Aggregation

- P2. Andness/orness-directedness. Conjunction and disjunction degrees are basic components of the decision process, and, thus, we need to select aggregation functions based on them. When we consider that andness is high, and some criteria are conjunctive, we need to select an aggregation function that is consistent with this requirement.
- P3. Full range from drastic conjunction and drastic disjunction. Drastic conjunction and disjunction are the more extreme cases of aggregation functions. In drastic conjunction when any criteria is not fully satisfied, the output of the aggregation is zero. Different applications need different degrees of andness and orness, and we need to use appropriate functions to accommodate them. From a mathematical point of view, the minimum has an andness of one, but there are operators more conjunctive than the minimum. They are called t-norms (we have mentioned them in Sect. 2.2.7). Similarly, while the maximum has an andness equal to zero, there are more disjunctive operators than maximum. They are called t-conorms (they are also mentioned in Sect. 2.2.7). Then, selection of appropriate t-norms and t-conorms can also be based on the andness degree. They are andness-directed t-norms [174] and t-conorms.
- P4. Selectable idempotency. Idempotency means that if all assessments for all criteria agree, the output of the function should also be this very value. Say, if all agree on an assessment of 0.8, then the output should also be 0.8. Mathematically speaking $\mathbb{C}(0.8, 0.8, \ldots, 0.8) = 0.8$. This is desirable in some applications but not always. We may consider reducing the output if no criteria is fully satisfied and, thus, $\mathbb{C}(0.8, 0.8, \ldots, 0.8) < 0.8$. Conjunctive functions (as the product) usually proceed in this way. Alternatively, we may consider increasing the output. If we consider that if all criteria are relatively well evaluated, the overall assessment should be really good. That is, $\mathbb{C}(0.8, 0.8, \ldots, 0.8) > 0.8$. This is the usual case of disjunctive functions.
- P5. Selectable annihilators. As we have discussed above, applications may require annihilators. That is, annihilator zero if criteria are mandatory, and annihilator one if one criteria may require the overall assessment to be one.
- P6. Adjustable andness/orness with respect to annihilators. Large andness degree usually implies annihilator zero. Similar with orness degree and annihilator one. The point in which a certain andness degree implies annihilators needs to be adjustable.
- P7. Importance weights. Aggregation functions need to be parametric to accommodate with different criteria with different importance. This is a key property. The importance of each criteria needs to be reflected in the output of the function. This requirement is in connection with the fact that each input has its own meaning or semantics (property P1).
- P8. Independence between importance and compensation degree. Both importance and andness/orness degrees are, in general, needed to implement decision support systems. For simplicity, users should be able to supply them independently, and then use a single aggregation function that takes both into account.
- P9. Simple soft computing propositional calculus. According to P1, aggregation corresponds to evaluation of logic expressions. To make decision engineering

simple, it is preferable to have a small number of aggregation functions that can deal with all the requirements. GCD [52, 53] is an example of an integrated framework that allows us to implement all these requirements. Approaches [174] based on OWA and WOWA [171, 172] are another example.
- P10. Simplicity, specifiability, and readability. Aggregation functions need to be simple, and with parameters easy to specify.

An Ideal Implementation

In an ideal process, the construction of a decision support system would consist on identifying the set of variables relevant for the assessment of the alternatives. In complex problems, the number of variables may be large, and we will need to build a structure with the variables. Say, an attribute tree as the one in Fig. 3.1.

The next step is to define the criteria by means of utility functions or membership functions (recall Figs. 3.2 and 3.3). Usually, we will have a criteria associated to each variable, and each criteria will have the associated function.

We also need to select the aggregation function that combines the assessments for the criteria we have defined. We need to select the appropriate function as well as its parameters. For this, following [55] we need to consider the following aspects of the function:

- conjunctive/disjunctive character,
- presence/absence of annihilators,
- presence/absence of idempotency,
- desired andness α,
- desired importance weights W.

If we have an attribute tree, or, in general, a structure with the variables and the criteria, we may need to select multiple aggregation functions, one for each level of the attribute tree (except for the basic criteria), each with appropriate parameters. Selection of the appropriate aggregation function at each level should be done based on the problem requirements.

3.4 Other Tools for Decision Support Systems

There are alternative ways in the literature for assessment and selection. For example, voting strategies can be seen as an alternative to aggregation. The two approaches are strongly connected. For example, we can consider a number of votes for each criteria and assessment, and then select the alternative that has more votes. The lower back pain diagnosis system [102] mentioned in Sect. 2.2.3 use a voting system in which the different diagnoses compete and the one with more votes is the one selected. When rules apply, they provide a number of votes to a possible diagnosis, and the

3.4 Other Tools for Decision Support Systems

number of votes depends on the term used to quantify the rule. For example, the rule already presented above

If observation shows patient age is between 30 and 40, then recommend diagnosis "Chronic Disc Degenerative" with a certainty level of "likely"

provides one vote to "Chronic Disc Degenerative" because they use the certainty level "likely". A certainty level "normal" provides zero votes.

There is also extensive literature on decision support systems based on preferences and pairwise comparison of alternatives. In short, some of these methods elicit expert knowledge by means of pairwise comparison of known alternatives, and then build the decision support system from these pairwise comparison. For example, we can build utility functions and select aggregation functions that are (partially) consistent from expert supplied information. These systems can then be applied to other yet unseen alternatives. An example would be to ask an expert to compare pairs of flats (or to ask about people for positions, computer systems, etc.), and, then, based on their advice find e.g. location preferences (or academic degree preferences).

In fact, from a historical perspective, it was John von Neumann and Oskar Morgenstern [185] who developed expected utility theory as a mathematical model for decision based on a definition of rational decisions. These decisions are pairwise comparisons, in the following sense: do you prefer this one or that one? They provide a formal definition of what a "rational decision" is. Then, when decisions are rational (in their sense), it was proven mathematically that it is possible to find utility functions that make the decision system to behave rationally. So, in their theory, rational decisions (pairwise comparisons) come first, and utility functions and aggregation come later. They are implicit in the way decisions are made. The discussion we have provided in this chapter is about starting from the utility and aggregation functions, with the goal of directly modeling the decision making process.

Exercise 3.5 Investigate the concept of expected utility.

Let us consider again "rational decisions". This means that sets of decisions cannot be arbitrary, but there are some constraints if they are rational. They need to satisfy a set of mathematical properties or axioms. One of these properties is called transitivity. Let us consider an agent that prefers ice-creams to muffins, and prefers muffins to cookies. Then, the only rational preference between ice-creams and cookies is to really prefer ice-creams to cookies. So, in other words, if the agent prefers cookies to ice-creams, then this agent is not rational. Utility theory is not for these type of non-rational agents.

Exercise 3.6 If we express our opinion on each criteria in terms of preferences, then aggregation of preferences is relevant. Investigate Arrow's impossibility theorem for aggregation of preference relations.

Experimental work has shown that original axioms for rational decisions are not always followed by people. Allais and Ellsberg paradoxes are examples of such

> Probabilities are set functions that are additive (see Figure 2.15). Because of that, it is easy to prove that for disjoint sets A, B, and C if we have
>
> $$P(A) < P(B)$$
>
> then, it is also true
> $$P(A \cup C) < P(B \cup C).$$
>
> Non-additive measures, also called fuzzy measures, monotonic games, and capacities are set functions that are not necessarily additive and, then, it is possible to have
>
> $$P(A) < P(B)$$
>
> but on the contrary have
>
> $$P(A \cup C) > P(B \cup C).$$
>
> This characteristic is exploited in conjunction with the Choquet and Sugeno integrals to deal with interactions. This characteristic also allows us to define Choquet expected utility theory that solves Allais and Ellsberg paradoxes.

Fig. 3.9 Choquet and Sugeno integrals, and non-additive measures

situations. This means that the original mathematical models cannot be used for modeling such human decisions, and this led to new research and to alternative approaches. Choquet expected utility is one of such alternatives. It is based on the Choquet integral we have already mentioned above, and that is useful when we have interactions between variables. In a very informal way, dealing with interactions we can solve some of these paradoxes. See for additional details Fig. 3.9.

3.5 Bibliography

Our description of decision support systems follows the common approach in multi-criteria decision making. Details of Logic Scoring of Preference (LSP) can be found in Dujmović's books [52, 53]. Main properties of aggregation functions and discussion on the selection of an appropriate function can be found in our works [55–57]. A mathematically oriented description of aggregation functions as well as of their properties can be found in our books [176–178].

Expected utility and Choquet expected utility, as well as a description of the Allais and Ellsberg paradoxes, can be found in the excellent book on decision under uncertainty by Gilboa [73]. Game theory has not been discussed in this book (we only mentioned monotonic games), but it is very relevant in relation to decision making. We can distinguish between cooperative and non-cooperative game theory. Cooperative game theory studies games (informally, set functions that model coalitions payoffs), which are related to non-additive measures and probabilities. So, topics briefly mentioned in this chapter. Non-cooperative game theory is related to games (with adversary) and search, topics we have discussed in Sect. 2.1. The textbook by Peters [130] provides an introduction to this field.

Chapter 4
Machine Learning at Work

Abstract Machine learning is the field that has brought AI to its success in the last years. Large language models and generative models, which are based on machine learning, have a large number of users. In this chapter we explain how machine learning models are built. We begin with simple models and then move into neural networks and deep learning that are currently the most successful ones. To illustrate that these are not the only existing models we also explain decision trees. They are a completely different type of model that are also effective in some applications. Then, we explain language models in terms of neural networks. The chapter finishes reviewing a few concepts connected with machine learning. We include concepts as outliers, missing data, bias, explainability, correlation, and causation.

TIMBER! TIMBER!

Groucho Marx, Go West, 1940.

Machine learning, and in fact also statistics, is about taking advantage of data in order to make decisions. There is a big distinction between the AI tools described in Chap. 3 and the ones we discuss here. In the previous chapter, we focus on building intelligent systems by means of codifying the experience and knowledge of people already making decisions in the field. For example, we want to reproduce the reasoning of a doctor assessing a patient, or we want to provide a fair ranking of patients for intervention based on expert knowledge about their medical situation and risks.

In contrast machine learning focuses on recorded data, and uses these recorded data to extract the relevant information needed for supporting a decision process. For example, a hospital has the historical data about the patients and the length of their stay. Then, when a new patient arrives to the reception, we can provide an estimate, as accurate as possible, of the length of stay of this new patient. This estimation is based on this historical data.

Machine learning precisely provides tools for building such predictive models. That is, use existing historical data to make a good prediction. Something similar to the example we have seen in the introduction. Given an age, predict the salary of a person as accurately as possible, based on the data already available. This data used to build (or train) a model is called training data.

There are two main types of prediction models. They are classified according to the type of variable to predict.

- Models for classification. This is about assigning a category or a class given some information about a person or a situation. For example, accept or not a loan, provide or not access to a social welfare program. In these examples, the number of categories can be more than one. For example, in hospital emergency departments some countries have 5 triage levels, other 4 levels. For a diagnosis system, several diagnosis may be possible. So, this corresponds to predicting a categorical or Boolean variable.
- Models for regression. This is about predicting a numerical variable given some information about a person or situation. For example, predict the number of days in the hospital, estimate the income of someone, predict the glucose level of a person, etc.

When such models are built from data, we call them data-driven models. It is the data that leads the construction of the model. In this case, our first concerns are the quality of the data, and the effectiveness of the model we build from these data.

When building a data-driven model, data is assumed to contain all relevant information. Then, we apply an inductive process to extract a predictive model from the data. Nowadays, the amount of data in most environments is extremely large, and, it is expected that this data is useful and enough for extracting the models we need to automatize, or at least support, decisions. Nevertheless, it is important to underline that existing data may not be enough. Relevant data for the models may be missing. We will discuss this problem in Sect. 4.6.2.

4.1 An Example of a Data Set

Data, in its simplest form, has a structure similar to the one we have seen in Table 1.1. The table is reproduced here as Table 4.1.

The data consist on the information supplied by 10 individuals concerning their age and income. Each row corresponds to a person, and we have for each person the age and the income. We have included an identifier for each person. Let us consider that we want to predict the income for some people for whom we know the age. So, we build a data-driven model from this data.

In real data sets, we usually have much more data than the ten cases displayed in the table. We may have a database of hundreds, thousands or millions of individuals (each represented in a different row in the table), and, instead of the two variables (characteristics or features) age and income, we may have tens of variables. In fact, hundreds, or even thousands of them may be available for analysis.

In order to make the example a bit richer, we expand the example considering four variables. More particularly, in addition to age and income, we consider also whether the individual is a woman, and whether the individual is national (both variables are

4.1 An Example of a Data Set

Table 4.1 A data set consisting of age and income for 10 people (artificial data)

Interview	Age	Income
i_1	24	1000
i_2	40	6000
i_3	30	2000
i_4	50	2000
i_5	40	3000
i_6	55	10000
i_7	33	2000
i_8	37	2000
i_9	26	1000
i_{10}	42	4000

binary ones). The data is artificial and for illustrative purposes only. A survey would be able to provide real data for the same variables in a real context. The data we are considering are listed in Table 4.2. Each row represents a person, and we have 40 rows associated to 40 people. The first 10 pople of the new table corresponds to the one in Table 4.1.

In machine learning, in order to be able to find models, we need to express the data in a mathematical way. We will use Y to represent the values of the variable we want to predict. So, in our example this is income. So, in Table 4.1, Y represents all the values in the column income. That is, Y represents the 10 values $Y = (1000, 6000, \ldots)$. If we focus on Table 4.2, then Y represents the 40 values in the column income. Then, we use X to represent the remaining information in the database. In general, X is a matrix of (usually) numbers with as many rows as people in the database and as many columns as variables we need to consider in our model as inputs. That is, variables that represent known information about the people. In the case of Table 4.2, we have a matrix with 40 rows and 3 columns. For Table 4.1 we have 10 rows and only 1 column.

In this data set, we have two variables that are numerical, and two that are binary. In other data sets we may have other types of variables, and even the structure of the data set can be completely different. Consider the case of sets of documents (so, texts), sets of images (e.g., photographs but also MRI), temporal data (as electricity consumption from households), videos, and the problem of classifying them as relevant or irrelevant for a given predefined task. For example, does the image suggest a tumor? What will be the consumption of this household tomorrow at 12:00? Please, complete the photograph filling the missing regions (i.e., predict the pixels of missing regions)? Also, consider the case of social networks and the goal of identifying people for targeted advertisements. Such data is commonly known as noSQL databases (for not only SQL), as an SQL database is one in which data is represented by rows (of individuals or objects) described in terms of a set of columns or variables, like in a spreadsheet. The approaches we explain in this chapter are regularly applied to these other types of data as well.

Table 4.2 Age, woman?, national?, and income for 40 people (artificial data)

Interview	Age	Woman	National	Income
i_1	24	Yes	Yes	1000
i_2	40	Yes	Yes	6000
i_3	30	Yes	Yes	2000
i_4	50	Yes	Yes	2000
i_5	40	Yes	Yes	3000
i_6	55	Yes	Yes	10000
i_7	33	Yes	Yes	2000
i_8	37	Yes	Yes	2000
i_9	26	Yes	Yes	1000
i_{10}	42	Yes	Yes	4000
i_{11}	22	No	Yes	1500
i_{12}	46	No	Yes	6700
i_{13}	32	No	Yes	4000
i_{14}	51	No	Yes	3000
i_{15}	49	No	Yes	4000
i_{16}	51	No	Yes	4000
i_{17}	31	No	Yes	2400
i_{18}	32	No	Yes	2400
i_{19}	24	No	Yes	2100
i_{20}	40	No	Yes	3700
i_{21}	23	Yes	No	900
i_{22}	41	Yes	No	5500
i_{23}	28	Yes	No	1900
i_{24}	51	Yes	No	2800
i_{25}	39	Yes	No	2950
i_{26}	56	Yes	No	7000
i_{27}	31	Yes	No	1800
i_{28}	38	Yes	No	2000
i_{29}	27	Yes	No	1050
i_{30}	43	Yes	No	3900
i_{31}	21	No	No	1500
i_{32}	47	No	No	6800
i_{33}	33	No	No	3900
i_{34}	52	No	No	3000
i_{35}	51	No	No	2000
i_{36}	51	No	No	1900
i_{37}	30	No	No	2250
i_{38}	33	No	No	2410
i_{39}	26	No	No	2110
i_{40}	41	No	No	2300

Neural networks and deep learning models, that we describe later, can be applied to such data as well. In particular, as we discuss briefly in Sect. 4.5, they are the basis of large language models (i.e., text processing).

4.2 Different and Competing Types of Data-Driven Models

As we have stated before (e.g., in Chap. 1), a model is an abstraction or a simplification. We use them here to establish a relationship between variables. It is important to underline that, in general, there is not such thing as *the correct model*. Because of that, for any particular application, we may need to consider alternative models. Researchers conceive, develop, and use different models based on different assumptions. There are assumptions on e.g. the data we have, and on the type of relationship there is (or is thought to be) between the variables. As models are simplifications, we can decide what to ignore about the data (e.g., ignore that the salary depends on whether the person is a woman, or whether is a national). Then, the models will be built following these assumptions (this is known as bias and will be discussed later).

Models are expressed formally. There are different approaches to define them. For example, we find statistical models, logical models, algorithmic models, and differential equations-based models. In this chapter, we focus on a few models. They are mainly polynomials, neural networks, and decision trees.

We have already seen in Sect. 1.1 two models for the same data. These two different models for the data in Table 4.1 are:

- income = $-4524.2 + 207.5 \cdot$ age.
- income = $127.59 + 50.44 \cdot$ age.

We want to underline here that these two models are both linear models (both base their prediction on a straight line) and are built (extracted or learned) from the data. Linear models mean, for this example, that when someone gets one year older, the prediction increases always the same independently of the age. I.e., the salary increase from 20 to 21 years is the same to the salary increase from 50 to 51. This increase is 207.5 euros for the first model and 50.44 for the second one. That models depend on data naturally mean that different data sets would produce different models, even if the type of model (its structure) is the same.

The first model above corresponds to a standard linear model, while the second one is a robust regression model. We have discussed them briefly in Chap. 1. The main difference between the two models is the influence that a rich person in the database may have on the linear model. In the second model, the influence of such people is reduced because, in a way, we are assuming that a very rich person is an uncommon case, and, thus, the particular income should not be reflected in the general trend of incomes with respect to ages. We can reformulate this explanation in a different way. We can assume that the information of any individual has the same relevance or importance when building a model. This is the case of the first equation. In contrast,

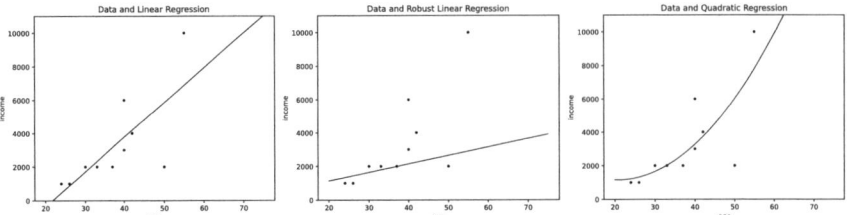

Fig. 4.1 The same data, three different data-driven regression models. Linear regression (left), robust linear regression (center), and quadratic regression (right)

in the second case, we are assuming that the data of some individuals may be more relevant than others for some reason. In particular, we consider that the people with *unusual or peculiar behaviors* are less relevant than the others. Here, we do not want to go into the details of what it means to be an individual with *unusual or peculiar behavior*, but, in our example, it mainly means someone that is significantly richer (i.e., larger income) than the others. In a way, we are inflicting some bias into the model (and in the prediction) when we are selecting the second approach. Note that, for the same reason, we are also inflicting some bias when we are selecting the first approach. We will discuss bias again in Sect. 4.6.4, in the context of model selection.

There are other assumptions implicit in these models. As we have said, in both types of models we are assuming that the relationship between age and income is linear. We are using a simple straight line to express how income changes when age changes. As we have explained above, when we use a linear relationship, a straight line, we implicitly state that if we get one year older our income will increase with a certain quantity independently of our current age. Of course, we can think that this is not the case and that people may have, in average, different increases at different ages. If we think so, the selection of this type of linear model is wrong. We should use something else. For example, we can use a polynomial of second degree to build our model. That is, we will use a non-straight line but a quadratic curve, a parabola. We plot a model of this form in Fig. 4.1 (left). In the same figure we include the other two models already discussed: standard linear regression (left) and robust regression (center). It is important to note that all three data-driven models have been built using the same data: the one in Table 4.2 and represented by dots in the figure. So, all three are simplifications or approximations of our real data in Table 4.2.

The mathematical expression of this non-linear model, properly, a quadratic model is as follows.

- income = $3530.13 - 230.87 \cdot \text{age} + 5.61 \cdot \text{age}^2$

Other models can be built as well. We will see some of them later. The three models we have considered are built using the small data set in Table 4.1 which has only two variables. One that is the one that we consider as input (age) and the other that we consider as the one to be predicted (income). Let us consider now the larger data set in Table 4.2 in which we have four variables. Let us consider building a model

4.3 How a Data Driven Model Is Built

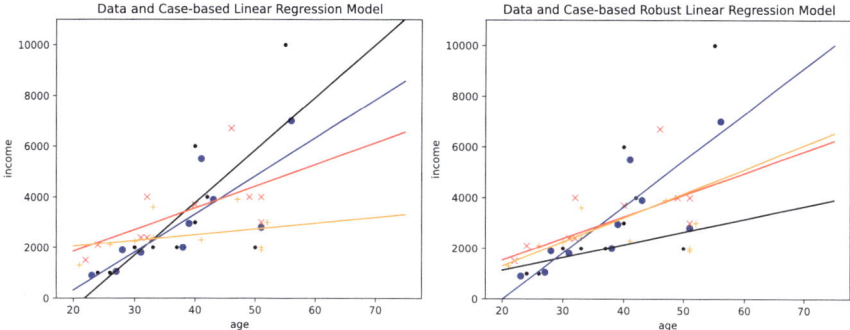

Fig. 4.2 The data in Table 4.2 and models based on four linear regression lines (one for each of the four combinations of the other variables). Linear regression (left), robust regression with Huber regressor (center) and with Ransac regressor (right)

for this data set. We consider three variables as input (age, woman, and national) and one as the variable to be predicted (income).

We provide an example of a model for this data set as well. Among all possible types of models, we consider the following one: we build four linear models, one for each combination for the pair (woman, national). That is, we have a straight line to model the relationship between age and income for the case that we know that the person is a woman and national, another for the case of a person that is not a woman but national, a third one for a woman that is not a national, and a fourth one for a person that is neither a woman nor a national. Figure 4.2 represents all data available as well as two models extracted from the data. One is based on standard regression (left) and the other on robust regression (right). As models are made by these four cases, the figures show four regression lines in the figure. The four data and the regression lines appear in four different colors to distinguish the four different cases. They are, black: (woman = yes, national = yes), blue: (woman = yes, national = no), red: (woman = no, national = yes), orange: (woman = no, national = no).

4.3 How a Data Driven Model Is Built

First we need a data set, which is called training data in machine learning literature. This corresponds to our Tables 4.1 and 4.2. Then, given this data set, a data-driven model is built adapting a generic type of model into one that fits the particular data available. This process is known as learning in machine learning and model fitting in statistics and statistical learning. We will illustrate this with the linear regression model because it is one of the simplest ones.

A linear model to predict income given age has this form:

- income = $\beta_0 + \beta_1 \cdot$ age

Here, β_0 and β_1 are two parameters that we need to set to actual numbers. In our first example we set β_0 to -4524.2 and we set β_1 to 207.5. The term *age* corresponds to the information we already know about the person, and *income* is what we are planning to estimate. Naturally, the parameters define the straight line. Then, for a given data set, we find the parameters β_0 and β_1 that set the line in the best possible position of the graph.

In order to know how well placed is a particular model (i.e., a particular straight line), we compute a numerical value that evaluates this model with respect to the data. That is, for any pair of values β_0 and β_1 we should be able to calculate a number that informs us about the suitability of these values. Mathematically, this is a function of the two values β_0, β_1 and the data set available. This function is called a loss function. We denote it by

$$L(\beta_0, \beta_1; X, Y)$$

where X, Y denote the data set (the values in the table: inputs X and values to be estimated Y). We may use $L(\beta_0, \beta_1)$ if the data set is clear, or simply $L(\beta)$.

This loss function is usually based on the error between the prediction of the model, and the actual data. For example, if we consider the 10 people in Table 4.1, we compute for each of the people the estimated income, and then compute the error between this estimated value and the correct one. Figure 4.3 (left) illustrates how the error is computed. E.g., let us consider the first person with *age* = 24. If we use our model with $\beta_0 = -4524.2$ and $\beta_1 = 207.5$ the estimation of her salary will be $\beta_0 + \beta_1 \text{age} = -4524.2 + 207.5 \cdot 24 = 455.8$. Nevertheless, the real income according to Table 4.1 is 1000. So, the error is $(1000 - 455.8) = 544.2$.

We use the square of the error. So, the value is always positive. For this person, the square of the error is, thus, $(1000 - 455.8)^2 = 544.2^2 = 296153.64$. In Fig. 4.3 (left) the error is represented with the blue line. I.e., the blue line is the distance between the actual data and the prediction (i.e., the corresponding position in the straight line.

Exercise 4.1 Compute the error for i_4 and i_5 using the same model above (i.e., same β_0 and β_1) and the information in Table 4.1.

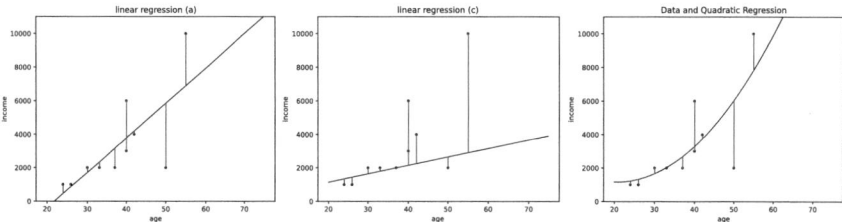

Fig. 4.3 Difference between the actual points and the prediction of a model. Three models are considered, two lineal models (left and center) and one quadratic model (right). Linear model with $\beta_0 = -4524.2$ and $\beta_1 = 207.5$ (left), and linear model with $\beta_0 = 127.59$ and $\beta_1 = 50.44$ (center)

4.3 How a Data Driven Model Is Built

Table 4.3 Database with age and income for 10 people, and the estimations of income using different linear models. Each model of the form $\beta_0 + \beta_1 \text{age}$. Last row corresponds to the mean squared error for the corresponding model, described by the pair (β_0, β_1)

Interview	Data		Prediction for (β_0, β_1)		
	Age	Income	(−4524.2, 207.5)	(−4520, 207)	(127.59, 50.44)
i_1	24	1000	455.8	448	1338.1
i_2	40	6000	3775.8	3760	2145.19
i_3	30	2000	1700.8	1690	1640.79
i_4	50	2000	5850.8	5830	2649.59
i_5	40	3000	3775.8	3760	2145.19
i_6	55	10000	6888.3	6865	2901.79
i_7	33	2000	2323.3	2311	1792.11
i_8	37	2000	3153.3	3139	1993.87
i_9	26	1000	870.80	862	1439.03
i_{10}	42	4000	4190.8	4174	2246.07
MSE	–	–	3193366.4	3193649.1	6995246.35

Mathematically, the loss function when we use the mean squared error (MSE) is expressed as

$$L(\beta_0, \beta_1) = MSE(y, \hat{y}) = \frac{1}{n}\sum_{i=1}^{n}(y_i - \hat{y}_i)^2,$$

where y_i corresponds to the real output (in our case, the real income) of the ith person as found in the database and $\hat{y}_i$ corresponds to the estimation of the output using our model (in our case, the expected income computed from the age of the ith individual based on the parameters of the model β_0 and β_1). Note that this mathematical expression is consistent with the notation we have given above where Y represented the whole column. So, y_i is the ith row of this column, and $\hat{y}_i$ is just an estimation of y_i.

In Table 4.3 (fourth column), we give the value we estimate for each individual using our model with parameters $\beta_0 = -4524.2$ and $\beta_1 = 207.5$. Then, we compute for each the error, we square it, and compute the average of these errors. This computation is called the mean squared error (MSE), and it is provided in the last row. This gives a measure of the quality of our model. A model will be perfect if the mean error is zero. Naturally, other model parameters will produce different values for MSE. So, as a matter of illustration, Table 4.3 provides the prediction and the mean error (i.e., MSE) for other model parameters (see fifth and sixth columns). Figure 4.3 (center) illustrates the errors for the linear model with $\beta_0 = 127.59$ and $\beta_1 = 50.44$.

The idea of using the MSE to evaluate models is naturally not restricted to linear models. It can be used for other models as well. To illustrate this, we show in Fig. 4.3 (right) the errors (blue lines) associated to the quadratic regression model we have given above. The figure shows that the errors (blue lines) seem to be lower in this case than for the linear model. We will return to this later.

If we have data, and a way to calculate how good a model is (the loss function or, here, the MSE), then, the next step is to find the model that is the best one. Machine learning algorithms look for the parameters that lead to a minimum loss function. So, for this example, they look for the β_0 and β_1 that combined produce a minimum squared mean error. We focus on this problem in the next sections.

4.3.1 The Parameters of a Data-Driven Linear Model

When the data-driven model is linear, and the loss function is the mean squared error, mathematics provide an easy way to compute the optimal parameters β_0 and β_1. There is a closed-form expression to obtain these two parameters. That is, an expression that permits us to compute the result with a finite number of basic computations. In fact, we can have an expression to predict Y with so many input variables as we have in our database X. So, in general, if we have n variables denoted by $x_1, \ldots, x_n$ and we look for a model $Y = \beta_0 + \beta_1 x_1 + \cdots + \beta_n x_n$ we can write a mathematical expression to find the parameters $\beta_0, \beta_1, \beta_2, \ldots, \beta_n$ from X that results into a minimum error when we estimate Y. This is provided in Fig. 4.4.

4.3.2 Gradient Descent

There are other ways to solve the same problem. One of them is the method of gradient descent. The main difference with the previous approach is that it is not a closed-form. This means that the number of computations we need to apply to have the exact solution can be, for some problems, infinite.

Why are we looking to this other approach then? Well, we will look to it, because the optimal parameters of most machine learning models cannot be found using a closed-form expression. It just does not exist. Then, we need to define algorithmic

---

If we have a database described by the pair X and Y, and we assume a linear model described in terms of matrices and vectors as $Y = X\beta$, and that X is invertible; then, the optimal parameters $\beta = (\beta_0, \ldots, \beta_n)$ that minimize the mean squared error are computed as

$$\hat{\beta} = (X^T X)^{-1} X^T Y$$

where X^T is the transpose of matrix X, and A^{-1} denotes the inverse of the matrix A. For the sake of simplicity, we are considering here that the leftmost column (which corresponds to β_0) in X is filled with 1s.

Fig. 4.4 Optimal parameters of a linear model using MSE as the loss function

4.3 How a Data Driven Model Is Built

approaches that find good enough approximate solutions. The gradient descent is one of them, and for a large number of problems they provide good approximations of the optimal parameters in reasonable time. Nevertheless, as it is not a closed-form, this means that for obtaining the only optimal solution, we may need in some occasions to have infinite time which, of course, we do not have.

How does the gradient descent work? The general idea is that we start from a (bad) solution and then we try to make it better, again and again, until we are satisfied enough. In other words, for our examples, we start with some initial values for our parameters β_0 and β_1, and then we update them several times (a kind of refinement) to improve them as much as possible. This is an iterative process (we repeat the improvement step), and it can go as long as we have time. If things go well, after some time, we will have appropriately good parameters, it may even happen that we have the optimal parameters. In some cases, things can go wrong, and we may get not so good parameters. Not only that, for some problems, things can go really, really wrong and the solution we find can be really bad.

Therefore, the key point in the gradient descent is how to update the model parameters. Or, in other words, how we improve them when we already have some numbers. For this, we use the loss function. As we have seen, the loss function provides a numerical value for any pair β_0 and β_1, and informs us about the quality of the regression line. In our example, how good is $\beta_0 + \beta_1 \cdot age$, with known β_0 and β_1 for our data. The larger the loss, the worse the solutions. The smaller the loss, the better. It is important to stress that the loss function allows us to evaluate any model, even a bad one. Note that in Table 4.3 we have already shown the loss function for three models. In that case as 3193366.4 is smaller than 3193649.1 and than 6995246.35, we can know that the first model is better than the other two.

To illustrate this, let us consider models with parameters β_0 in the interval $[-100, 0]$ and β_1 in the interval $[-100, 300]$. For example, $income = -50 - 70 \cdot age$. Note that these models are weird and wrong as we estimate that all people have negative salaries that even decrease when they get older. Figure 4.5 plots the

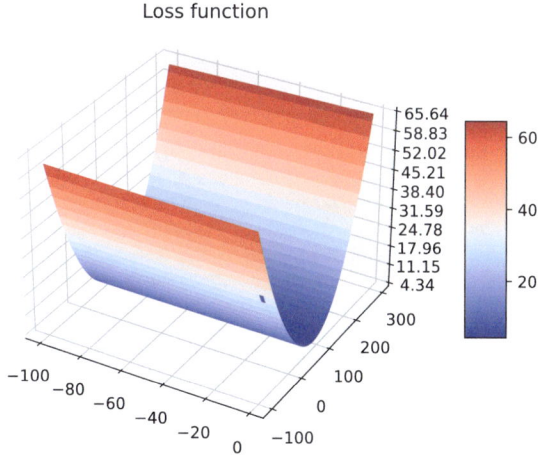

Fig. 4.5 β_0 in the interval $[-100, 0]$ and β_1 in the interval $[-100, 300]$

loss functions for these parameters. More concretely, we have the value of the loss function for each pair (β_0, β_1) with β_0 in the interval $[-100, 0]$ and β_1 in the interval $[-100, 300]$. Naturally, the loss is much higher than for the optimal model.

Let us go back to the gradient descent and see how it works. We will start on a position (defined by a pair of β_0 and β_1). Then, we can evaluate its quality using the loss function. Once we know its quality, we need to move to another position (another pair of β_0 and β_1) with a smaller loss. That is, we need to descent from the current position to a lower position. We denote the next position by β_0' and β_1'. We can repeat this last process as many times as we want. We go from β_0, β_1 to β_0', β_1', then to β_0'', β_1'' and so on.

So, the procedure is as follows:

- Start with a pair β_0, β_1
- Find a descending direction and move to β_0', β_1'
- Find a descending direction and move to β_0'', β_1''
- ...

So, in each step we need to find for any position the descent direction. Mathematics provides a tool for this. The gradient of a function at a point provides information on the descent direction. So, this gradient is what is used, and that is why the method is called the gradient descent. In Fig. 4.6 we show an analogy of this problem of finding a minimum of a function of two inputs.

Let us illustrate this method on our example. Figure 4.7 shows the loss function for values of β_0 in the range $[-4970, -4090]$ and values of β_1 in the range $[188, 227]$. This figure can be computed and drawn because our model consists of only two parameters, because we know the loss function and we know which part of the function to plot. In general, this is not possible, the number of parameters is large, the possible values are infinite, and we do not know were are the good ones to look to.

The optimal values, i.e., the best solution, are in the center of the figure. They are, as we have already seen before $\beta_0 = -4524.2$, $\beta_1 = 207.5$, and correspond to a loss function of 3193366.4. If we start from any pair of values β_0 and β_1 (e.g., from $(\beta_0 = -5000, \beta_1 = 190)$) and we proceed by improving these values, which means

> The problem of the gradient descent applied to a convex surface can be seen as similar to the problem of finding the lowest point of a perfect crater. How can we find this point? We can proceed as follows: we start in a random position inside the crater, then we walk one step in a descending direction. From the next position, we move again one step in a descending direction. We do this again and again, until we actually find that there is no descending direction. So, we are at the lowest point.
> In our case, the positions on the crater are defined by (β_0, β_1), the loss function defines the shape of the crater (i.e., the height for any position), and the gradient provides the information necessary to find the descending direction.

Fig. 4.6 The minimal on a convex surface and on a crater

4.3 How a Data Driven Model Is Built

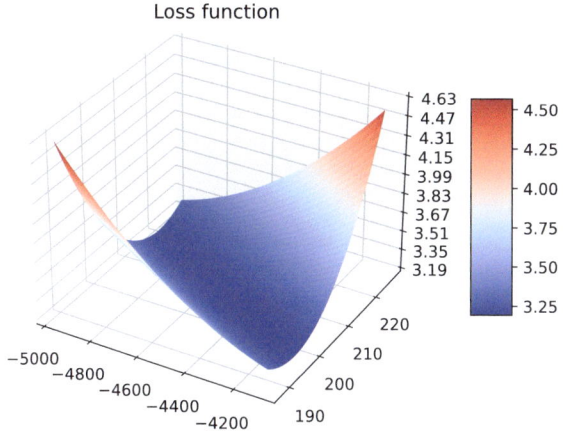

Fig. 4.7 Loss function associated to the linear regression problem for β_0 in the interval $[-4970, -4090]$ and β_1 in the interval $[188, 227]$

decreasing the loss function, we will reach this minimum or will be near enough to it.

We will use β^0 to denote the parameters when we start. Say, $\beta^0 = (\beta_0 = -5000, \beta_1 = 190)$. Then, β^1 denotes the parameters after the first step, β^2 the parameters after the second step, and so on, so, β^n are the parameters at the nth step and β^{n+1} the parameters at the $n + 1$th step. Then, as it is customary, we use $\nabla L(\beta^n)$ to denote the gradient of the loss function L at the nth position β^n.

The gradient gives the direction, but, in fact, it points to the ascend direction and as we have been repeating, we should go in the descending direction. So, we should reverse the gradient sign. I.e., we need to go towards $-\nabla L(\beta^n)$. In fact, $\nabla L(\beta^n)$ not only informs about the direction but also how steep is the function there.

With all this, we can express the rule to update the parameters. Nevertheless, something is still missing. We have to go to the descending direction, but how much? Well, this we really do not know. If we advance too much, it may happen that we get to a place that is worse than our current position. If we advance too few, it may happen that it will take forever to reach to the best place. In our programming, the size of the step is controlled by a parameter that is called η. This parameter is known as the learning rate.

Then, the rule for updating the parameters β is

$$\beta^{n+1} = \beta^n - \eta \nabla L(\beta^n),$$

which mainly means, that the new position is the previous position (β^n) plus a step proportional to $\nabla L(\beta^n)$ (proportional to η) but in the opposite direction of ∇L (so, downwards instead of upwards).

The gradient descent uses this rule from an initial β^0 and computing then, β^1, β^2, ..., until we are satisfied with the solution.

The selection of an appropriate parameter η is sometimes difficult, and we will not discuss this here. Nevertheless, in Fig. 4.8 we illustrate how different values of η

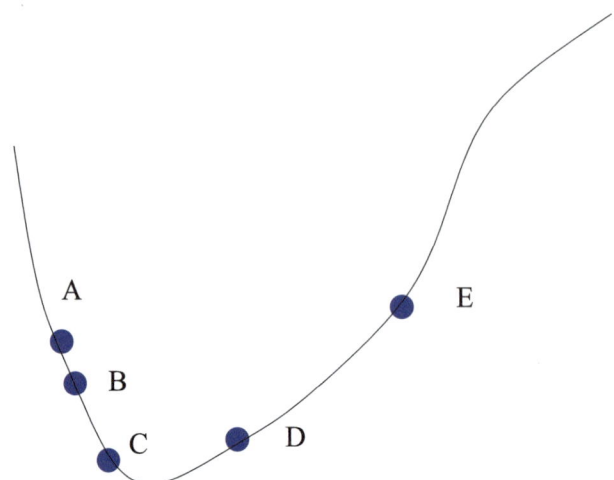

Fig. 4.8 Loss function and the selection of the learning rate. Depending on the value of η we may move too slowly to the optimal value or we may even move to a point with worse loss function

may affect the result. Consider that we are now in point A and the curve is the loss function. As the figure shows, the loss goes up again. If η is too small, then we move to a position (say B) that is too near to the current one and it will take long to get to the minimum. If η is appropriate we may move to a better position (say C). If it is too large we can go beyond the minimum (say, positions D and E) and even to a point that is worse than the current one (say E) as the loss function is larger there than at the actual position (i.e., the loss at E is larger than the loss at A).

4.3.3 A Graphical Representation of Linear Models

We have seen the description of a linear model in which we estimate a variable (the income) given another one (a given age). We give now a graphical representation of this model in Fig. 4.9 (left). The graph includes circles or nodes, and lines or edges. Each circle or node represents the input data, or a computation or (partial) result. The edges represent transmission of information, and edges have associated a parameter (β_1 and β_0 in the figure).

More particularly, we have that the node in the left represents the input variable x (in our example age), and the one in the right the output variable y (in our example income). The node in the center combines the information that comes from the left (i.e., x) with the parameter β_1 together with β_0 and transmits the result (i.e., $\beta_0 + \beta_1 \cdot x$) to the right (i.e., to y).

If our model consists of two inputs instead of one (e.g., *age* and *national* = Yes), we can just add another node for the second variable and the corresponding edge

4.3 How a Data Driven Model Is Built

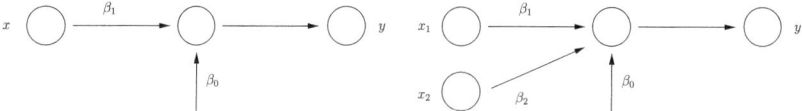

Fig. 4.9 Graphical representation of a linear model with one input and one output (left), and two inputs and one output (right)

with its parameter. If we use x_1 and x_2 to represent the two input variables and β_1 and β_2 to represent the corresponding parameters, then we have a model such as

$$y = \beta_0 + \beta_1 x_1 + \beta_2 x_2,$$

which means in our case

$$income = \beta_0 + \beta_1\, age + \beta_2\, national$$

and its corresponding graphical representation is given in Fig. 4.9 (right).

Similarly, we represent the case of an arbitrary number of inputs (see Fig. 4.10). In this case, we have n nodes for variables $x_1, x_2, \ldots, x_n$ on the left, each with its own edge to the center node with a parameter $\beta_1, \beta_2, \ldots, \beta_n$. The computation of y corresponds in this case to

$$y = \beta_0 + \beta_1 x_1 + \beta_2 x_2 + \cdots + \beta_n x_n.$$

We can consider more complex models with the same type of structure. The neural networks we discuss next can be seen from this perspective.

4.3.4 Neural Networks and Deep Learning

Neural networks and deep learning are models originally inspired by the neurons of the brain. They are composite computational models with their basic unit, called a neuron, computing a numerical output value from several numerical input values. Neural network jargon also follows the one of biology.

The inputs represent the strength of the signal to the neuron, and then the output is activated or not depending on these signals strength, and an activation function. Input signals can have positive and negative effects on the activation of the neuron. That is, they help to activate the neuron or prevent its activation.

Computationally, the neuron receives a number of inputs (say n) and produces one output. Each input will provide a number. Then, in addition, each input has associated a weight. The sign of the weight, positive or negative, permits to represent whether the signal has a positive or a negative impact in the activation. More particularly, if the weight is positive, the larger the input, the more the neuron is activated. In

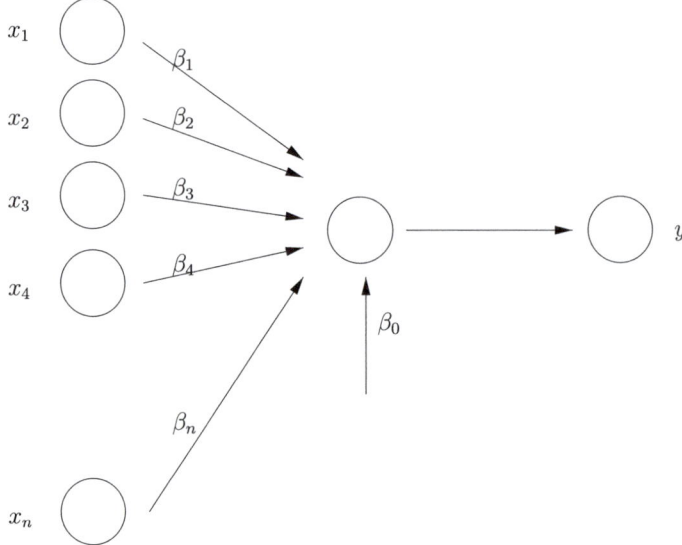

Fig. 4.10 Graphical representation of a linear model with n inputs and one output

a way, the input signal is propagated to the output. In contrast, if the weight is negative, the larger the input the more the neuron is deactivated, and the activation of the neuron is prevented. That is, the input is not propagated to the output and can prevent the propagation of other outputs as well. Weights can be large or small, depending on the importance or relevance of the input. In addition, each neuron has associated an activation function that finally regulates the output based on all the internal calculations.

As a single neuron can already be useful for some calculations, we will use one to illustrate how a neuron computes. Let us consider the problem of having very simple images with solely $3 \times 3 = 9$ pixels. Figure 4.11 illustrates three examples of these very tiny images. For simplicity we consider only two possible colors in each pixel. We illustrate a cross (left), horizontal bars (center), and vertical bars (right).

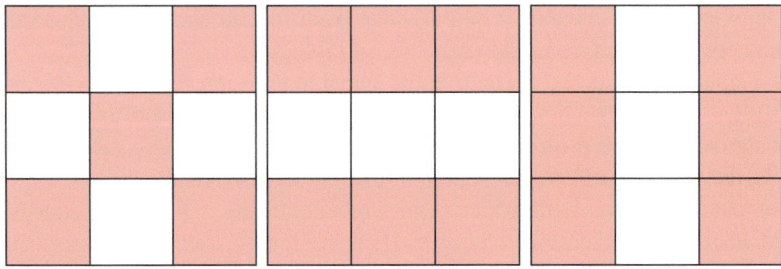

Fig. 4.11 Example of three different red and white images: a cross (left), horizontal stripes (center), and vertical stripes (right)

4.3 How a Data Driven Model Is Built

+1	−1	+1
−1	+1	−1
+1	−1	+1

+1	+1	+1
−1	−1	−1
+1	+1	+1

+1	−1	+1
+1	−1	+1
+1	−1	+1

Fig. 4.12 Codification of three different red and white images using the values +1 for red and −1 for white: a cross (left), horizontal stripes (center), and vertical stripes (right)

How this is actually codified? As we have only two colors, for simplicity and convenience, we represent red as +1 and white as −1. We illustrate the representation of these three images in Fig. 4.12 (left), (center) and (right). Formally, we can represent the cross in the memory of the computer as follows (where the first three numbers correspond to the first row, the next three to the second row, and the last three to the last row):

$$[+1, -1, +1, -1, +1, -1, +1, -1, +1]$$

In actual applications, it is usual to use other codifications for the images (as e.g., RGB. Then, for RGB a similar process is applied but other weights and computations are required to accommodate the RGB codification.

Now, let us consider that we want to detect with our neuron when a given image is a cross. Say, we have an image, and we want to detect when it corresponds to the one in Fig. 4.11 (left).

To achieve this, we use a neuron with 9 inputs. This corresponds to one input for each pixel. Each input will provide the strength of the *signal* in the pixel. In our case, the *strength* just indicates if the pixel is white or red, so, if it is −1 or +1. Then, using the corresponding 9 inputs the neuron computes an output. Figure 4.13 (left) represents the neuron that takes 9 inputs and produces an output. Our goal is that this neuron *activates* when these 9 inputs represent a cross.

Here, *activates* means that if the figure is a cross, the output should be +1 or positive, and if not, then the output should be −1 or negative. If the figure is *similar* to a cross, then we would expect something close to +1.

So, this means, that when the image is the cross, with five positions activated (in red in the figure) and four positions not activated (in white in the figure), the output neuron is also activated (so, also in color in the figure). A graphical representation of this process is provided in Fig. 4.13 (left). To make the computation simple, we can use a linear model for the neuron, which mathematically corresponds to the following using the notation in Fig. 4.10:

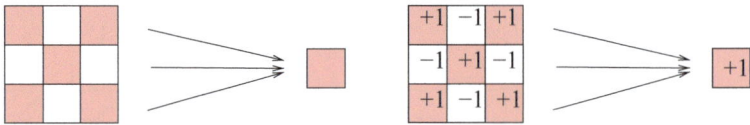

Fig. 4.13 Neuron to detect a particular 3 × 3 image (left), and weights associated to each input to detect a cross (right). Formally speaking, the weights are associated to the edge or connection between the input and, in this case, the output

$$\beta_0 + \sum_j x_j \beta_j$$

This means that we take the value of each pixel (i.e., x_i) and we multiply by a weight (i.e., β_i) which states whether the pixel contributes or prevents the detection of a cross.

How are these weights assigned? We will have positive weights associated to the inputs that form the cross (i.e., to positions in the corners of the figure and the central position). In contrast, we need negative weights for the other ones. This is illustrated in Fig. 4.13 (right), with positive and negative weights.

Let us consider again the images in Fig. 4.11 with their codification in Fig. 4.12. Then, we compute for each image the output of the neuron using the weights in Fig. 4.13 (right). As we have written above, the formula to compute is this one:

$$\beta_0 + \sum_j x_j \beta_j.$$

We are using $\beta_0 = 0$, and the x_j and β_j are the inputs (values in the pixels) in Fig. 4.11 and the weights in Fig. 4.13 (right). They are aligned, so, we do not need to worry with the subscripts.

Let us start with the figure that is actually a cross (i.e., Fig. 4.12 (left)). We need to multiply each input (value of the pixel) with each weight. We start with the first row

$$(+1) \cdot (+1) + (-1) \cdot (-1) + (+1) \cdot (+1)$$

then, the second one

$$(-1) \cdot (-1) + (+1) \cdot (+1) + (-1) \cdot (-1)$$

and, finally, the third one

$$(+1) \cdot (+1) + (-1) \cdot (-1) + (+1) \cdot (+1).$$

So, adding all together we get

$$+1+1+1 \quad +1+1+1 \quad +1+1+1 = +9.$$

4.3 How a Data Driven Model Is Built

Let us now compute the same for the horizontal bars (i.e., Fig. 4.12 (center)). The weights are the same, but the inputs change. So, if we compute the three rows we have (first element of the product corresponds to the pixel in the image) the following:

$$(+1) \cdot (+1) + (+1) \cdot (-1) + (+1) \cdot (+1)$$

$$(-1) \cdot (-1) + (-1) \cdot (+1) + (-1) \cdot (-1)$$

$$(+1) \cdot (+1) + (+1) \cdot (-1) + (+1) \cdot (+1).$$

So, in this case, we will have

$$+1 - 1 + 1 \quad +1 - 1 + 1 \quad +1 - 1 + 1 = +3.$$

We observe that the output is positive but not as much as for the cross.

Finally, let us consider the vertical bars (Fig. 4.12 (right)). In this case, the computations are as follows

$$(+1) \cdot (+1) + (-1) \cdot (-1) + (+1) \cdot (+1)$$

$$(+1) \cdot (-1) + (-1) \cdot (+1) + (+1) \cdot (-1)$$

$$(+1) \cdot (+1) + (-1) \cdot (-1) + (+1) \cdot (+1),$$

which produce

$$+1 + 1 + 1 \quad -1 - 1 - 1 \quad +1 + 1 + 1 = +3,$$

which is the same as for the horizontal bars.

So, we see that the output is more activated (i.e., has a larger value) for the cross than for the other two images. So, with a larger activation, our tiny neural network informs that Fig. 4.11 (left) is more a cross than Fig. 4.11 (center) and (right). Naturally, this is what we want.

Exercise 4.2 Compute the output of a 3×3 image that is the reverse of Fig. 4.12 (left). That is, a white cross instead of a red one, replacing $+1$ by -1, and -1 by $+1$.

In Fig. 4.13 (left) we have the weights to detect a cross. In an application we would learn these weights. We would use several images each of them with a label "it is a cross" or a label "it is not a cross", and using gradient descent we would adjust the weights. With this 3×3 in red and white there are not many images, but the same applies to large images that require thousands or millions of weights.

We have seen in these examples that while inputs where either $+1$ or -1 (i.e., each pixel value), the output is not. In neural networks it is usual that after the computation of the summation of the products, we apply a function that moves back the output

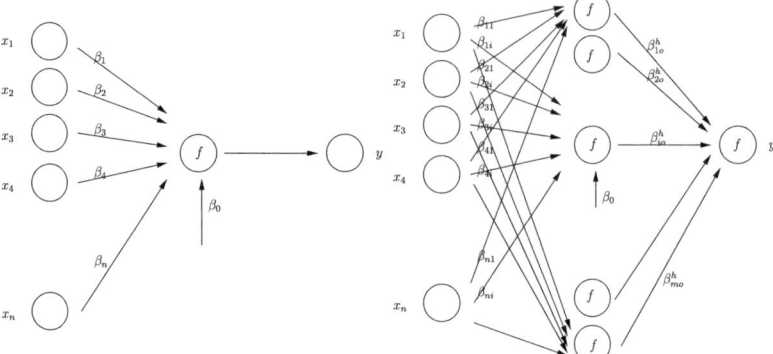

Fig. 4.14 Graphical representation of a non-linear model with n inputs and one neuron in the hidden layer (left), and with n inputs and m neurons in the hidden layer (right)

into the original range of values. In this case, we would move the output to $[-1, +1]$. This function is known as activation function. If we use f to denote this function, the actual computation of the network corresponds to:

$$f\left(\beta_0 + \sum_j x_j \beta_j\right).$$

A very simple one in our case would be to divide the output by 9. Then, with weights in $[-1, +1]$, all output values will be always also in $[-1, +1]$. In practice, other functions are used (as the sigmoid, tanh, and ReLU).

Figure 4.14 (left) corresponds to a graphical representation of this computation. Figure 4.14 (right) shows an example of a more complex network. It has multiple neurons that, in parallel, combine the inputs and are activated under some conditions. Then, the outputs of these neurons are further combined. We have only three layers in this network, but we may have more. In deep learning we may have e.g. 10 layers of neurons.

Some technical words are used in neural networks and deep learning. As we have seen, we usually have different layers. We distinguish the input layer (in our example, the one in which we have associated pixels of the image), the output layer (the one that corresponds to the final computation), and the hidden layers (in Fig. 4.14 there is only one of these layers).

Then, we have the concept of kernel. This corresponds to a pattern of weights that is replicated in the network. Say that we have a large image (instead of our simple example of 3×3) and we still need to detect 3×3 crosses in the large image. Then, we could copy the structure and weights we had in Fig. 4.13 (right) multiple times to find these crosses in multiple regions. This is a kernel. We would proceed similarly to detect other patterns.

The whole structure of the network is known as the architecture. We need to define, of course, the number of neurons in the input layer and in the output layer. This is based on the problem. E.g., if we are going to classify images of 1024 × 768 pixels, we need 1024 × 768 = 786432 inputs. If we have RGB, then we may need to multiply this number by 3. Then, about the output, if we have a classification problem that is binary, we will have one or two neurons in the output (e.g., one neuron that represents with $+1$ that the image is a dog and -1 that it is not a dog). The architecture also defines the number of hidden layers and the number of neurons each. Complex problems need more neurons, and usually are distributed in several hidden layers.

Learning in deep learning corresponds to find the weights associated to the neurons. This is usually done for a given architecture. So, first, given the problem, we need to define the appropriate architecture. Then, we use an algorithm to learn the parameters of this architecture. For this, we need a training set. In the learning step, we usually start initializing the weights at random (or using some heuristic) and, then, in a succession of steps we improve the weights so the outputs for our training data get closer to the desired output. Gradient descent and related approaches can be used to optimize the weights.

Exercise 4.3 In gradient descent for neural networks, why can an improperly chosen learning rate cause the loss function to increase rather than decrease?

Exercise 4.4 An important property of feedforward neural networks is that they are universal approximators. Investigate what it means to be a *universal approximator*.

4.3.5 Classification Problems

In this section we have focused on regression problems. As we have defined at the beginning of this chapter, there are two main types of predictive models: classification and regression. In regression, we predict a numerical variable. In contrast, in classification problems we predict a category or class.

The machine learning models we have seen so far can be used (with some modifications) for classification. In particular, neural networks and deep neural networks are applied to classification. In a way, our discussion about the detection of a cross can be seen as a classification problem. I.e., is the 3 × 3 image in Fig. 4.11 (left) a cross? In the general case we can proceed in the same way for Boolean problems and, in general, problems with only two classes. One class can be represented by $+1$ and the other by -1. Another alternative is to use an output layer with multiple output units. More specifically, to have as many output units as classes or categories. Say, we want to assess if an image is a dog, a cat, or an elephant. Then, we construct a neural network with three output neurons, one that activates if the image is a dog, another that activates when the image is a cat, and a third one that activates if the image is an elephant.

In order to evaluate the quality of the model in regression we used mean squared error. In the case of classification problems, loss functions are based on coincidence on the class assigned by the model and the one in the training set. Cross-entropy is an example of loss function for classification problems.

We will see in the next section decision trees that is a type of model that is specially suited for classification problems.

Exercise 4.5 Three culinary experts have tasted 100 different Panettone produced in the city of Milan. They compiled a database with the main information about the ingredients and each step of the baking process. The joint opinion of the experts about each Panettone is also recorded. Each Panettone falls into one of the following categories: "excellent taste", "not good enough", or "disagreement". We will use these data to build a machine learning model that predicts the opinion of the experts, based on the releveant information

Decide which of the following statements is true.

- This is a regression problem
- This is a classification problem
- This is an unsupervised learning problem
- This is a clustering problem
- None of the other statements is true.

4.4 Decision Trees

Decision trees are another type of models that focus on categorical data. Therefore, its main use is for classification problems. The model is defined by a set of chained tests, that leads to a final outcome for the output variable. Figure 4.15 shows an example. We have built it using the data in Table 4.2, but the output has been made binary and only states if the income is above or below 2500. So, we have two possible values as output "Salary above 2500', which we represent as "T"; and salary below, which we represent as "F".

This type of structure is known in computer science as a tree. It can be understood as a tree upside-down. The block or node in the top of the structure is known as the root of the tree, and then we have branches or edges that go down in the figure until we reach an end. An end block or node is known as a leaf of the tree.

Then, naturally, the goal of the model is about predicting whether the salary of someone will exceed 2500 or not. Say, we want to estimate whether Liam, who is a national, 25 years old, earns less than 2500 or more than that.

There are several blocks (or nodes) in Fig. 4.15. Each represents a test on an attribute. The first line in a block represents the test. So, the first block on top questions whether the age is below 38.5 years old. Then, the block includes two arrows. If age is below or equal to 38.5 we should move to the block on the left, and if it is above 38.5 we should move to the block on the right.

4.4 Decision Trees

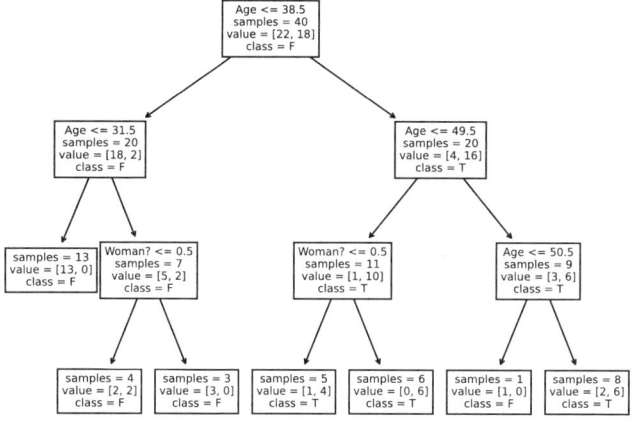

Fig. 4.15 A decision trees built from the data in Table 4.2 using the Gini index. Solution built using Python scikit-learn with max_depth = 3

The decision tree has been learned with the data in Table 4.2, which includes information on 40 people. Some of this people has a salary below 2500 and some above. Each block includes information on the number of people (samples, or records) in this data set that are associated to the block. The block also includes information on how many of them are in each class (i.e., with a salary below or above 2500). The first block shows that we have 40 people represented there (i.e., the line "samples = 40"), and among them 22 have a salary lower than or equal to 2500, and 18 with a salary larger than 2500. This is provided with the line "value = [22, 18]". The 22 corresponds to the class "F", and the 18 to class "T". The prediction if we don't go down in the tree would be "F". This is provided in the line "class = F". The value selected for a block is the one that is majority in the block. There may be ties, however.

In our case, when we consider Liam's information, we would move to the left as the age of 25 is <38.5. Then, the next test asks again about age, and whether it is smaller than 31.5. This is the case of our data about Liam, so, we move again to the left. Then, the next block does not include a test. It is a terminal block (or node). As we have said above, using the notation in computer science, this is a leaf of the tree. The block states that the class is "F", so, this is what we infer, that Liam has a salary below 2500. The block also shows that this outcome is based on the data in the database, and, in particular, that there are 13 people in the database associated to this block (i.e., to people below 31.5 years old) and all are in the class "F".

We can also see that if the age would have been larger than 31.5 (i.e., between 31.5 and 38.5), we would have been asked in the test if the person was a woman. In the block, the test is written as "Woman? <= 0.5". If the value of the variable Woman? is "yes", then we should go to the right (as a "yes" is codified with one) and if the variable Woman? is "no", then we should go to the left (as "no" is codified with zero).

If we look to the information in the blocks, we can also see that there is a leaf with 4 samples and a distribution [2, 2] that assigns "F". It corresponds to people between 31.5 and 38, which are Men. If we search for these people in the database, they are individuals denoted by i_{13}, i_{18}, i_{33}, and i_{38}. The first two are nationals, and the two last ones are not. It can also be seen that among the nationals, i_{13} has salary above 2500 while i_{18} is below, and among the non nationals i_{33} has a salary above 2500 while i_{38} not. So, there is no way to distinguish among them. That is, no existing variable in the database allows us to distinguish about the two classes. That's why the decision tree cannot be developed further.

4.4.1 Learning the Tree

Machine learning is about finding the model from the data. This also applies to decision trees, and then the goal is to build a tree that is as small as possible. Small means that the number of tests that are required to classify a new case is as small as possible. In short, ask the few relevant questions to make a decision.

Therefore, the goal is to select the variable that better distinguishes between the two classes on top. If we were lucky, and such variable existed, we would be able to distinguish perfectly the "T" and the "F". Then, the solution would be a single test, and we would finish there. If this is not so, we select a *good* variable, and then we do the same to both left and right.

So, the key for a machine learning algorithm is how to select which is the best variable to include in the test (i.e., should we use now age?, woman?, or national?). Then, we also need to decide which are the conditions for this variable. Decision trees are usually built for categorical variables or binary/Boolean variables (as woman and national). If this is the case, we have one edge or arrow for each alternative (as in the case of the variable woman in Fig. 4.15. In contrast, if we have a numerical variable (as in the case of age), we need to find a cutting point (as the value 38.5 on the top block, or the value 31.5 on the block on the second row, left). We will not go into the details, but decision tree learning software tries to find a good value for classifying the records.

Finding the optimal tree is not easy, and can be too time consuming. So, as an alternative, there are algorithms that select variables for a test based on some indices. These indices, in general, produce good (small enough) trees. Different indices produce different decision trees. They are not optimal but lead to good enough results.

The Gini index and information gain (based on entropy) are examples of these indices. As we have said, constructing decision trees based on these indices do not always produce the optimal tree, and, thus, they can produce different trees for the same data. We illustrate this showing two different trees obtained from the same data we have used in this section. They are in Fig. 4.16. The one on top is built using the Gini index, and the one on the bottom using information gain. As the data set is small, and has only three variables, the difference between the two trees is small. With

4.4 Decision Trees

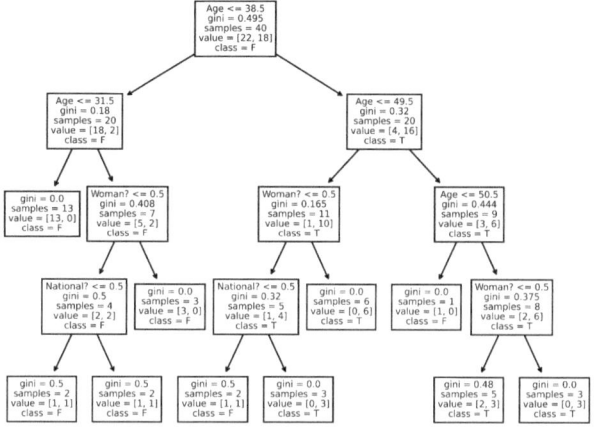

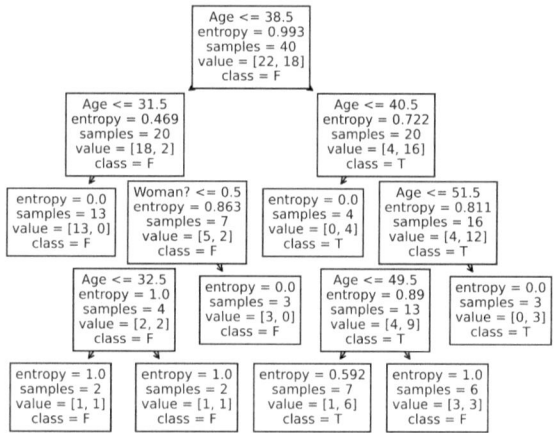

Fig. 4.16 Two decision trees built from the same data set (Table 4.2) but using different criterion: Gini index (top) and information gain (bottom). Solution built using Python scikit-learn with max_depth = 4

larger data sets with larger number of variables, the differences could be larger. So, in summary, these two figures illustrate that the same training data set can produce different trees when different criteria are used.

We want to highlight that the decision tree in Fig. 4.15 and the one in Fig. 4.16 (top) are both built using the Gini index. Nevertheless, they are different because although we have applied the same algorithm to the data, we have provided a different parameter to the algorithm (max_depth). This parameter controls the size of the tree.

4.5 Language Models

Language models are based on neural networks. Their goal is to produce sentences (patterns) that are similar to real sentences as found in real documents. In short, the model learns existing sentences from sets of documents and tries to produce text that is consistent with these sentences. Naturally, the goal is not to memorize the sentences but to follow the same patterns.

In order to have good performance, the size of the neural networks is very large. Improved versions of ChatGPT have been produced increasing the number of parameters. In other words the corresponding neural networks are larger and larger, containing more nodes and edges, with the corresponding weights. Note that one weight is one parameter. GPT-1 is said to have 117 million parameters, GPT-2 to have 1.5 billion parameters, ChatGPT-3 to have 175 billion, and GPT-4 1.8 trillion parameters. So, that is why they are called *large* language models.

GPT stands for generative pre-trained transformer. The goal of a transformer is to predict the next word. Consider an unfinished sentence in English, and the goal is to predict which is the word that follows. Then, we can output a word based on this prediction. Then, we can do this again, and again. In this way we can write a whole sentence. Then, a whole paragraph, finally, a whole text. If the initial text is a question, we will be (probably) producing an answer.

The prediction at any time is based on the previous text. Mathematically, we can understand the process of learning in a deep learning model for text as learning the probabilities of having a word given the previous ones. Then, the prediction is conditioned to the previous text. In this way, the output does not need to be deterministic (i.e., given the same input we obtain the same output) but randomized taking into account prediction probabilities.

Transformers are based on a concept called attention. Internally, in the neural network we have a representation of the meaning of words. This representation is built during the learning process and corresponds to vectors of numbers. The success of transformers rely on the fact that the representation of a word (i.e., the vector of numbers associated to it) changes with the context of the word. So, the word *spring* in the two following sentences will have different internal representations.

- Spring has arrived and all flowers bloom.
- I disassembled the watch and now the spring is lost.

Language models are trained with text documents. The set of texts used is called corpus. An example of documents used for training is wikipedia, which is said to have been used for GPT-3. Say that we use the page of wikipedia for "Spring (season)" (as of 15 June 2025) which starts "Spring, also known as springtime, is one of the four temperate seasons, succeeding winter and preceding summer". Then, in the training we give consecutive pieces of this sentence to the neural network so that it learns what it comes next. For example, we provide

- "Spring, also known as springtime, is one of the four temperate X"

  and we make it to learn that X is season.

These pre-trained models often do not include domain-specific knowledge. This is so because they only have a general knowledge that has been obtained from their training using an open access corpus. In this way, we incorporate this information into the model. When we need that the answers of our system include domain-specific knowledge bases (e.g., proprietary information related to our business as well as information found in our corporation reports), or legal documents and regulations, we use retrieval-augmented generation (RAG) technology. E.g., Perron et al. [126] explain about the use of RAG in the context of social work, so that the system replies better to questions in this context.

4.6 Some Additional Concepts in Machine Learning

The introduction to machine learning has been focused on what it means building a model. In particular, we have explained that we look for a model that approximates as good as possible some data. Actual construction of models, as well as their application poses a number of problems that need to be considered as well.

First, models strongly depend on the data we use for their training. So, some concepts related to data are of relevance here. Data needs to be obtained, maybe collected on purpose, or, alternatively, retrieved from existing databases. Before learning the model, we need to do data preprocessing which includes aspects as feature selection (selecting attributes or variables that are relevant), data cleaning (e.g., correcting errors and handling missing values), and data transformation (as e.g. encoding categorical and ordinal values, scaling using normalization or standardization). We do not discuss this preprocessing here, but it has an important effect on the quality of the models. Missing information goes beyond missing values in some records (e.g., because some patients do not have results of some analysis, answers have not been recorded, sensors were not working). We will discuss in this section the important concept of missing or dark data. Once a data-driven model is built, before its use in a real-world environment, we need to have guarantees that the model performs well. A way to check its performance is to use some data and see how good are the results. Nevertheless we cannot use for this purpose the same data we have already used for training. Our analysis would be too optimistic. We will define below training, test, and validations data sets. They are different data sets to assess better how good the model is.

Second, there are important concepts related to the optimization problem. We have explained that we use gradient descent in the learning process. Well, sometimes this method does not work well. We have already mentioned this inconvenience. The effectiveness of gradient descent depends on the shape of loss functions. We discuss this problem below. We have also discussed that there are different types of models. How can we know which to select? Usually, there is not a clear answer to this question. Nevertheless, for some problems, bias and variance provide some help with this selection. We include a discussion on error, bias, and variance below. We also include sections on fairness, explainability, correlation and causation, and privacy.

4.6.1 Training, Test, and Validation Data Sets

In this chapter we have discussed learning from a data set. We have called it training set. In practice, it is usual in machine learning to use also a validation set. This set is expected to have similar properties as the training set but e.g. about other people or objects. The validation set is used to select among different models.

For any machine learning problem, performance measures establish how good is the model on unseen data. In regression problems we can use mean squared error on validation sets as such performance measure. In the case of regression, we can use measures as accuracy and F1-score that assess if the class that the model assigns to instances or records in the validation set coincide with the actual ones.

The validation set is used to know if the model has an appropriate generalization capability. Informally, if the model is good, the error on the training set and the error in the validation set should be similar or comparable. If not, it is better to try another type of model. We will give additional details on this problem below, discussing over-fitting and under-fitting.

Finally, once the model is decided and learned, a test set can be used to estimate the performance of the model. This is called the test set. So, the test set is only used once when we have already the model to be used.

Note that in the literature, sometimes the names of test and validation sets are interchanged.

4.6.2 Missing Data

The development of data-driven models require data. Internet and extensive data storage seems to provide the key component for the algorithms to run and produce the machine learning models that are used later to make decisions. Nevertheless, existing data in internet, and private and public databases are not the whole picture. There is information that is missing because it is not recorded. Data-driven models may fail and decisions may be wrong if this unavailable data is not taken into account.

4.6 Some Additional Concepts in Machine Learning 101

Obviously, if we use only internet data, we only have represented those people and organizations that have a presence there, and, mainly, have an active role there. Those that do not access internet (e.g., elderly, without resources, or internet-averse) are not represented. Similar cases can be found in other contexts. David J. Hand in his book [84] calls these data that are missing dark data. Data analysis and data-driven models need to be done taking into account this information.

Once a local public library I know published a survey. Library users answered about their preferences and providing satisfaction degrees on different questions. One was about the schedule and most of the respondents answered with a very high satisfaction degree. The library is closed on holidays and weekends, and it is difficult to access outside school hours. So, I was wondering who was happy with such short schedule, but, of course, the ones that actually can visit the library may be very satisfied with it!

Depending on the purpose of the survey missing data may be crucial, and the conclusions may be wrong. In general, dark data can cause wrong decisions.

Hand [84] classifies dark data in 15 different types. They include from data we know that are missing, to data we don't know that are missing. A real-world example [84, p. 33] is about the construction of scorecard for predicting defaults of bank repayments. Existing data is about actual people who had already a loan granted and either they failed or not (yet) the repayment. Nothing was available about those that applied and had no loan granted, and let alone information about them failing or not a repayment if the loan would have been granted.

Dark data is not so easy to deal with, because it is not always possible to *correct* what is available, to take into account what is not. For example, consenters and unconsenters differ in unpredictable ways, which makes data correction difficult [84, p. 52].

Another example about the problem of missing data is explained by Eubanks [66, p. 147] in relation to a system for the Allegheny County Office of Children, Youth and Families. The system Allegheny Family Screening Tool (AFST) forecasts child abuse and neglect. The system has access to data collected from public programs, and has no access to data from private services. In particular, no information is available about parents accessing private drug treatments, nor private mental health counseling. Therefore, prediction is fundamentally biased.

4.6.3 On the Surfaces Defined by Loss Functions

We have explained that in neural networks and other optimization problems, we apply gradient descent to find the optimal parameters. If the surface defined by the loss function is convex, it is relatively easy to find the optimal solution. That is, it is easy to find the best point if the surface defined by the loss function is similar to the example of the crater we have seen in Fig. 4.6, or as a bowl. For this type of surfaces, there is only one global minimum, and if we always descend, we will be able to find

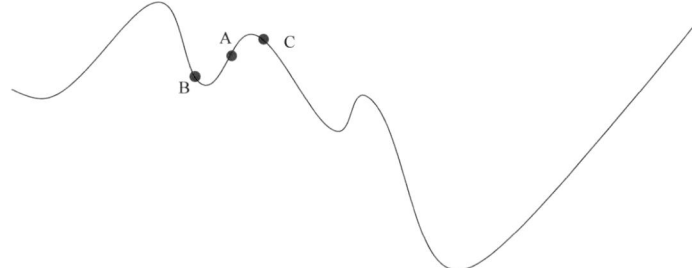

Fig. 4.17 Example of simulated annealing. Point A moves to point B with some probability p, and to point C with some probability $(1 - p)$

it. Then, we can start at any point at random and we will probably reach this global minimum after some steps.

Nevertheless, not all problems are like this. We may have a surface with several ups and downs. Say, like a mountain range with several valleys, and peaks (see Fig. 4.17). Then, it is not so easy to find the point which is the global minimum. If we start at a random position and we use the gradient descent we may got stuck in a position that is not the global minimum but only a local minimum. For example, we can finish in a tarn or a mountain lake, instead in the lowest valley of the region.

It is not uncommon that AI and ML optimization problems with lots of parameters have loss functions that are not convex. In this case, the gradient descent does not work and alternative solutions have been developed to find good enough solutions. An example is simulated annealing. In short, we move to a lower position with some probability, but also with some probability we can move to a higher position. If we consider again the example of the mountain range, if we are near the mountain lake (say in position A in Fig. 4.17), we may be moving downwards with some probability p (e.g., to position B in the figure), but also with some probability $(1 - p)$ we may move upwards and, thus, be able to jump to another valley (say to point C).

4.6.4 Error, Bias, and Variance

We have stated before, and repeated, that a model is an abstraction or a simplification. This is important in machine learning because data contains a lot of detail, including particularities of individuals, and all kind of errors, and when we build models from data, we want that these models learn the general trend. E.g., maybe someone is the owner of a bakery and has a larger salary than usual for her age. Say, she is 39 and earns 2950, which corresponds to record i_{25} in the file. We do not want models to learn data specifics.

Let us consider the data about age and income. We are interested in the general trend, but not the details on the data. To make our point clear, let us focus on the data in Table 4.2 for women who are not national. Then, let us build a model for these

4.6 Some Additional Concepts in Machine Learning

data. Nevertheless, we have seen that there are lots of options. Selecting one model implies that there are characteristics of the data that we can learn, and some others that we cannot. We have discussed this in Sect. 4.2.

To make things *simple* we only consider 6 models that are polynomials of different degrees. We use polynomials of degree 2, 3, 4, 6, 7, and 9. Mathematically, they are the following polynomials.

- income $= \beta_0 + \beta_1 \cdot \text{age} + \beta_2 \cdot \text{age}^2$
- income $= \beta_0 + \beta_1 \cdot \text{age} + \beta_2 \cdot \text{age}^2 + \beta_3 \cdot \text{age}^3$
- income $= \beta_0 + \beta_1 \cdot \text{age} + \beta_2 \cdot \text{age}^2 + \beta_3 \cdot \text{age}^3 + \beta_4 \cdot \text{age}^4$
- income $= \beta_0 + \beta_1 \cdot \text{age} + \beta_2 \cdot \text{age}^2 + \beta_3 \cdot \text{age}^3 + \beta_4 \cdot \text{age}^4 + \beta_5 \cdot \text{age}^5 + \beta_6 \cdot \text{age}^6$
- income $= \beta_0 + \beta_1 \cdot \text{age} + \beta_2 \cdot \text{age}^2 + \beta_3 \cdot \text{age}^3 + \beta_4 \cdot \text{age}^4 + \beta_5 \cdot \text{age}^5 + \beta_6 \cdot \text{age}^6 + \beta_7 \cdot \text{age}^7$
- income $= \beta_0 + \beta_1 \cdot \text{age} + \beta_2 \cdot \text{age}^2 + \beta_3 \cdot \text{age}^3 + \beta_4 \cdot \text{age}^4 + \beta_5 \cdot \text{age}^5 + \beta_6 \cdot \text{age}^6 + \beta_7 \cdot \text{age}^7 + \beta_8 \cdot \text{age}^8 + \beta_9 \cdot \text{age}^9$

Then, in the learning process we look for the polynomial that is better fitted to the data. In other words, we set the parameters of a given polynomial so that it is as close to the points as possible. As we did above with the regression we can formalize this "as close to the points as possible" in terms of the mean squared error (MSE).

It is important to highlight that when we increase the degree of a polynomial, the polynomial can adapt better to the points. It would be a better fit (and the error will be lower) if we use a polynomial of degree 2 (a parabola) than one of degree 1 (a line). If we have a polynomial of degree 1, the line cannot pass through all the points, unless they are aligned. Nevertheless, the larger the degree, the more we can fit the polynomial to the points. So, for a polynomial of degree 2 (a parabola, Fig. 4.18 top, left), we have more freedom but does not fit perfectly. If we increase the degree enough (same figure moving left to right, and top to bottom), we fit better and better the data. That is, the curve is nearer and nearer to the points. We see in the figure that when we increase the degree of the polynomial, the error between the model and the data tends to zero. The model with degree 9 seems to have almost zero error. This is true. More precisely, the mean squared error for this polynomial is $8.56 \cdot 10^{-08}$. So, for most of us, this is actually the same as zero.

Nevertheless, as we have a common understanding of how salary changes with age, it is very clear that the model with degree 4 (Fig. 4.18, second row, left) shown in the figure behaves incorrectly. Observe that in this case, the estimation of the salary of a 20 year old person starts around 3000, then *decreases* and from about 25 years old starts to increase again, *decreasing* when the person is 40 years old, and then increasing largely from about 50. If we consider larger polynomial degrees, models have a more disturbing shape. For degree 7, the model provides negative salaries for several ages. E.g., negative incomes are estimated for people about 25 years old, about 35 years old, and between 45 and 50. Nevertheless, as we have already underlined, with these high degrees, the models are very close to the data.

So, we have that low degrees seem to provide better information about the trends, with larger error. In contrast, large degrees miss the trend completely, and have no

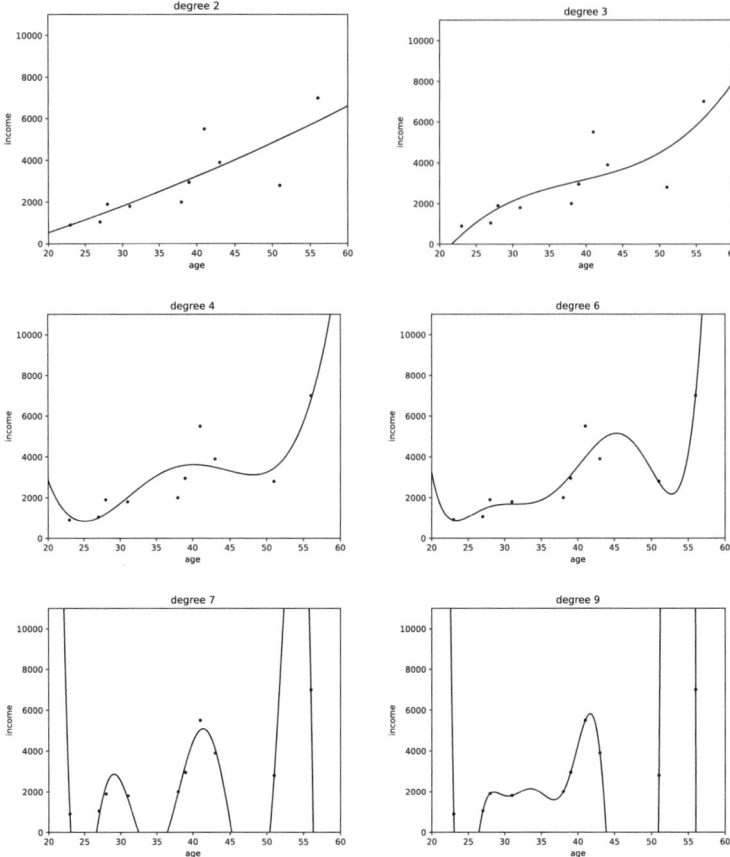

Fig. 4.18 Models built from the data in Table 4.2 but restricting it to national = no woman = yes. Top to bottom and left to right models correspond to polynomials of degree 2, 3, 4, 6, 7, and 9. In the center of each figure we can distinguish the point corresponding to record i_{25}, the bakery owner who is 39 years and has a salary of 2950

error. So, we need to select an appropriate degree that provides good information about the trend, with a reasonable error. Among the models in the figure, degree 2 and degree 3 seem to be good.

From a machine learning and statistical perspective, we have two conflicting interests. Too low degrees provide what is called under-fitting, as the model does not properly learn the trend. The error is too large, but also the model is too simple. In contrast, too large degrees provide what is called over-fitting. The model learns not only the trend but also the irrelevant details on the data. See that for large degrees, the polynomials representing the model tend to be closer to the point representing the bakery owner (record i_{25}, 39 years and a salary of 2950). The model is learning

4.6 Some Additional Concepts in Machine Learning   105

the actual salary of this person. Then, of course, if we need to estimate someone else salary with a similar age, estimation will be wrong.

This problem is also known as the bias-variance trade-off. In short, bias is what the model can learn, and what cannot. It is impossible for a model based on a polynomial of degree 2 to learn so much ups-and-downs as found in the larger degree polynomials. So, there is bias error. In short, variance, is related on how changes on the data change the model. Say, what happens if we change a single point. Low degree polynomials and under-fitted models do not change significantly when a single data point changes. Nevertheless, large degree polynomials and over-fitted models would change. So, there is a lot of variance on the models when data changes.

To illustrate this, let us take the data in Table 4.2 and let us modify i_{22} (as has been fired and moved to another company) and now the salary is 1010. Then, we retrain the models. We provide in Fig. 4.19 the model for degree 3 and for degree 7. It can be seen that the model with degree 3 is very similar to the one in Fig. 4.18. It has changed, but not so significantly. On the contrary, the model with degree 7 is absolutely different: the ranges where before we had large values, now we have small or negative; and the ranges where before we had low values, now we have large values. Observe the case of 25 years old and of 40.

Of course, these figures are made on purpose, and two particular cases do not prove mathematically that this is always the case. Nevertheless, it is true that large degree cause larger variance. Lower degrees provide more stable models.

The use of both training and validation data sets can be used to find a good bias-variance trade-off. When the model complexity increases (i.e., the polynomial has a higher degree), the bias error decreases. The model is better fitted into the data: the difference between the variable in the original data and the predicted value decreases. This is what is observed in Fig. 4.18. Nevertheless, for validation data, when the complexity increases first the error decreases but after a point the error increases again. This is because first the model is better and is learning the common trends that are found in both training and validation sets. Nevertheless, when complexity increases more, we are capturing specificities that exist only in the training data set (i.e., the particular salary of the 39 years old woman). We had first under-fitting, then we had a good model with good generalization capability, and finally we had over-fitting.

Exercise 4.6 Investigate how the ideas explained in this section apply to neural networks architecture, and in decision trees. In particular, what does it mean *complexity*?

Exercise 4.7 How can overfitting take place in decision trees? Relate overfitting with model complexity in decision trees.

4.6.5 Models, Predictions, and Outliers

We have just seen in the previous section that some models produced really bad results for some of the points. Our data included the bakery owner, that has an income that

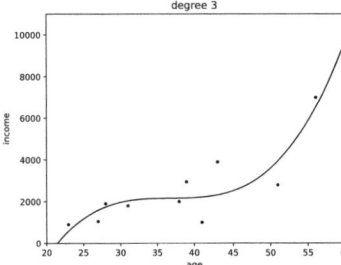 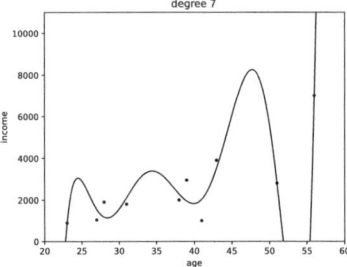

Fig. 4.19 Two new models built from the data in Table 4.2 but restricting it to national=no woman = yes, and replacing the salary of i_{22} by 1010. Models correspond to polynomials of degree 3 and 7

is larger that what is expected for her age. Depending on the type of model we learn, points like this may affect strongly the model.

A point (e.g., a record corresponding to a person) that differs significantly from the others is known in statistics as an outlier. We could consider that i_{25} is an outlier. This is an informal definition of outlier. To make it more formal, we would need to define what are *normal* observations.

Outliers and data with uncommon characteristics (people with uncommon or unique properties) when used in the training process can cause wrong outputs in the models. We have already seen in Fig. 4.18 that for models with a degree larger than 3 we have a peak on the income for those people around 40 years. This is caused by the bakery owner. Some machine and statistical learning algorithms try to reduce the effect of outliers. As we have already discussed above, robust regression is an example of such tools. Their goal is to produce results that do not depend so much on a single point, and, so, reduce the effect of such uncommon data.

It is relevant to highlight here something that has been implicit in all our discussion. Once we learn a model, the model produces outputs for any input we give to it. In most of the cases, we do not know how good is the output for the particular case under consideration.

That is, say that our machine learning algorithm has produced one of the models in Fig. 4.18. Then, say, we have a 42 years old friend, and we want to estimate her income. We use the system and get a number. Naturally, the system computes the output using 42 and the model itself. Nevertheless, some (most?) models do not provide information on how sure is the model itself on its prediction. If we *force* the model to give an output, the model will provide it. Note that this is also the case if we ask the model to predict the salary for another friend who is 75 years old. Note that in this case, there is not even data in the database for people at that age, and, thus, the model would be probably wrong, and, in any case, it is for sure unreliable. The concepts of interpolation and extrapolation (see Fig. 4.20) relate to this problem.

> Interpolation. It is an estimation or prediction of a value between already known values. In our example in Figure 4.18 we can see prediction of incomes between 23 and 56 year old people as interpolation. Here, different polynomials produce different interpolations. Note that often, with interpolation we expect that the model goes through the actual data points.
>
> Extrapolation. It is an estimation or prediction of a value outside the range of actual points. In our example in Figure 4.18 any prediction for people below 23 years and above 56 years is an extrapolation.

Fig. 4.20 Interpolation and extrapolation

4.6.6 Fairness in Machine Learning

Data-driven models are built from data. Nevertheless, this does not imply that they are objective. We have seen that the selection of the type of model has strong effects on the predictions. We have seen this in Sect. 4.6.4 where a *wrong* model selection causes peaks of income for 40 year old women, or even negative incomes for some people. Then, in Sect. 4.6.5 we have discussed the effects of data itself in the model. Once the type of model is fixed, the presence or not of a record (e.g., a person) can have effects on the data-driven model and its prediction. In particular, outliers may have strong effects in the models. In the same way, missing data, as explained in Sect. 4.6.2, can cause (with its absence) important effects on the decisions made. Recall the case of the AFST system described by Eubanks [66] and explained above. The system may not raise a child neglect warning for families not using public services.

Other aspects that naturally affect data-driven models are the variables we have in the database, and the ones we actually select to be used as inputs in our system. Note that the fact that the variables are selected automatically by a feature selection process does not prevent bias. Consider the case of a decision tree for loan approval where the first node asks whether the client is a man or a woman, or a system that uses as input the race of the client. This may be considered unacceptable practices. The fact that the decision tree is built by the software and the variable in the root is selected *automatically* does not make the system fair. Which variables are actually used by a system need to be carefully studied. Note that some variables may be considered as safe but they can be a proxy of problematic ones. This is the case of using ZIP code in a model for loans. ZIP can be just a proxy for race, and, therefore, the system can produce biased results.

The area of fairness in AI, mainly fairness in machine learning, studies how to build intelligent systems that are not biased. From a technical perspective [26, 109] there are multiple definitions of what fairness means (defined by different metrics), and there are different ways to mitigate the problems (e.g., modify training data, modify the learning process, and adjust conclusions of ML models).

Implementation and deployment of AI-powered systems, and software systems in general, can also cause bias and inequality in the society. They can perpetuate and even increase existing inequalities. For example, not all citizens may be equally able to use and take advantage of a new app. For example, because it is implicitly targeted to some population segments. Consider the case of applications with intensive use of internet, applications only for mobiles, applications using codes mainly used by young people, and applications continuously updated, which case difficulties to the elderly. Software systems that require last generation mobiles also introduce bias in their use (e.g., restricted to people with a certain economical status). Eubanks [66] explains some of these cases.

The fact that AI systems are not always fully autonomous, that they only provide recommendations, and that final decisions are left to humans does not necessarily avoid bias. It has been shown that even in these cases, decision makers may question [66, p. 141] their own judgment, and just use model's recommendation as a final decision.

4.6.7 Explainability

When a model is simple, why it produces a given output may be easy to understand. This is the case of a linear regression model with a few variables. For example, if we only have age, then we know the effect of each year in the output. It is the parameter associated to the variable age. If there are a few variables, it is straightforward to see the effect of each variable. The same applies to decision trees if they are not too large (i.e., their depth is small). We know how the decision is made, because it is based on the data and then traversing the structure from the top using the queries and values. For example, if we know that someone is 28 years old, the tree in Fig. 4.15 will give as output F because when we traverse the tree we finish in the leftmost case, which corresponds to an F. Models that are easy to understand by inspection are often call interpretable models.

Nevertheless, when models become large, then the reason of why it has produced a given output is not easy to know. Neural networks and deep learning models have this problem. We input the data and we obtain a result after a large number of computations using a large number of parameters. Therefore it is difficult to know why this is the output and not another one, and which were the factors that caused the model to produce that particular output. The reason why a model makes decisions is of course important. Ribeiro et al. [136] built a system to distinguish between images of wolves and Eskimo dogs (huskies). The system worked well but they proved that the system was not focusing on the animals but on the background. So, the system was detecting whether the background was white or not.

The field of explainability in AI studies this problem, and develop tools to help to understand how decisions are made. For example, some tools provide measures of the relevance of variables in the actual output, others provide very similar examples that lead to a different outcome (or which changes in the input would produce a different outcome).

4.6.8 Correlation and Causation

Machine learning and statistics build models based on relationships between variables. In the most simple case, with one input variable and one output variable, we build a model that explains how the output variable changes for changes in the input variable. This was our example with income and age.

If we have two highly correlated variables, a linear model will produce good results. Nevertheless, that two variables are correlated does not imply that the values that one variable take are a consequence of the values of the other. That is, it does not imply that there is a causal implication. In our example, we may consider that the salary is a "consequence" of age, so, there is a kind of causality. Nevertheless, if we build a model to predict age based on salary using the same data set, this "consequence" does not apply.

So, in short, correlation does not imply causation. A typical example in the literature is the icecream consumption and number of drowning incidents. When we have data about these two variables, we may have correlation between them. That is, the more icecream consumption, the larger the number of drowning incidents. And the less number of drowning incidents, the less consumption of icecreams. Nevertheless, it is of course false that eating icecream implies drowning, or in the other way round. The fact is that hot weather is the cause of both to increase or decrease.

Machine learning and statistical models are built trying to find relationships, and they can be good at that. These models alone, however, do not help for finding causal relationships.

Causal modeling [124, 125] has as objective the representation of causal relationships. Then, causal inference is about determining the actual effect of a variable or phenomenon. For this, we can use statistical tools, but we need more than that. It is very important to highlight that the whole analysis of causality scapes from what a machine learning or statistical model is or can do. Note that in any machine learning model, when we update the inputs (e.g., we change age from 20 to 25), the output is updated. Nevertheless, this change is not due to an actual causal relationship. The same applies if we divide by half the number of icecream consumptions. Our model will decrease the number of drownings. Nevertheless, it should be very clear that any public policy for decreasing the number of icecreams eaten in beaches in summer will not necessarily decrease the number of drownings.

4.6.9 Models and Privacy

We have just discussed that outliers can affect the model. Data about people with unique characteristics, or uncommon characteristics, may have strong influence on the model. This is not only a problem for model performance, but can be also a problem from a privacy perspective. Machine learning and statistical models can have traces of the data we have used for training, and these traces can lead to the disclosure of sensitive information. We will discuss this problem in more detail in Chap. 5.

4.7 Machine Learning Beyond Prediction

In this chapter we have focused on prediction, first on regression and later on classification. Machine learning for prediction is one of the types of machine learning: supervised machine learning. There are others. It is usual to divide machine learning into three categories. Let us review them.

- Supervised machine learning. In the training database we have a variable that we distinguish from the others because is the one that we want to predict. Then, we build a model for this particular variable. In statistics, this variable is known as the dependent variable (the others are the independent ones).
- Unsupervised machine learning. In this case there is no distinguished variable. The goal for a machine learning algorithm is to discover structures or patterns implicit in the data. Clustering algorithms are typical for unsupervised ML. They try to find similarities between the objects in the database, and establish structures with them. For example, in a database with clients, we can use clustering for their segmentation. We will group together all those people with similar characteristics, or behavior. Clustering algorithms differ on the types of structures they build from the data. The most common structures are partitions (or non-overlapping clusters) of objects, and hierarchies of objects or clusters. Other types of tools relate to dimensionality reduction.
- Reinforcement learning. This is a completely different type of approach, and usually apply to AI systems. In short, a system receives feedback of its performance, which can be just positive if system's outcome is good and negative if system's outcome is bad. A simple example is reinforcement learning for games. Consider a system that plays a game, then when the system wins, it receives the positive feedback. In contrast, if the system loses, it receives the negative feedback. Then, the system uses the received feedback to adjust its behavior and improve its performance.

Exercise 4.8 We regularly travel from Umeå to Skellefteå. Over the past three years, we have recorded all our trips in a database. For each trip, we have stored information about the weather (rain, cloudy, sunny), temperature (from -30 to $+30$), month (January–December), arrival time, and means of transportation (car, bus, or bicycle). Let us build a decision making model that decides the means of transportation for us. What kind of machine learning should we use? supervised or unsupervised? Why?

4.8 Bibliography

Machine learning is such a hot topic that there are plenty of resources in the web, including explanations of algorithms, concepts, as well as software. For a book reference, Hastie et al. [85] is a good one. There are two additional versions with applications in R and Python.

Chapter 5
Security and Privacy

Abstract Security and privacy are important components of any software system. The same applies to intelligent systems and machine learning applications. In this chapter we explain the main concepts related to security and privacy for databases, secure communications, and machine learning models. In particular, we discuss, authentication, authorization in access control, secure communications, data integrity, and privacy for both databases and machine learning models. The chapter finishes explaining what is security and privacy by design.

> ningú del volt li sap la medicina
> i ningú li coneix el pensament.
> Però el que dins li mou una baralla
> i tot el mal que ve d'avall i amunt,
> prou que ella el sap i no diu res i calla
> i entre les altres va aguantant el punt.
>
> Josep M. de Sagarra, El comte Arnau, 1928 [142].

Nowadays, security and privacy is a key component of any software system. The same naturally applies to any AI system. Security and privacy by design is about building systems so that they satisfy the requirements because they have been included in the specifications of the software.

In this chapter we will present the main concepts related to security and privacy that are relevant for accessing and using databases (authentication and authorization in access control), transmitting information (secure communication and data integrity), and building and using machine learning models. We also show by means of examples that security mechanisms are not enough to avoid the disclosure of sensitive information, and that privacy mechanisms may be necessary. Concepts as privacy models are also explained with some examples.

Artificial intelligence and machine learning are commonly used tools to detect attacks in software systems, and mechanisms based on machine learning have also been defined to prevent these attacks. These topics are not explained because they are beyond the scope of this book.

5.1 Security and Data Protection

Access to the data needs to be restricted to authorized personnel. Two main concepts are used for this authentication and authorization.

Authentication consists on proving that you are who you say you are, and, thus, you can ask for authorization to access the resources or services you need. There are several ways to verify that the identity claimed is actually the one actually associated to the entity that claims such identity.

Authorization consists on defining access rights (i.e., policies) to resources and services. Then, authorized users can have such rights granted. Access control provides different ways (so called access control models) to grant this access.

We describe them below in more detail.

5.1.1 Authentication

In computer systems, different approaches are used for authentication. Each of them is called a factor, and while in the past a single one was typically used, it is nowadays common to use multi-factor authentication to increase the security level. The most used factors are the following ones.

- Something the user knows (knowledge). This usually corresponds to a password or a personal identification number (PIN), but security questions can also be used (as e.g. mother's maiden name, and birthplace).
- Something the user have (possession). In this case, a physical object is used to verify the identity. Typical objects include an ID card, a USB security token, and your mobile phone.
- Something the user is (inherence). The verification of the identity uses some user's physical property. This is usually a biometrics. For example, fingerprints, and iris, but it can also be based on other characteristics as voice recognition.
- Location. The actual location of the user is taken into account in the verification process. E.g., access is only granted within the premises of the company.

In two-factor authentication, at least two mechanisms of different factor types are required for authentication. For example, to log in to a system, you may need a password. In addition, you must have your mobile phone at hand, as some information is sent to it, which you need to provide to the system before gaining access. Multi-factor authentication is to provide better security guarantees and avoid security breaches if one of the factors is compromised. E.g. it is not enough for intruders to hack your password or stole your mobile phone. They need both to impersonate you.

In the European Union, there is a payment directive (Revised Directive on Payment Services—PSD2, Directive (EU) 2015/2366) which asks for "strong customer authentication" (SCA). This is defined in terms of multi-factor authentication.

5.1.2 Authorization in Access Control

When a person is authenticated, the system recognizes who claims to be. Then, what can this person access? There are different ways to grant access to services, i.e., to provide authorization. The main ways to grant access are the following ones.

- Discretionary access control. Access to objects (as e.g. files) are granted by the owners of these objects. This type of access control is usual in cloud storage and file sharing systems. For example, if I create a file with the slides of a talk, I decide who can access them and provide individual permissions to only those that need them.
- Mandatory access control. The security policy is centrally controlled by a policy administrator. Access to objects are granted for a user only if there is a rule or policy that grants the user this access. This type of access control has been used in security and military systems.
- Role-based access control. The security policy is centralized but access to objects are not granted individually to users but to groups of users based on their roles.

  Roles are defined by a name and sets of privileges. These privileges can be of different types. Typical examples are access to files, printers, and resources; right to modify a file (e.g., update some fields or the whole file); execution of programs. Users are then assigned roles into the system.

  For example, in a computer system for schools, Alice can be either a "teacher", a "student", a "coordinator", a "director", or an "IT technician". Then, roles have authorizations associated to their privileges. For example, "students" have access their own marks, the schedules of their courses, etc. In contrast, "teachers" have access to the marks, and also the privilege of their modification. That is, "students" can not modify their marks but "teachers" can. The "academic director" can modify students assignments to courses. It is a centralized manager from the IT department who assigns access rights to roles according to security policies and school requirements. Then, authorization for a particular user is based on the assigned roles. In our example, whether Alice can update or not a mark in the computer system solely depends on the roles she has been assigned. If the only role she has is "student" she will not be able to do so. In contrast, if she is a "teacher", then she may be able to change some marks. Multiple roles can be assigned to the same user, according to the organization needs.
- Break-glass access control models [24, 131]. In emergency situations (as in health care and disaster management) some flexible access control may be required to override access control restrictions on demand. The break-glass model is used for this type of situations and permits, with correct access control privileges, to grant access to restricted data, services and resources. As under normal functioning access to such data and services is not allowed, the usage of these exceptional rights are logged for later audits and reviews. That is, the usage of break-glass access is monitored so that after the situation is back to normal, an analysis of the actions performed can be done and misuse punished.

5.1.3 Secure Communication

Secure communication usually refers to protecting the content of a message so that unintended recipients (someone else than the expected receiver), as message sniffers, cannot read it. Encryption is the standard way to provide this service. More particularly, local encryption in your device and decryption in the recipients device.

Encryption is usually implemented using public-key cryptography. In public-key cryptography each agent (or person) needs two keys that complement each other. One is private and only the agent (or the software) knows it. The other is public and everybody can know it. These two keys are built in such a way, that any of them can be used for encryption and for decryption.

Say that Agnès wants to send a message to Brianna. To make things simple, Agnès wants to send Brianna a single letter. Say this letter is in this case A. How this can be done? Both Agnès and Brianna have two keys, one is private and the other is public. So, Agnès has a private key that only she knows and another one that everybody can know. Let us use Pr_A to denote the private key (and the private encryption) that only Agnès knows, and Pu_A to denote the public key (and the public encryption) that everybody can know. Similarly, we use Pr_B and Pu_B to denote the private and public keys of Brianna.

These two keys can be used for two different things. One is sending private messages (secure communication). The other is to sign one owns message. We can even do both things: sign our own message and make it private so that only the recipient can read it.

Let us say that messages are single letters, and letters are codified with numbers using the ASCII/UTF-8 codification as listed in Table 5.1. Then, for example, if we want to transmit the letter A we take its value 65 and this is the number we will transmit. We will encrypt then 65 and give another one to the recipient.

Let us now consider the two scenarios when Agnès wants to send the message containing the letter A to Brianna.

- Agnès sends the message m to Brianna that only Brianna can read. To do this, Agnès takes the message m and uses Brianna's public key, and produces a new message. Here $m = 65$ as she is transmitting A. Mathematically this is to compute $Pu_B(65)$. Let us say that the computations result into 10. So, Agnès sends 10 to Brianna. Then, Brianna receives a 10. Then, Brianna using her private and secret key Pr_B computes $Pr_B(10)$ and gets 65. Only the private key of Brianna can help

Table 5.1 Codification of some letters and symbols in ASCII/UTF-8

Codification	64	65	66	67	68	69	70	71	72	73	74	75	76	77	78	79
Symbol	@	A	B	C	D	E	F	G	H	I	J	K	L	M	N	O
Codification	80	81	82	83	84	85	86	87	88	89	90	91	92	93	94	95
Symbol	P	Q	R	S	T	U	V	W	X	Y	Z	[	\	]	^	_

to go back to 65. A wrong key will produce another letter. Therefore, this message can only be read by Brianna, no one else can correctly decrypt it.

- Agnès sends a message m to Brianna so that Brianna knows that only Agnès may have produced it. To do this, Agnès takes the message $m = 65$ and uses her own private key to produce its encrypted version. Mathematically, this is to compute $Pr_A(65)$. Let us say that this results into 21. Then, Brianna receives this 21 and using the public key of Agnès (i.e., computing $Pu_A(21)$) gets the 65. Only Agnès that knows her own private key may have produced a message that can be properly decrypted using Pu_A. Here, the message is signed by Agnès. All know that only Agnès may have produced it, but all can read it.

If someone wants to sign a message and send it to someone so that only this someone can read it, then we need to apply both encryptions, and the reader will need to apply both decryptions. Say Agnès sends a signed message to Brianna, then, Agnès signs first it with her private key (i.e., encrypts $Pr_A(m)$) and then encrypts with Brianna's public key:

$$Pu_B(Pr_A(m)),$$

and the resulting message is transmitted.

As in this example a message is a single letter, incorrect pairings of private and public keys may still produce a *valid* message (i.e., a letter) although an incorrect one. In general, when the message is a long text, decryption would produce gibberish text.

How this actually works in practice? There exist different implementations that allow to build private public-key cryptosystems. One of them is the RSA cryptosystem. Here RSA stands for Ron Rivest, Adi Shamir, and Leonard Adleman who described the algorithm in 1977. This system was also developed independently by Clifford Cocks in 1973 in England, but it was classified until 1997.

The system is based on prime numbers. The key element for security is that multiplying two prime numbers is computationally easy, but, in contrast, when we have a large number it is difficult to find their factors even if we know that it is the product of only two prime numbers. We will explain here how this works with small numbers (small prime numbers), but in practice we need very large numbers to have guarantees of security. See Fig. 5.1 about the meaning of large.

Recall that prime numbers are those natural numbers greater than 1 that are not a product of two smaller natural numbers (see Fig. 5.1).

Let us build a simple RSA cryptosystem for Agnès. To start, we need to consider two prime numbers p and q. We will use small numbers. Let us take $p = 11$ and $q = 23$. Then, we multiply them obtaining the number n_A (we use n_A as it corresponds to Agnès). So, $n_A = 11 \cdot 23 = 253$. We also compute the so called Carmichael function from n_A (or from p and q). We denote it by $\lambda(n_A)$ as p and q are prime and n_A is the product of p and q, the computation of this function is computationally easy. In this case, it is the least common multiple of $p - 1$ and $q - 1$. So, the least common multiple (lcm) of 10 and 22. This is 110. Mathematically, $\lambda(n_A) = lcm(p - 1, q -$

Prime numbers are those natural numbers greater than 1 that are not a product of two smaller natural numbers. The following are the prime numbers up to 150:

2, 3, 5, 7, 11, 13, 17, 19, 23, 29, 31, 37, 41, 43, 47, 53, 59, 61, 67, 71, 73, 79,
83, 89, 97, 101, 103, 107, 109, 113, 127, 131, 137, 139, 149.

Two numbers are coprime if the only positive integer that is a divisor of both of them is 1. If two numbers are prime, they are also coprime. So, 61 and 67 are coprime. But also, 9 and 10 are coprime even they are not prime.

Number theory is the branch of mathematics that study integers and arithmetic functions. Prime numbers are a key concept in number theory. The fundamental theorem of arithmetic establishes that every natural number greater than 1 is either a prime itself or can be factorized as a product of primes that is unique up to their order.

Large numbers in cryptography are usually described in terms of the number of bits we need to represent them. Numbers in a computer are represented in binary (i.e., only 0 and 1 are used), and then we need much more bits (binary digits) than standard decimal digits. E.g., 1, 2, 3, 4, 5, 6 and 7 are represented in binary by 1, 10, 11, 100, 101, 110, and 111. So, they need 1, 2, or 3 bits. Numbers from 8 to 15 need 4 bits. Since 2015 it is recommended to use numbers with 2048 bits in cryptography. That is, a sequence of 2048 zeroes and ones. Such a long binary number is translated into the usual decimal numeral system into a number with 617 digits.

Fig. 5.1 Primes, coprimes, and large numbers in RSA cryptosystems. What is large?

1). For $p = 11$ and $q = 23$, we have that $\lambda(n_A) = 110$. The values p, q and $\lambda(n_A)$ are kept secret.

Now, we need to choose a number that is smaller than $\lambda(n_A)$ and such that it is coprime with $\lambda(n_A)$. Two numbers are coprime if the only positive number that is a divisor of both is 1 (see Fig. 5.1). There are several of such numbers smaller than 110. For example, the number 101 has this property. Let us take it. Then, this number is the public key for Agnès. So, using the notation above, $Pu_A = 101$, and Agnès publicly announces this number. The value of n_A is also part of the public key, so, Agnès also publicly announces it.

The next step is to compute the private key. To do so, we need to solve a problem called the modular multiplicative inverse. In short, we need to find a number that is a kind of inverse of the number we have just defined. That is, the multiplicative inverse of 101. We will not go into the details of this computation, but we give some of these details in Fig. 5.2. For the number $Pu_A = 101$ we obtain $Pr_A = 61$.

As a summary, the public key for Agnès is the pair (n_A, Pu_A) and the private key is Pr_A. So, $(n_A, Pu_A) = (253, 101)$ and the private key is $Pr_A = 61$.

Then, Agnès can encrypt any message m with a key e as follows:

The problem of modular multiplicative inverse consists of finding a number d that when multiplied by e results into 1 modulo s. In our setting, e corresponds to the public key, so $e = 101$ and s corresponds to the number that is coprimer with $\lambda(n_A)$

Then, our goal is to find a number d that multiplied by 101 results into 1 modulo 110.
The solution is 61 because when we multiply $61 \cdot 101$ we obtain 6161, and if we divide 6161 by 110 it results 56 and the remainder is 1. So, 6161 modulo 110 is 1.

Fig. 5.2 Modular multiplicative inverse of 101 modulo 110

5.1 Security and Data Protection

- Compute m^e and apply modulo n_A.

Recall that modulo (for positive numbers) returns the remainder of a division. So, in short, Agnès computes m^e and then divides the result by n_A and takes the remainder.

Decryption uses the same schema. That is, using the decryption key d, and with the received encrypted message m', we would obtain the original message as follows:

- Compute m'^d and apply modulo n_A.

This is so because mathematically, combining encryption and decryption pairs we obtain the original message m. This is expressed in mathematics

$$(m^e)^d \text{ modulo } n_A = m^{e^d} \text{ modulo } n_A$$
$$= m \text{ modulo } n_A$$

This is for Agnès, and the same needs to be done for Brianna. So, Brianna needs first two prime numbers, and she selects $p_B = 17$ and $q_B = 19$. Then, she multiplies them and obtains $n_B = 323$, and computes the Carmichael function and obtains $\lambda(n_B) = 144$, as this is the least common multiple of 16 and 18. Then, selects a public key that is coprime and smaller than $\lambda(n_B)$. She selects $Pu_B = 109$. The final step is to compute the private key with the modular multiplicative inverse. She gets in this way the number $Pr_B = 37$. Now, Brianna has the public key $(n_B, Pu_B) = (323, 109)$ and the private key is $Pr_B = 37$.

Using the keys above, we can revisit the two cases of Agnès and Brianna we have considered above. In both examples we consider that Agnès wants to send a letter A which corresponds to transmitting the number 65 (according to Table 5.1).

- Agnès sends the message m to Brianna that only Brianna can read. So, Agnès wants to transmit 65; and to do so she uses the public key of Brianna, so, this is 109. Therefore, the computation is:

$$(65)^{109} \text{ modulo } 323 = 141.$$

Therefore, Brianna receives the number 141. To decrypt this message, Brianna uses her private key $Pr_B = 37$ and computes

$$(65)^{37} \text{ modulo } 323 = 65.$$

So, it knows that Agnès sent an A.

- Agnès sends a signed message m to Brianna so that Brianna knows that only Agnès may have produced it. Agnès takes the 65 and uses her own private key $Pr_A = 61$ (with $n_A = 253$) and computes

$$(65)^{61} \text{ modulo } 253 = 21.$$

Agnès sends this 21 to Brianna. Then, Brianna decrypts the message using Agnès public key. That is, $Pu_A = 101$. It computes

$$(65)^{101} \text{ modulo } 253 = 65.$$

So, it knows that Agnès sent an A.

Exercise 5.1 Compute the message Agnès will transmit if she wants both to sign it, and that only Brianna can read it.

As we have explained, this approach works because the decomposition of a large integer in its prime factors is computationally very costly. If we take the number $n_A = 253$ it will be very easy to find 11 and 23 that multiplied produce 253. Nevertheless, a large number will take too much time to factorize.

5.1.4 How Can We Attack Agnès' Message?

If Agnès uses small primes, then factorization of the number is easy, and a successful attack is possible. If we focus on Agnès, the goal is to know her private key Pr_A, from the public information $(n_A, Pu_A) = (253, 101)$.

First, we look for the factorization of $n_A = 253$ which are (of course) the two primes 11 and 23. When this is done, it is trivial to compute the Carmichael function from n_A because we know that is based on p and q, and the least common multiple of $p - 1$ and $q - 1$. In this way, we obtain $\lambda(n_A) = 110$. With all this information, we can compute Pr_A as the solution of modular multiplicative inverse from Pu_A and $\lambda(n_A)$. This problem is not so computationally complex. Therefore, we can get easily the private key of Agnès Pr_A. This is what we have computed in Fig. 5.2.

Nevertheless, as we have said above, these numbers were secret and Agnès should not disclose them. If the prime numbers are large then the factorization of their product is not easy, and the attack fails. So, the factorization is key in the attack. For example, consider that Agnès considered $n_A = 629107$ instead of 253, then, the unique factorization of this number takes more time that the one of 253. It will still take more time if Agnès selects 40378981, and even more if Agnès selects $n_A = 33701025973$. Nevertheless, these numbers are really small.

The factorization of these numbers are as follows:

- $631 \cdot 997 = 629107$
- $5099 \cdot 7919 = 40378981$
- $65537 \cdot 514229 = 33701025973$

These factorizations in a regular laptop take less than a second (in my laptop the last factorization takes in average 0.00139 s). So, these numbers are too small for real protection. We need very large primes. Nevertheless, something like

1331520515757964429726536183024432862323571784665691685492498174409486833572310989222278345

is still not big enough. If Agnès uses this number, its factorization into the two primes

- 37547332574898624019733579791287730
- 354624529745721749359044919174854645800559518766197637100

takes much longer in my laptop. In fact, I abandoned this factorization after a few hours. Nevertheless, it is still not secure enough. An attacker could factorize the number in a more powerful computer and then easily compute the Carmichael function, and, thus, break her secret messages.

If the two primer numbers are really large, their product, of course, will be still larger and, then, the factorization is not possible in *reasonable* time. Without the factorization, it is not possible to compute the Carmichael function, and therefore we cannot solve the modular multiplicative inverse for Pu_A and $\lambda(n_A)$. So, we cannot find Pr_A.

That's why we need to use very large numbers. As computers are becoming faster, we need to have large enough numbers so that it takes a while to build powerful enough computers to break the encryption. Note that we want to ensure our encryption to be safe not only now but also in the future. E.g., that our private documents are not decrypted by someone in 10 years. The RSA-250 number (a number with 250 decimal digits) is an example of a large number that has already been factorized. That's why the current recommendation is to use numbers with 2048 bits (617 decimal digits).

5.1.5 Data Storage and Integrity

Encryption is not only appropriate for communications, it is also useful for storage. If we encrypt the data before storage in our own computer, then, only us can read them properly when we decrypt them with the decryption key. An intruder able to access the files will not be able to actually read their content.

Cryptography is also used to guarantee data integrity. Data integrity is about ensuring that no one makes unauthorized modifications to the data. If we have data in our computer (or in the cloud), how can we be sure that no one else has accessed the files and modified its content? For example, has someone modified the account number for bank transfers without us noticing it? The same applies to software that we download from a repository. Is the software we download the same that was upload by the creators? or someone has made modifications to it to add some malicious code? Cryptography provides tools for data integrity. Hash functions combined with digital signatures are used for this purpose.

A hash function is a mathematical function that takes usually a big chunk of information and produces an output of a given size. SHA-256 is one of these hash functions that takes a text and produces a string of 256 bits. The functions are built with two main properties:

- a small change in the input (i.e., a small change in the file) will produce a very different output with a high probability, and
- given the output of the function (e.g., the 256 bit summary) it is very difficult to compute the input (i.e., the original file).

In addition, we expect that the probability of any output is the same.

As an example, we can consider SHA-256 applied to two sentences. The first sentence "I live in a big town" represents the information we actually stored in a file. When we store the file, we compute the hash function of the file and store its result in a secure way (e.g., signed/encrypted). Then, let us consider that an intruder accesses the file and replaces "b" by "p"! Nevertheless, when we need to use the file, the first thing we do is to compute again the hash function. So, we apply SHA-256 to the file "I live in a pig town". Then, we obtain something else (very different indeed) and when we compare it with our securely stored original hash we know that the file has been modified!

For illustration, we give these two SHA-256 values for the two files.

- "I live in a big town."
  Its SHA-256 representation is:
  '2c54526ed5e479a6596a54ace176aaeb7f42eabf109ad5f445b793a7e24b6555'
- "I live in a pig town."
  Its SHA-256 representation is:
  '056d325820fc45d37f9821c34bb3114ed333708573f8b712146765608faeba25.'

5.1.6 Quantum Computers

Quantum computers are not yet there, but their fundamental properties are different to the ones of current computers. Their different way of processing data make them a threat to some existing security technologies. In particular, to RSA. In 1994 Peter Shor developed an algorithm for quantum computers that would be able to provide a factorization for an integer. If such a computer can be effectively built, then an efficient algorithm can be implemented in it. This would break RSA cryptography and, therefore, is a threat to existing systems currently in use in the world.

Nevertheless, at this point, it is unclear if such algorithm can be built in practice. Current technology for quantum computers has not been developed enough to solve small problems. Let alone for problems as factorization of large integers. In addition, Shor's approach is based on assuming a quantum computer that has no errors/noise, while actual current quantum computers have high error rates. So, quantum computers do not seem to be a threat in the short term. Nevertheless, there is research to overcome this problem. Post-quantum cryptography focuses on algorithms that would be safe even if such computers are ever made.

5.2 Privacy for Databases and Machine Learning

Regulations (as GDPR in the EU) have made clear that privacy is a right, and that the digital world is not exempt from privacy requirements. Access control, and secure communications provide tools so that only authorized people access the information either in corporate databases or in communications. Nevertheless, this is not enough to guarantee that disclosure does not take place in the digital world.

When data is collected, and shared, even when controls are properly implemented, unappropriate disclosure of sensitive information can take place. Data privacy techniques, may be required. Naive anonymization may still lead to disclosure. Here, with naive anonymization we mean removing information that is clearly personal as names, identity card numbers, address and so. This type of anonymization is usually not enough.

Why this is not enough if authorization and access control are properly implemented? The problem is that those that access (or receive) the data, even if they are authorized to have access to such data, can learn information about other items of interest that they should not know. That is, they can infer from the authorized data some information that they should not learn. It is better to explain this with an example.

Let us consider that we have a database with information of all the people that has attended our unit in the last years. This database is provided in Table 5.2. The database includes personal information as name and address of a contact person (variables/columns: name, address, and nationality). We may also have here, names of other adults in the household, identity card numbers, telephone numbers, etc. (not displayed in Fig. 5.2). Then, we have information about the first time these people contacted our unit (column: first contact), as well as about the children in the household (column: children) and the number of children we support with the service we provide (column: children supported). Finally, we also record in the database the

Table 5.2 Database with the information about the attendees to our unit

Name	Address	Nationality	First contact	Children	Children supported	...	Service provided
DEJ	Examensvägen	Swedish	9 October 2024	1	1	...	B
IBC	Marievvägen	Italian	18 October 2023	2	2	...	A
JEH	Rymdvvägen	Swedish	14 January 2025	2	1	...	A
JAG	Planetvvägen	Swedish	17 April 2024	3	2	...	A
SHE	Strandvvägen	Swedish	16 September 2024	8	3	...	C
GRW	Hvällvvägen	Swedish	28 May 2024	2	1	...	C

service we provide (column: service provided). Other information may be included as well, depending on the type of service we provide, as salary/income, illnesses, etc.

Let us now consider that we need to share this database with someone else for some data analysis. This can be a person from another unit of the same department, another department of the same organization, an external researcher or a data scientist at a research institute. They need the data to do some analyses about the people that use our services, and intend to publish these analyses to the general public.

Let us consider that we have a rough idea of the purpose of the analysis but not the details. Note that if we knew exactly what they want to compute, another option would be (maybe) to provide them with the results they need. The fact that we compute the results ourselves and provide them to the researchers do neither exclude completely disclosure risk problems, as we discuss later.

It is important to underline that the problem is not about access control or about intruders, or unintended recipients receiving a copy of the database. The problem is all about authorized people accessing authorized data. We are assuming that the receiver of the data has all appropriate authorizations for these required data analyses. Just for the sake of illustration, computations of interest may include mean number of children, information about the mean income of people requiring some economical support, relationship between children supported and service provided, etc.

A first inspection of the database shows us that there is information that these data scientists do not need at all for their computations (e.g., name). The same applies if we have information about identity card numbers, telephone numbers and the like. Then, there is some additional information that is clearly problematic, as full address. In addition, other variables (fields, or columns) can also be seen as quite sensitive. We have e.g., nationality. Sharing data that includes nationality can be problematic. So, we may decide that this information is sensitive. Observe that there is only one Italian household in the database. So, after this analysis we decide to remove these variables and provide only the other variables (columns) of the database. Table 5.3 provides the information that would be available to the data scientist. This information is only part of the full database, and, using the jargon in computer science and databases, it is called a view (a view of the original database).

Table 5.3 View of the original database for the data scientist, with only some of the information about the attendees to our unit

First contact	Children	Children supported	...	Service provided
9 October 2024	1	1	...	B
18 October 2023	2	2	...	A
14 January 2025	2	1	...	A
17 April 2024	3	2	...	A
16 September 2024	8	3	...	C
28 May 2024	2	1	...	C

5.2 Privacy for Databases and Machine Learning

The fact of sharing this reduced view of the database can still be problematic. It can lead to undesired disclosure. We can illustrate two cases.

- The date of first contact may be too informative. The data scientist remembers well that precisely on Tuesday 14th January, while she was celebrating her birthday in a cafeteria near the social service office, she saw two parents of the school of her own children that precisely have two children. So, she is identifying the case in the database and can also infer which is the service this family has. It is a service of type A.
- There is a case with a family with 8 children. This is a small town, and families have only a few children. The number of children can give enough information to identify the family. Again, the data scientist can use this information to know what service this family receives. It is a service of type C, and they started attending the office on 16 September 2024.

In the first case we have used only one attribute, in the second case another. In bigger databases or on data of large towns, one or two attributes may not lead to disclosure, but a combination of them, can do. In the example above, we may use that we know a family of two children and that they are attending the office since 2023 to infer that they have a service of type A.

In general, two types of disclosure are possible.

- Identity disclosure. It is when we are able to find someone in the database. We identify a record or case in a database and relate with a real person. In the example above, this is what we have done first. Say, the data scientist knows who is the family that attended social services on Tuesday 14th January 2025.
- Attribute disclosure. It is when we are able to learn something about someone from the information in the database. In the example above, this is what happens when the data scientist learns that the service the social service provides to the family is of type A. The most common situation is that identity disclosure causes some attribute disclosure, as in this example. Nevertheless, we can have any type of disclosure without the other.

Data privacy studies techniques to reduce or limit disclosure. In this example we can reduce the information of first contact. Instead of providing the whole date, we can provide only month and year, or just year. This process mainly corresponds to reducing the quality of the data. Protection of the variable number of children is also possible but can be more difficult. We will discuss this later.

Sharing data without protection is problematic, as we have seen, because it can lead to disclosure. Sharing summaries and computations from the data can also be problematic, even if we do not share the data themselves. Summaries can include traces of the original data that can help us to infer sensitive information.

Consider the case that we do not share the database but we will decide to share only some summaries. For the database above we can consider, for example, the following summaries: (i) for the variable first contact, how many families attended the service every year, (ii) for the variable number of children in a family, the mean

Table 5.4 Summaries of the view of the original database on the attendees to our unit. Data to be published

Summaries				
First contact	Children	Children supported	...	Service provided
2023: 1	Min: 1	Min: 1	...	A: 3
2024: 4	Mean: 3	Mean: 1.66	...	B: 1
2025: 1	Max: 8	Max: 3	...	C: 2

number of children, as well as the minimum and maximum number of children; and (iii) for the services provided, a count of each type of service. If we proceed in this way, we will have the summary we provide in Table 5.4.

The publication of this summary can be problematic, and lead to disclosure of sensitive information. This is so even if we only publish this summary instead of the full protected database. Consider again that we live in a small town where there is only one family with 8 children. Then, naturally, the summary clearly shows that this family has attended the social services.

We wrote before that summaries can contain *traces* of the original data that can leak sensitive information. Our example illustrates this situation with information about the family of 8 children clearly reproduced in the summary. Similar situations appear with other types of functions. For example, mean values can also lead to disclosure. A typical case is when we have salaries of people (e.g., salaries or income of people/families attending a service). When all salaries are kind of *usual* salaries, the mean will be another *usual* salary. Note that this applies to both low, medium, and high salaries. Nevertheless, if the database contains an extremely large salary (and very different than the others), the mean can be oddly large. In this case, the mean salary would also show traces of the original data. In this case, we could infer that someone we know (who is rich) is attending the service.

The problem of disclosure associated with a summary is found also in machine learning when applied to sensitive data. A model built from sensitive data can have traces of the original data. In machine learning, there has been research to identify these models and to solve this problem (see Fig. 5.3), it describes membership inference attacks that focus on quantifying the risk of problematic models. More particularly, can we know that a record was used to train the model?

Summaries and models need to provide us information, but ideally this information should not be too tightly associated to particular records. Then, these attacks and disclosures are not possible.

5.2.1 How Can We Provide Privacy Guarantees?

If sharing data can cause unintended disclosure, and if summaries and machine learning models can also cause disclosure, how can we have guarantees that privacy requirements are met?

Privacy models are computational definitions of privacy that help in this process. That is, they specify what kind of privacy we require, and then we can develop the appropriate solution (i.e., a program) and, thus, implement a software system with appropriate privacy guarantees. There is not a single privacy model, as there are different ways to understand disclosure, and different ways to ensure that a type of disclosure does not take place.

Privacy models are associated to disclosure, and to ways intruders or attackers can use shared information to learn unintended information about someone. When designing an application, we first need to understand the type of disclosure than can take place, and that is not desirable, this helps to select the privacy model that applies, and then use the appropriate software that provides a solution that is compliant with the privacy model. For each privacy model, there can be different software solutions. In the particular case of protecting a database, these solutions will provide different types of protected databases. These software solutions may differ on the quality of the solution (i.e., quality of the produced data), the computational cost of building the solution, and other properties of the software.

To illustrate privacy models we give some examples. We will also provide different protected versions of the database above.

Privacy from Re-identification

When we share a (protected) database, the goal of the privacy model "privacy from re-identification" is to avoid intruders to find someone they know (or someone they have information about) in the database. The proportion of correctly identified re-identifications (or a probability of re-identification) is a measure of risk, and it can be estimated quantitatively applying record linkage algorithms (see Fig. 5.4).

Let us consider the case of having a database with some records (as in our example in Table 5.2), and a data-driven model built from this database (e.g., a machine learning model that predicts the type of service using family's data).
A membership inference attack (MIA) is a way to quantify in what extent the data-driven model contains enough traces from the data to know whether a particular record was used to build it. E.g., can we "proof" with some certainty that the record of the family with 8 children was actually used? Membership inference attacks are built using machine learning itself. In particular, we build MIA models that say "yes" if they estimate that a record was used to build a model and "no" if it was not used. Then, we take a record of a family, we take the output of our data-driven model for service prediction, and apply our MIA model to this information. Then, its outcome is: "yes" it has been used/"no" it has not been used to training the model.

Fig. 5.3 Membership inference attacks

> Given two different databases that contain records with information about the same people, *record linkage* is the type of software used to find the correct linkages between these records. Say, if both databases includes records about Maria, which are these two records? Record linkage algorithms are used for database integration (e.g., in corporations having large databases that need to standardize). Is this Maria Carlsson living in rue de Molière in file A the same as Marie Karlson in file B also living in rue de Molière?
> Record linkage is also used to attack protected databases. To do so, we proceed as follows. On the one hand we take the protected database as file A. On the other hand we build a database with any information an intruder may have (e.g., public information or information gathered from other sources) about individuals. This is file B. Then, we apply record linkage to link the records in both files. The algorithm suggests possible links between the two files. Some are correct, but some are not.
> If we are the office that protected the file, we know which are the correct links. So, we know how good intruders can do with their information and the record linkage algorithm. We have a proportion of correct links, which can be seen as the probability of having a correct re-identification. Say, as in our example, we have 8 records in the shared file A. Then, the intruder builds a file B with data from her acquaintances and then applies record linkage. To make things simple, there are 8 acquaintances in her file. She gets 8 suggested links (i.e., they relate the 8 anonymized records with her 8 acquaintances). If we know the real data, we can know how many of these suggested links are correct. Say, only one is correct. Then, the risk is 1/8. This value is an estimation of intruders performance, and a measure of the risk.

Fig. 5.4 Record linkage for risk assessment

To avoid re-identification, software for data protection typically reduces the quality of the database to make re-identification no longer possible. For example, we increase the age of some people and decrease the age of others. Reducing the quality of the database implies that the protected database is less useful than the original one. There is some information loss and data utility degrades.

To make re-identification no longer possible may require unacceptable information loss. We may need to modify a record too much to avoid re-identification (e.g., we update so much the ages that they are no longer useful). If the database contains people with very unique characteristics, data protection may cause a big damage into the data utility. Because of that, we may accept some re-identification risk. In other words, one may be able to accept some probability of re-identification, if it is low enough, if this can provide also a good data utility. Finding a good balance between disclosure risk and data quality is the cornerstone of the field of data privacy.

Methods for data protection are developed to find this good trade-off between data utility and disclosure risk. They are called masking methods. Some of the most common masking methods for data protection are generalization, suppression, swapping [40, 41, 72], noise addition [22], and microaggregation [45, 50]. Most methods can be classified into two broad classes. They are perturbative and non-perturbative methods. We explain them below.

- **Non-perturbative methods**. Detail on the data is reduced but no error is introduced into the original data. In our database, we can replace the date of first contact which includes (day, month, and year) by (month, year) or just (year). This reduces the quality but nothing is incorrect. Similarly, we can update the columns giving information about the number of children considering some intervals for those not so frequent values. As we expect several families with 1, 2, or 3 children we may use these values without modification, and then use the intervals [4, 5] children, and [6 or more] children. Suppression of problematic records, or problematic values is also an option.

Replacing numerical data by intervals is a very common solution. In the case of categorical data (as e.g. towns, zip codes, or professions) it is usual to replace the categories by broader categories (as e.g. counties and regions, zip codes with less digits, and groups of professions). In this case, again, the detail of the data is reduced but no error is introduced.

We provide a protected version of the view in Tables 5.4 and 5.5. These modification may be enough to avoid re-identification. Note that now we cannot longer find with certainty the 8 children family.

Appropriate masking or anonymization needs to be implemented, and this requires an analysis of the process. For example, if the 8 children family is the only family in town with more than 6 children, then, re-identification is still possible, and protection insufficient. Similarly, if we only suppress the number equal to 8 in the column children because this number is problematic, from the fact that the number is suppressed the attacker may be able to infer that it should be an 8, and, thus, this leads to the same disclosure.

- **Perturbative methods**. In this case data is modified producing data that actually contains errors. For example, we can modify the number of children increasing or decreasing the actual number we have in the database. Swapping is also a common way to protect the database. We can apply this approach to the column first contact. Then, we swap the values we find there between the first and the fourth record, between the second and the sixth, and between the third and the fifth.

In this way, none of the protected records is an actual record of the original database. Of course, the process reduces the quality of the data and causes some information loss. Nevertheless, if the distortion (noise) is introduced with care, the data can still be useful for our purposes.

Table 5.5 Protected version of the view of the original database using a non-perturbative approach

First contact	Children	Children supported	...	Service provided
2024	1	1	...	B
2023	2	2	...	A
2025	2	1	...	A
2024	3	2	...	A
2024	[6 or more]	3	...	C
2024	2	1	...	C

Table 5.6 Protected version of the view of the original databases using a perturbative approach

First contact	Children	Children supported	...	Service provided
17 April 2024	2	2	...	B
28 May 2024	3	1	...	A
16 September 2024	1	1	...	A
9 October 2024	4	2	...	A
14 January 2025	7	3	...	C
18 October 2023	1	1	...	C

Let us illustrate this approach providing the protected version of the database in Table 5.3 according to what we have just explained. We include it in Table 5.3. Recall that we applied swapping to the first column (first contact), and increased or decreased (or left unmodified) the second and third columns (children, children supported).

As we have applied a perturbative approach none of the records we have in the protected database is a real record. Therefore, no exact re-identification is possible. That is, in general, if we have information about a family we will not be completely sure about finding them in the shared file. Nevertheless, in general, this does not fully exclude re-identification. A mild protection can produce records that are similar enough to the original ones. Also, even if we are producing kind of *fake* records, the information in the database may be good enough for our analysis. For example, the dates we have in the database are real so we can study if there are periods with more visitors to our offices. Also, we have modified the number of children in a way that the mean number of children is not modified. It was 3 in the original database and it is still 3 in the protected database. Similarly, the number of children supported is 1.66 in both original and protected databases.

Note that Tables 5.5 and 5.6 are two different protected versions of the same database. Their disclosure risk and data utility would be different, and which is to be selected would depend on the application.

k-Anonymity

The privacy model called k-anonymity also focus on avoiding identity disclosure and re-identification when we share a database. The key idea is protecting individuals by means of hiding them into groups of at least k identical people. To implement this idea, we will need to modify the original database to create these groups (or clusters) of identical people.

The idea of k-anonymity was introduced by Pierangela Samarati [145] (see also their reviews [43, 44]). Its formal definition is based on the concept of quasi-identifier. A quasi-identifier is the set of variables that an intruder knows (e.g., public available information, or information you can have if you know the person) and can make someone unique or distinguishable. In the example above, the number of children

5.2 Privacy for Databases and Machine Learning

Table 5.7 Protected version of the view of the original database. This database satisfies 2-anonymity for the quasi-identifiers (children, children supported)

First contact	Children	Children supported	…	Service provided
9 October 2024	[1, 2]	[1, 2]	…	B
18 October 2023	[1, 2]	[1, 2]	…	A
14 January 2025	2	1	…	A
17 April 2024	[3, 8]	[2, 3]	…	A
16 September 2024	[3, 8]	[2, 3]	…	C
28 May 2024	2	1	…	C

would belong to the set of quasi-identifiers, as this is unique for a family in the town. Other variables as neighborhood or town (if in the file) would also probably be quasi-identifiers. In contrast, we may assume that the variable first contact is not. It is only known by the people and the office. Similarly, we consider that the service provided is not a quasi-identifier. This is a confidential variable only known by the family and the service. Identifiers (as identity card number) are not considered here as the common policy is not to include them in the protected file (or encrypt them).

The usual way to protect a file so that it is compliant with the idea of k-anonymity is to make groups of at least k people that are similar enough. Then, we update their characteristics so that they are actually the same. In Table 5.7 we provide an example of a protected version of Table 5.3 that satisfies k-anonymity for $k = 2$ when we consider as quasi-identifiers the variables children, and children supported. This file is 2-anonymous because for each combination of these variables, we have at least two records that are the same. Then, even if we know someone that we think that is in the file, there is always some uncertainty on which is the corresponding record. For a 2-anonymous file we will always have two possible records. In particular, we have two possible records in the case of the 8 children family. In this case, they have different first contact date and different service provided. So, for example, we don't know the service of the family of 8 children.

We will not go into the details of explaining how a k-anonymous file is actually built. Nevertheless, it is worth to mention that there are different ways for this. One of the differences between approaches is about how to make the groupings (formally, the clusters) of the records. Another is how to make the k records the same. In the example above we have replaced numbers by intervals. So, as the first family had one child and the second 2, we have used the interval [1, 2]. A simple alternative (much used in practice) would be to write the mean, and, thus, use 1.5 children in the file.

Differential Privacy

In this case protection does not focus on data but on computations from data. That is, we will not share the data but only provide some summaries (as in Table 5.4). As we have already discussed above, summaries may be sensitive. They can be used to infer confidential information.

Differential privacy is a privacy model to avoid disclosure from computations. Informally, a computation from a database should be quite invariant to the fact of having or not having an individual. That is, a summary should be basically the same for two databases that differ in a single record. Differential privacy was introduced by Cynthia Dwork in 2006 [58] (see also the survey [59]).

For example, if we have a large database of individual incomes in Sweden and we want to compute the mean income in Sweden, the outcome should be basically the same whether or not we have left one person out of the file or we have included this person in the file.

Similarly, the mean number of children per family supported by the social service should be a number that does not depend much on a particular family having attended or not the service.

The formal definition of differential privacy is based on randomness. That is, instead of considering just the function (say the mean of the number of children) we use a randomized version of it (say the mean of the number of children plus some random error). The idea is that if the error is not so large, then the outcome will be still valid for analysis and at the same time we have better privacy. Say, it is mainly fine if instead of 3 we provide 2 or 4 as the mean number of children.

Differential privacy works well for large databases and computations that change little when actual values change. In this situations, the noise or error we add into the actual solutions is not so much. For very small databases and computations that can change significantly with a variation of a single value, we may need to add a lot of noise to have an effective protection. In our case, the database is very small, and the function maximum may change significantly when a single value in the database changes. Note that if we have in the database a family of 12 children, the output changes to 12 in Table 5.4.

5.2.2 Data Has Different Forms

We have used so far very simple examples in what concerns to data. Our examples were based on a database containing records representing people which had either dates, numbers (i.e., children), and categories (i.e., service provided). In practice the type of data can be very diverse. E.g., we may have even text documents, images, voice recordings, etc.

From a privacy perspective, complex data increase the risk of disclosure. Anonymization is also possible for these data but we need to make an appropriate analysis of the risk. For example, let us consider a photograph that includes a few people. Naturally, the faces of the people may allow us to re-identify them. Blurring the faces may then be an option (even if some analysis have shown that a simple blurring may still not be safe enough). Nevertheless, even perfectly blurred faces may lead to disclosure. Background information can provide enough information

5.2 Privacy for Databases and Machine Learning

Table 5.8 Friendship between students in a class

Student	Friends
Alba	Baura, Clàudia, David
Baura	Alba, David, Elisenda
Clàudia	Alba, David, Elisenda
David	Alba, Baura, Clàudia
Elisenda	Baura, Clàudia

about the place, the people, etc. E.g., a family photograph in front of their home. In addition, tags and information in the image file (geo-tagging, creator name, date, etc.) may still be there after *anonymizing* people faces.

Similarly, voice recordings can lead to disclosure. Disassociating voice recordings with the names of those recorded, as well as other clearly identifiable information (as time and place of the recording) is usually not enough. Voice can be re-identified. Also, background noise can also help on this. A train passing by, a clock, etc.

Data protection for documents strongly depends on how the document will be used later. Document sanitization consists on removing sensitive information from a document producing a new document that contains as much information as possible from the original one. To do so, it is usual to look for sensitive and identifiable information in the document. This includes names, but also illnesses and treatments. Detection in a document of well established concepts (as names or illnesses) is relatively easy and there is software to do so. Nevertheless, document sanitization is difficult because other information present in the text can lead to reidentification and can be sensitive. Note that patient records can contain all kind of annotations that can lead to identification. For example, information about parents' illnesses, treatments related to genetic disorders, and hereditary diseases can lead to identification of a patient. Other information relevant for both treatment and disclosure may be international travels.

The data in our examples (as e.g. in Table 5.2) follow a structure that is very common in databases and spreadsheets: records about people described by columns. Nevertheless, not all information in digital form has this type of structure. Documents, voice recordings, and images have not this structure. We have already mentioned some of their privacy-related problems. The structure of the data found in social networks neither follows this structure. For example, friendship relationships between people in a social network cannot be properly processed (e.g., anonymized/protected) as if it was a standard file (with this spreadsheet-like form). This is so because, if Alba and Baura are friends, the rows of Alba and Baura are not independent. We illustrate this in Table 5.8, where we list friendships between 5 students in a school. We need to take into account the relationships in the data protection process. Say, if we delete the friendship between Alba and Baura in one row, it should also be deleted in the other one.

A graphical representation of friendships is given in Fig. 5.5. There, each node or circle represents a student (e.g., A for Alba, and B for Baura), and each link or edge

Fig. 5.5 Representation of the information in Table 5.8 about friendship between students in a class in a graphical form. Each node (or circle) represents a student. A is for Alba, B for Baura, C for Clàudia, D for David, and E for Elisenda. An edge or link between two nodes represent they are friends

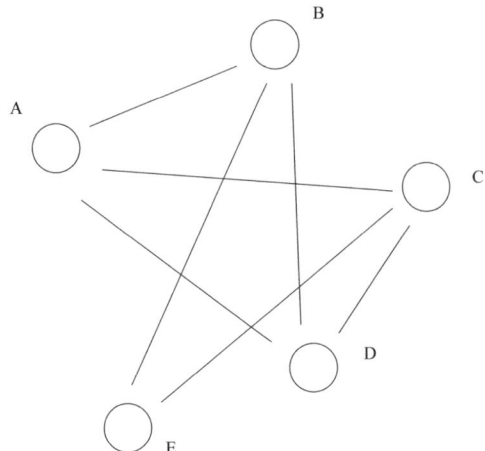

represents a friendship relationship between two people (the edge between nodes A and B represent that Alba and Baura are friends).

We will not go into the details of how protection needs to be dealt with to avoid problems due to dependencies in the information. It is important to mention that the same type of discussion on the type of disclosure, and similar approaches for protection apply here (i.e., disclosure risk, privacy models, masking methods).

The problem of dependencies between data objects (as in the case of friendships) can also appear in a standard database. Say that we have databases about people, and there are several of them which are members of the same household. Then, there may be similarities in their information. In fact, we may even have the same information duplicated in different rows. Proper anonymization needs to take these relationships (correlations, dependencies, duplications) into account. The same occurs when we have several cases corresponding to the same person (see e.g. in Clayton et al. [34, p. 23], the case of a child that is involved in multiple cases across time, or multiple siblings). Not taking these cases into account will lead to privacy breaches.

To illustrate the problem of dependencies, consider the case that the database contains as two different cases the attendance of the two parents in a family. They visited independently the office the first time and independent records were created. From then on, the records mainly contain the same information, including the service provided. We reproduce in Table 5.9 the corresponding view (same as Table 5.3 but with two new rows corresponding to this family). It is easy to see, that, for example, if we use a k-anonymization model with $k = 2$ without taking into account that there are dependencies, we will combine the last two records and, this will not provide any protection to this family.

Exercise 5.2 Apply the same approach we used in Table 5.7 to provide a 2-anonymous version of Table 5.9. Discuss an alternative grouping (clustering) of records to achieve a proper 2-anonymization.

Table 5.9 View of the original database including two non-independent records corresponding to two parents from the same family

First contact	Children	Children supported	...	Service provided
9 October 2024	1	1	...	B
18 October 2023	2	2	...	A
14 January 2025	2	1	...	A
17 April 2024	3	2	...	A
16 September 2024	8	3	...	C
28 May 2024	2	1	...	C
15 April 2025	7	1	...	B
18 March 2025	7	1	...	B

5.2.3 Synthetic Data

Synthetic data has boomed in the last years. Synthetic data stands for data that is similar to real data but it is fake. Say, we have population data about user consumption in one economic sector. For example, we have records about the books that people bought in our retail shops. That is, each person and each sale, the list of books they bought. If this is an online platform, we can also have available what these people browsed and the ratings they gave to the books they bought. Then, we can use these data to build similar shopping carts but that don't correspond to real customers. This is synthetic data. Similarly, we can produce synthetic images (e.g., synthetic faces or synthetic paintings), synthetic audio recording (e.g., synthetic songs), and synthetic video.

Why synthetic data? One of the reasons is to avoid disclosure of sensitive information and circumvent privacy regulations. Some argue that synthetic data is not bound to privacy regulations, and therefore they can be shared and used without restrictions. Note, however, that the degree in which synthetic data is really private is a matter of disagreement and discussion. It ultimately depends on how similar the fake data is to actual one, and, in particular, to the not-so-average individuals, so, it relates to uniqueness and re-identification. Another reason is that obtaining real data that satisfies our requirements may be difficult or even impossible. For example, if we need to train a data-driven model to detect objects in uncommon conditions, real available data may not include enough of such cases. Then, we can build a synthetic model that reproduces the uncommon conditions and produce as much data as we need. E.g., foggy conditions in streets, animals crossing streets and roads, children running into the road after a ball, etc.

Synthetic data can be built in different ways. One is to build them using some kind of models constructed by us. For example, we can build a physical model of the street with cars and pedestrians, and move them at will. Physics simulations can help on building such models, as objects should follow the laws of physics. Multibody system dynamics [6, 90] provide computational methods that can be used for simulations. These types of models are not only used for building data for machine learning, but they can also be used for other purposes as e.g. robots, virtual reality, and games. Another alternative is to build synthetic data from a model build from real data. Neural networks and deep learning is one of the approaches, but alternatives exist using other machine learning and statistical approaches.

In some type of applications, the construction of data-driven models using synthetic data seems to produce models with acceptable quality.

Nevertheless, the long term effects of synthetic data is not very clear. First, depending on how data has been produced, synthetic data can produce implausible or impossible data. Say, a synthetic data generator for households produces families with a negative number of children. Some of these errors can, of course, be easily corrected but others are not because they are difficult to detect. Second, synthetic data may reduce data to their most usual characteristics. Therefore reducing their complexity and removing real but not so usual cases. Models based on these data will reproduce the patterns found in the synthetic data, and their extensive use can have long term effects.

Disclosure risk and privacy requirements are one of the problems that synthetic data try to solve. Nevertheless, synthetic data is not necessarily compliant with privacy requirements. Observe that if we use real data that is sensitive, and build synthetic data that is very much similar to the real data, these data can be sensitive as well. We may have *fake* households that are almost equal in characteristics to the real households. Privacy-preserving synthetic data mechanisms need to be implemented so that privacy leakages do not take place.

We will discuss the effects of synthetic data in art in Sect. 7.7.

5.3 Security and Privacy by Design

The importance of security and privacy cannot be overstated. Software needs to be secure, and data as well. We have highlighted in this chapter aspects as authentication and authorization. We have also discussed how to ensure secure communications, and the use of cryptography to ensure that data is not forged by intruders. That is, ensure data integrity. We have illustrated that securing data is not enough to avoid undesired disclosure, and that there are privacy solutions (e.g., masking methods) that provide guarantees against some types of disclosure.

Security and privacy requirements need to be considered when software is planned and developed. Security and privacy by design is about developing software solutions in which these requirements are considered as important as other requirements about the functionalities of the software, and, thus, need to be taken into account from the initial steps of any project.

Privacy by design was introduced by Ann Cavoukian [27], who proposed seven principles. Since then, several strategies have been proposed [27, 83, 88] to implement these principles. I consider that a key principle for privacy is data minimization.

That is, collect only the data that you need (minimize collection), keep them as short time as required (minimize retention), and anonymize/mask the data instead of keeping them in their original raw form (minimize disclosure).

5.4 Bibliography

Most cryptographic tools mentioned in this chapter are described in texbooks on cryptography as e.g. Katz and Lindell [93]. The discussion on privacy is based on our book [175].

Chapter 6
AI Applications in Social Sciences

Abstract This chapter describes some examples of applications of artificial intelligence in social sciences. We first present an overview focusing on types of tasks, from data extraction from documents to predictions and recommendations. We also mention tools related to work design and workflows. Then, we focus on some specific branches of social sciences and discuss some examples of applications, as well as some of the difficulties we encounter to build AI systems. In particular, we focus on work management, public administration, social services, and criminal justice. A brief section on AI in economics closes the chapter.

> Diners de tort fan veritat,
> e de jutge fan advocat;
> savi fan tornar l'hom orat,
>   pus que d'ells haja.
>
> Anselm Turmeda, Llibre de bons amonestaments, 1398.

Artificial intelligence (AI) has been used in different types of applications in social sciences. In this chapter we discuss some of these applications. We begin with a description of tools based on the typical classification we use within AI and machine learning. That is, the classification is based on the type of application, and not on the branches in social sciences. We want to highlight that there at present several reviews focusing on AI in social sciences [97, 191, 192], as well as on social sciences of AI [192]. Then, in the second part of the chapter we will add a discussion on applications on some of the different branches.

6.1 From Data to Decisions

AI-based systems are applied in all type of processes within both public and private corporations. They are used from data extraction and analysis, to decision making (including prediction and recommendations). Decisions can apply to clients (patient, families, elderly) and to employees (reducing workload, optimize resource allocation). We review these type of processes here.

6.1.1 Data Extraction

Machine learning tools and language models, can be used for information extraction from native digital documents but as well as from digital versions (e.g., scanned files) of physical documents. They can also help on the integration of distributed databases, and on information extraction from them. For example, to combine the information gathered by different departments using different software systems, so that information extraction is possible. This is the case of integration of health data, and financial/income data, within social services.

6.1.2 Data Analysis and Visualization

Machine learning can help on data analysis and visualization, and complement standard statistical methods for quantitative analysis. For example, it can help to establish complex relationships between variables, extending the type of models that are standard in statistics. The advantage of using AI is, first, that we can consider much more data than before; second, that we can consider more complex models establishing more complex relationships between variables; and, third, that we can consider other types of data than just simple numerical or categorical variables.

Data analysis of large amounts of data can detect risk factors, and can be the basis of the construction of data-driven models which will be used for prediction (predictive analytics) and recommendation. We discuss this below and we mention a system for assessing risk of homelessness.

Machine learning can be used to analyze textual data. This can be long texts (e.g., books or articles), but also posts and even short posts including emoticons. Natural language processing tools can help on this purpose. Also, machine learning can analyze multi-modal data consisting not only on texts, but also on images, recordings, and videos all together (as they are commonly shared by users in social media). Note that AI tools are valid not only to help in the quantitative analysis of online social networks, but also of offline social ones. The interplay between online and offline social interactions has also been studied. See e.g., the discussion by Lieberman and Schroeder [101] and references therein.

Sociology takes advantage [99] of these tools to study human social activity. Similarly, there are applications of these tools in e.g. psychology [9] and political science [148].

6.1.3 Assessment and Decision Support Systems

In some branches of social sciences there is a need to assess people for a variety of objectives. Examples include risk assessment in relation to children neglect or abuse, and violence suicidal, screening in hospital intake, and highest potential in rehabilitation [64].

6.1.4 Predictions and Recommendations

There are predictive models that are used to advise about individuals. E.g., social workers and other professionals can get recommendations from AI systems with the goal of preventing crises before they occur. AI systems may include alerts for timely interventions.

There is naturally a relationship between data analysis (as mentioned above), assessment, and prediction. As we have already stated, data analysis and data-driven models are often used for understanding risk factors and for making predictions.

For example, there are predictive models about re-entry into the child welfare system, drug addiction [166], payment failures [19], risk of homelessness [19, 166], crime recidism [68], etc. Then, there are recommendations about which is the best type of support [64] someone needs. This includes personalized recommendations about medical treatment and therapies. Machine learning can also help to plan more effective interventions in e.g. long-term care.

For example, Clayton et al. [34] describe 8 different AI systems for child protection, all about prediction. For example, the aim of one of the systems is to predict whether a child's case would escalate wihin 12 months. Here escalating means the child being on a child protection plan (CPP) or being looked after (CLA). Looked after corresponds to the case the local authority placing the child somewhere other than their legal guardian.

6.1.5 Gadgets and Accessibility

Software applications can help impaired people and increase their accessibility on different types of tasks. In addition, electronics and robotics provide a large number of physical gadgets that can be also useful in a variety of contexts. All these objects include embedded software that uses some type of AI for their functioning. From hearing impaired devices that use AI to process sound, to smart walkers for mobility-impaired people that have some learning capabilities to adapt their behavior to people's usage. We can underline among the gadgets, robots for older people for unwanted loneliness and for people requiring therapy (e.g., robots as Paro that interact with people), robots for other purposes (e.g., medicine-dispensing robots, robotic wheelchairs), wearable devices and other kind of gadgets for building smart ecosystems (so that they are able to detect falls and injuries, and to manage medication). These systems include all kind of sensors including cameras to sense the environment.

Some of these products have been developed to increase accessibility. Examples include screen readers, text to speech, and hearing aids. They are all examples of AI powered tools that help accessibility.

6.1.6 Workplaces, Work Design, and Workflows

In addition to those systems and applications directly focusing on people (patients, families, clients, etc.), there are also tools that focus on the workflow in social services. There are tools to forecast demand of social services, optimize resource allocation [100], minimize caseloads and clerical work. Language models can also help in reducing clerical work helping on writing reports. Some of these tools have their origins in profit-driven corporations, with the goal of maximizing productivity.

6.1.7 New Challenges

Digitalization, AI, and machine learning provide tools for already existing problems, but they also introduce new problems and makes some issues more acute. For example, the extensive use of online social media increases the number of fake news, the speed of their propagation, and also introduces new forms of manipulation and political persuasion [47, 101], as well as new tools for information wars [36]. They are also the cause of new addictions.

Human-computer interactions increase, as AI becomes pervasive, and AI-based software is everywhere. Tisseron states that "the psychology of the 21st century will be the one of the interactions between humans and machines" [169].

When AI enters corporations and the public administration, it impacts [13] how jobs are performed and work experience. Employees use new tools, processes change, and managers have additional information on employees activities and performances, as well as tools to deal with them. Technological changes do not automatically imply well-being nor an increase of productivity. Therefore, implementation of artificial intelligence affects work design. In human service organizations, implications [167] go beyond employees as AI also affects users (e.g., clients, patients, students).

An example of the difficulties of incorporating AI is provided by Lu-Myers, Myers and Patil [104, 123]. They discuss the problem of using AI in medicine, with new tools that need to be mastered, and professional's obligation to make the best possible decision for the patient.

Implementation of process automation have also their own challenges, some of them already discussed by a number of authors. In the context of social services, we find e.g. Toll [170], Ranerup and Henriksen [134], and Svensson [163]. They underline collaboration difficulties between stakeholders, each with different perspectives, and resistance from employees. In relation to employees, they mention problems as work meaningfulness, and in relation to the automation, factors as what exactly needs to be automated, who is responsible, what are the benefits (e.g., while cost saving is one of the driving forces for automation, software "can be costly and require tedious maintenance" [170]). As an example of factors to be taken into account, Asatiani et al. [8] provide a checklist for deciding robotic process automation (RPA). These works focus on the public administration, and mainly on RPAs. A discussion on the differences between the automation in private corporations and public administration is provided by Asatiani [7]. Decisions on which interventions are best can be based on the Multiphase Optimization Strategy (MOST) [35].

Exercise 6.1 The Luddites were a movement of English workers who opposed automated machinery in the 19th-century. Investigate this movement.

6.2 AI in Social Sciences

Let us now focus on specific branches. We will mention some existing systems, but also discuss the particular difficulties that researchers need to take into account when building AI systems.

6.2.1 AI for Work Management

In Human Resource Management (HRM), AI tools are used for staffing, recruitment and omboarding, performance management, payroll and worktime management, and administration [127]. Examples includes creation and publication of job descriptions, pre-screening of applications, matching candidates to positions, chatbots to replace human interviewers, and video-interviews. Robotic Process Automation (RPA) automates actions on software systems. It has been applied to Human Resource Management (HRM) for paperwork [91].

There are tools for automated reporting. They build reports or infographics automatically combining information from multiple sources. These documents can contain text and graphics (extracted from corporate databases). This can be done on-demand or at fixed schedules. In relation to reports, language models [126] can, of course, be used to retrieve information as well as to generate all kind of reports. Retrieval-Augmented Generation (RAG) are used in combination with language models trained with open documents for domain expertise.

Other tools include AI task-scheduling, that combine information from to-do lists and calendars found in different platforms. They send reminders for tasks, and can reschedule tasks if they are not completed. Some can translate emails into tasks in the schedule. AI-based ones estimate the time for tasks and provide task categorization. Guay [81] provides a comparison and analysis of these tools.

6.2.2 AI in the Public Administration

Automated Decision-Making (ADM) correspond to automated decisions mainly in the public administration [139] (it is also known as Automated Administrative Decision-Making (AADM)). For example, on September 2023, Finland introduced an automatic post-decision monitoring [111] of student residence permits. In general, student resident permits are granted for several years. The system uses information from national registers, and, based on such information, assesses whether the requirements are still met. If this is not the case, the residence permit may be withdrawn. The decision of residence withdrawal is not done automatically but is done by an official of the Finnish Immigration Service.

6.2.3 AI in Social Services

We have already mentioned above some of the tasks related to assessment. For example, risk assessment in child protection (e.g. to determine children neglect or abuse) and eligibility assessment for social services. Other examples using predictive analytics include predicting re-employment [182], and homelessness [19, 166]. Wykman [191] provides a review on AI in social work, and Ohlenburg [117] provides a discussion taking into account the social protection delivery chain: assessment, enrollment, provision, and monitoring and management.

Some of the difficulties of building these systems in practice can be found in Landau et al. [96]. Among them, we highlight the bias, little systematic nationwide evidence about risk factors, as well disparities on definitions of assessment and diagnosis (the authors state that different average rates of child maltreatment cases between US states are probably due to different definitions, prevailing culture, child welfare resources, and reporting practices, and evaluting performance of ML models). Also, it is difficult to convey into the model all the knowledge that experts use in their decision. E.g., van den Berg et al. [182] show that "self-reported (and to a lesser extent caseworker) assessments sometimes contain information not captured by the machine learning algorithm". We have discussed bias in data and of ML models in Sect. 4.6.6.

Bias in social services is not a new problem, it was already there before AI. For example, Denmark and Greenland governments agreed on 2025 on stopping [61, 87] the parenting competency test (forældrekompetenceundersøgelse, FKU). It was used to decide foster placement of children with Greenlandic background. These tests were controversial and were considered cultural and linguistic biased, and also the cause of a different percentage of out-of-home care between ethnic Danish children and Greenland-born children.

In the context of social services, it is important to highlight the difficulty of a correct assessment of AI systems' performance. Eubanks [66, p. 169] writes in the context of violence prevention: "A family scored as high risk by the AFST will undergo more scrutiny than other families. Ordinary behaviors that might raise no eyebrows before a high AFST score become confirmation for the decision to screen them in for investigation. A parent is now more likely to be re-referred to a hotline because the neighbors saw child protective services at her door last week".

It is important to highlight that bias can have dramatic consequences in applications related to social services.

6.2.4 AI in Criminal Justice

Criminal justice is very broad, and, thus, there is a broad type of AI-based applications that are regularly used. For example, facial recognition [113, 155] is used for law enforcement and surveillance practices, and applied to both video and still images. Recognition can be done live (live facial recognition, LFR) and with surveillance footage (retrospective facial recognition, RFR).

Tools for data analysis are also used for extracting information from large databases, that may include information associated to criminals. A report mentions [10] the intensive use of data sources in pursuit of law-enforcement objectives. Extracted information from databases includes travel patterns [12] and tracking financial transactions [67, 120]. Automatic transaction monitoring is applied to identify suspicious patterns, and e.g. prevent money laundering and terrorist financing. Oztas et al. [120] (in 2024) explain in their report that they conducted interviews with anti-money laundering experts, and that interviewees use rules-based transaction monitoring within their institutions. Some mention that they are moving to systems with "advanced capabilities such as entity resolution, machine learning, and graph analytics". There are tools that analyse information in social media but also in the dark web (see Fig. 6.1). This includes posts and images. For example, software has been used [16] to flag possible sexualised images of children.

Predictive policing (crime forecasting) is to identify potential criminal activity. Data analysis and machine learning have an important role in this process. Note also the ethical issues of predictive policing (which include privacy intrusion, inaccurate predictions, etc.). The report [10] written by the Alan Turing Institute Data Ethics Group lists some of these ethical issues. This was related to the project "National Data Analytics Solution-Violent Crime" for West Midlands Police. Because of the relevance of data analytics in policing, offices and boards have been created (see e.g. the National Data and Analytics Office (NDAO) in UK).

In addition to AI for database information extraction, there are AI-based algorithms useful in other contexts. E.g., for DNA analysis [137], gunshot residue analysis [108], and gunshot detection from audio files [137].

> The dark web refers to the part of the internet that requires specific software or authorization (e.g., password) to access. Tools for anonymous communication (as e.g. Tor) that are able to hide who requests some information and provides a way for this person to get the required information are useful to access the dark web. It is used by hacking groups, black markets (e.g. selling sensitive data from ransomware attacks) and pornography, but it is also used for avoiding censorship, and for privacy.
>
> The deep web refers to the part of internet that is not indexed by web engines. Examples include unlinked web sites that can only be accessed knowing the URL, or that are password-protected. An example is a web-based mail service and online banking. The dark web is a part of the deep web.

Fig. 6.1 The dark web and the deep web

Actuarial Risk Assessment (RA) tools [20, 39] in criminal justice are statistical methods to assess the future risk of violence or recidivism (or reoffending). They are typically based on risk predictors. Machine learning is being incorporated [17] in this setting exploiting historical data.

In relation to the use of AI in justice, as AI evidence, the document "AI for judges" [12] points out relevant questions about the actual expertise of data-driven models. They include the methodology of building the systems, and issues as "error rates", maintenance and monitoring (including database updating, and asking whether the machine "is not learning bad habits"), and bias ("critics argue that risk assessment tools not only have, or could have, racially biased results, but also, through the process of machine learning, exacerbate racial inequalities in the criminal justice system" [12, 14]). In addition, the document also discusses a problem that has also been reported by others: "such algorithms can generate their own reinforcing and circular logic. The algorithm predicts criminal conduct, police patrols are increased, and additional arrests occur, validating the accuracy of the algorithm" [12]. Note that this last comment is similar to the discussion by Eubanks [66] in the context of violence prevention, which we have reproduced in Sect. 6.2.3.

The above mentioned document [12] also discuss some problems related to the use of AI in sentencing. They include aspects as wrong predictions because historical data can only partially match the current case. This can be because there are not similar previous cases, or because most similar previous cases are outliers (quite different to the present case with a complete different sentencing), and, thus, the prediction is completely different that what be otherwise be sentenced. The case of outliers and prediction quality, as well as the problem that systems often produce results independently of their own prediction capability, has been discussed in Sect. 4.6.5.

6.2.5 AI in Economics

The field of econometrics studies the application of statistical methods to economic data. Regression models are commonly used to establish relationships between variables. In the last years, the use of machine learning models for similar problems [28] is increasing. Different type of data related to economics can be of relevance. In addition to static databases with information at a given time, databases with temporal component are of relevance. This corresponds to time series. That is, numerical data that changes with time due to different types of factors. Examples include unemployment and stock exchange. As these two examples illustrate, time series can have different time scales.

The use of machine learning in finance is also very important. Stock markets are digitalized, and there are AI-based trading bots for automated trading, analyzing patterns, and making decisions about buying and selling stocks [121].

Econometrics [129] for risk analysis is also of relevance. For example, in insurance, accurate predictions are needed. Then, machine and statistical models are used to predict e.g. mortgage repayments. Relevant problems here include the need to model rare events. They are events that have a very low probability of occurrence, but that they may have a very huge economical impact. It is also important to highlight that databases may not contain historical data about these rare events, and not even enough data about common situations. We have already discussed in Sect. 4.6.2 the case of missing data or dark data (data that is not in the databases but it is actually needed to build a model). We illustrated it with the example of models about failing repayments. People that did not get the loan approved cannot fail a repayment. Also, databases are unbalanced. That is, the proportion of people that fail repayments and the ones that succeed in their repayment is different.

Exercise 6.2 Investigate other uses of AI within the field of economics.

6.3 Bibliography

This chapter has been written based on the articles mentioned in the different sections. Eubanks book [66] influenced the critical tone. While aid and humanitarism is not a topic considered in this book, the book by Sandvik [146] is very interesting in showing how technology has affected this field, changed practices, and shifted power. Finally, we need to mention also Pardo-Guerra's book [121] on automating finance, and the handbook edited by Elliot [62] on AI and social sciences.

Chapter 7
Ethics, Society and AI

Abstract Artificial intelligence (AI) systems are used in a social context. They are socio-technical systems. In this chapter we discuss some of the relationships between AI and society. The chapter contains a diversity of topics, woven with the interplay between AI and society. We begin with the question whether AI is really possible in a machine? An old question, in fact. The notion of agency follows. Then, we discuss trustworthy AI. The chapter follows with topics related to social and environmental costs of AI (energy, labor-intensive AI, art).

> Your future hasn't been written yet. No one's has.
> Your future is whatever you make it. So make it a good one.
>
> Doc Brown, Back to the Future III

The long term effects of digitalization, machine learning, and artificial intelligence in our society are a matter of concern. Nevertheless, already now, development and usage of AI raises several ethical and societal questions. Most questions have no clear answers. Therefore, they cannot be seen as check-boxes or compliance requirements.

The field of trustworthy AI, which provides requirements for AI systems based on ethical principles, highlights the need to consider AI systems in the social context. It stresses that AI systems are in fact a socio-technical system.

In this chapter we discuss topics concerning the relationship between AI and society. The topics are very divers, and the chapter is written in a quite unstructured way. It is a hotchpotch of topics. We focus on questions like is AI possible? Will AI surpass human intelligence? Will AI produce art? Is AI affecting jobs, and salaries? Is AI producing safe systems? Are there ecological costs of the use of AI? We do not discuss, however, topics as AI for good and related initiatives that want to foster proper and ethical uses of AI. Nor do we discuss the use of AI for war (analysis of data and images for military purposes, selection of targets, and AI embedded in robots, drones, and weapons).

We begin discussing the problem of whether AI is possible in a machine, and the question of agency in relation to intelligent systems. The following section is about trustworthy AI. Then, we have sections discussing environmental costs of AI, and on the relationships between AI and labor. Finally, we have a section on AI, generative data, and art.

© The Author(s), under exclusive license to Springer Nature Switzerland AG 2026
V. Torra, *AI for Social Sciences*,
https://doi.org/10.1007/978-3-032-07216-0_7

7.1 Is AI Possible in a Machine?

One of the roots of AI is computation theory. This field, that belongs to theoretical computer science, studies which problems are solvable with which computing models. Here, computing models are seen as theoretical models of computation, and, therefore, with different theoretical computing capabilities. Theoretical models and computational capabilities link with the Chomsky hierarchy [30, 31], defined by the linguist Noam Chomsky. In this hierarchy, we have different types of formal languages, and there is an association between types of formal languages and theoretical models of computation.

In the 1930s, three different computational models were proven to be equivalent, and they are now known to correspond to the most general type of formal languages. They are the Turing machines, introduced by Alan Turing [179] in 1936, the λ-calculus, introduced by Alonzo Church [32, 33] in 1936, and the general recursive functions, introduced by Kurt Gödel [42, 74] in 1933. This work led to the Church-Turing thesis, which can be expressed in different equivalent ways depending on the computational model used [37, 150]. We use the one as it appears in Shagrir [150].

> Any effectively computable function (of positive integers) is Turing computable.

This does not answer the question if an artificial intelligence is possible. In short, we do not know if intelligence is an effectively computable function. Nevertheless, the questions are connected by Alan Turing himself. After these works and during the Second World War, Turing was involved in code-breaking German encrypted messages, and after the war, he proposed the *imitation game*, now commonly known as the Turing test. As we have discussed in Chap. 1, this is one of the ways to define artificial intelligence. In fact, in his paper [180] introducing the imitation game, he also discusses computation, and contrary views to the questions "Can machines think?" and "Are there imaginable digital computers which would do well in the imitation game?". Among the arguments considered, we find the "Theological objection" and the "Continuity in the Nervous System" (nervous systems are not discrete-state machines).

This was a theoretical work, that appeared more or less in parallel to the first computers. Since then, computers and digitalization have changed society, and AI has become pervasive in the society, with a real impact in our life. Whether artificial intelligence is possible in a machine is still an open question

The question whether computers and programs are enough for intelligence appears again and again, Vinge [184] in his 1993 paper writes about a workshop to investigate "How We Will Build a Machine that Thinks" where "there was general agreement that minds can exist on nonbiological substrates and that algorithms are of central importance to the existence of minds".

While the discussion of whether AI is possible is still not answered, some state that the point in which AI will surpase human intelligence is near. The *singularity*, a term used by Vinge in his above mentioned 1993 paper [184], is the time in which this will happen, and, then, there will be an *intelligence explosion* (using I. J. Good's words [76] from 1965) because improvements will accelerate. While Vinge predicted singularity before 2030, Kurzweil that popularized it in his book [95], predicted 2045.

7.2 AI, Autonomy, and Agency

We have discussed in Chap. 1 that systems built using AI techniques can have different levels of autonomy, and we have seen in Sect. 1.2 what autonomy means, as well as the different autonomy levels associated to autonomous vehicles. Agency is a concept that is also relevant when developing AI autonomous systems. Agency is defined by Nyholm [116] as "a multidimensional concept that refers to the capacities and activities most centrally related to performing actions, making decisions, and taking responsibility for what we do", and by Boddington [21, p. 342] based on Taylor's [168] as "performance—of adaptive behavior seen as accomplishing some goal". Nyholm considers different kinds of agents depending on their agential capacities. They are the following ones [116, Sect. 3.3].

- Domain-specific basic agency. Pursuing goals within certain limited domains.
- Domain-specific principled agency. As above, but in a way that it is regulated and constrained by certain rules or principles.
- Domain-specific supervised and deferential principled agency. As above, but in addition, the agent can be supervised by an authority who can stop it or to whom control can be ceded.
- Domain-specific responsible agency. As above, but in addition the agent understands criticism of its agency, and is able to defend or alter its actions based on its own principles or on principled criticisms of its agency.

This latter definition is in agreement with Oshana [119], who states that responsible agency is about satisfying "certain epistemic conditions and certain social and psychological conditions of control". Here, the "epistemic conditions guarantee that the responsible agent is self-aware, that they are rational, that they are not ignorant of the circumstances in which they act, that they are cognizant of and able to act within established moral guidelines, and that they are responsive to reasons to adjust or amend their behavior in light of these guidelines". Achieving this type of agency would be a step towards moral agents [21, Sect. 11.5.2] and [119, Sect. 2.1].

A self-driving car would be able to satisfy the first three kinds of agencies [116, Sect. 3.4], as they can pursue the goals, follow rules and prohibitions, and transfer vehicle control to the driver if required to do so. Nevertheless, to achieve the fourth is not within the goals of the automotive industry. Self-driving cars are not expected to justify or discuss about their driving, nor alter it based on these discussions. Changes in driving will only happen when new software is deployed in the vehicle. So, agency, in the above sense is not in the picture. Explainability for AI can be seen as loosely connected with justification of actions and decisions, but responsible agency goes well beyond this.

7.3 Trustworthy AI

AI systems are part of a socio-technical context. In work design, socio-technical systems [63] recognize the interaction between people and technology. It is well known that the effects of technological advances are not always positive, and that, for example, adoption of new machines in a factory does not necessarily increase production (see Trist and Bamforth [181] in the context of coal mining). For Baxter and Sommerville [15], socio-technical thinking means that "systems design should be a process that takes into account both social and technical factors that influence the functionality and usage of computer-based systems". This discussion naturally applies to AI [49].

The EU guidelines for Trustworthy AI [3] were introduced as a tool for the development, deployment and use of AI systems, taking into account this socio-technical context. Then, they state that AI systems are trustworthy if they comply with applicable laws and regulations, adhere to ethical principles and values, and they are robust from a technical and social perspective. In short, if they are lawful, ethical and robust. Ethical principles are translated into seven requirements. These requirements, which are also included in the EU AI Act [65] (see e.g., Recital 27), are the following ones.

- Human agency and oversight. Systems are to serve people, and need to be controlled by humans. The proper construction of an AI system in this way is not always trivial. People tend to adapt to AI systems, and even revise or update their decisions to the one of the AI system (see [66, p. 141]). We have discussed agency and autonomy in relation to AI systems in Sects. 1.2 and 7.2.
- Technical robustness and safety. Systems need to be protected against vulnerabilities, and should be safe and not cause damage (even if used in unexpected situations).
- Privacy and data governance. Development and use of AI and ML systems should care individuals' privacy. Special attention needs to be taken for data (both for databases used to build ML models and for data entered/recorded by systems during their life-time). Data access control, and privacy measures need to be properly implemented. Data governance is about the policies about data. We have discussed in Chap. 5 privacy and security.
- Transparency. This relates to traceability, interpretability, and explainability. Users need to know that they are interacting with an AI system. In addition, when decisions are made by AI systems, users should be up to a certain extent be able to understand these decisions (e.g., criteria behind AI system outcomes). It is also important to make clear the limitations of AI systems. We have discussed briefly interpretability and explainability in Sect. 4.6.7.
- Diversity, non-discrimination and fairness. AI systems should avoid discriminatory and unfair biases prohibited by the law. It is important to recall that biased data usually produce biased data-driven machine learning models. Aspects to be taken into account include diversity on the data, participation of different stakeholders when system requirements are made explicit and during the process of building the system, and finally ensuring non-discrimination when the system is in opera-

tion. The problem of bias and fairness in machine learning has been presented in Sect. 4.6.6.
- Environmental and societal well-being. Development of AI systems need to take into account people's wellbeing. Moreover, not only individual impact, but also societal impact needs to be also assessed. Critical examination of environmental impact can also be assessed.
- Accountability. When AI systems are deployed and in operation, they can behave incorrectly, and cause harm. Responsability need to be assigned to liable parties. See e.g. [103, 115] about accountability and answerability in AI.

The consideration of AI as socio-technical systems is key in the consideration of ethics in AI. Ethics cannot be implemented in AI systems. We can include AI guardrails in AI systems so that they are compliant with some security, privacy, legal, and ethical requirements. Nevertheless, these requirements need to be clearly identified and properly formulated. It is the socio-technical system that can be evaluated in ethical terms. "Does the job recruiting system fairly distribute job advertisements? Does the parole system that determines which convicts are eligible for parole do so without discrimination? Do social services decide the eligibility of applicants accurately?" [187].

Exercise 7.1 In Chap. 1, we reviewed alternative definitions of AI. Does the concept of trustworthy AI challenge or support any of those definitions.

7.4 AI, Computation, the Cloud, and Energy Consumption

The constructions of AI models are made by algorithms that are computationally costly. As we have explained in Chap. 4, their goal is to look for the parameters that optimize the output (provide the best output) for a given input according to the data we have available (the training data set). Learning a model is achieved applying an iterative process, and in each step parameters are updated. The number of parameters can be huge, the rule to update them may require costly computations, and the number of steps in this iterative process required to achieve the desired results can also be large. All together, the construction of a model can take long.

Of course, all depends on how large is the training data and on the number of parameters. A relatively small data set of hundreds or thousands of records with a few variables can produce linear models or simple models with a few parameters in a very short time. In contrast, large language models trained on large corpus of documents take months. Also, the simplest models can be computed in a small computer or laptop while large models are trained in supercomputing and high performance centers. They require multiple processors working in parallel to optimize the millions of parameters.

For example, ChatGPT-3 is said to have 175 billion parameters, and ChatGPT-4 1.8 trillion parameters. The Swedish large-scale generative model GPT-SW3 is offered in versions between 126 million parameters and 40 billion parameters. Technical description of ChatGPT-3 and its training was provided by Brown et al. [23].

Just to illustrate these numbers, let us consider that we are able to find one optimal parameter in 1 s, then, when we have 1 billion parameters (i.e., 1000000000 parameters), we would need 31.70 years to optimize all of them if we do this optimization sequentially (i.e., one parameter at a time). That is,

$$1,000,000,000 \frac{1 \min}{60\,s} \frac{1\,h}{60\,s} \frac{1\,day}{24\,h} \frac{1\,year}{365\,days} = 31.70979\,years$$

and, if instead of a billion of parameters we have a trillion, then we need 31 millennia. If we are faster, and we can compute 1000 optimal parameters in a second, then for one trillion parameters we are back to *only* 31 years.

Parallelism allows to compute and update several parameters at the same time using multiple processors. In this way, and using the fastest machines, time can be very much reduced. It is said that the training of ChatGPT-4 required *only* a few months.

In contrast, the storage requirements for these models seem more standard in terms of actual computer hardware. A model with 175 billion parameters require *only* 700 GB, if we use 4 bytes for each number. A two hours film in Full HD requires about 16 GB, and in 4K UHD about 60 GB. So, this amount of memory requirements is similar to storing 10 films, and naturally fits in a 1 TB disk. The model with 1.8 trillion parameters require 7200 GB, which is about 10 times larger. These are the sizes of the models when we store their parameters for optimizing the model outputs (i.e., in the learning process). Nevertheless, when the models have already been trained, their size is often reduced, as we do not need as much precision when applying them than for learning them. So, instead of 4 bytes for each parameter, we use only 2 bytes. This means reducing their size to half.

While the storage requirements for models is not so large, actual stored data is. Just the weight of an average web page has been multiplied by 115 between 1995 and 2015 [132, p. 75], and the computing requirement for editing a text is multiplied by 2 every 2 or 3 years. Software becomes more complex and require more computational power for similar tasks.

While most data in the past were stored locally, now they are in data centers. Industry, including social networks and media, as well as administrations transfer most of their data to data centers. These centers also offer computing services. For example, computationally costly AI learning algorithms can be executed there.

Data centers have enormous electricity costs for their daily operation. Electricity consumption is needed to run servers and storage systems. In addition to that, centers have a large number of machines, which produce heat. Then, cooling systems are needed, which need in general high electricity consumption. Overall, the energy consumption of data centers in the world is enormous and increases yearly. As an illustration, in 2023, the energy consumed in data centers in U.S. was 176 TWh which was the 4.4% of the total of U.S. electricity consumption. Several countries have smaller energy consumption than just data centers in U.S. To compare, in 2023, Sweden [196] consumed 503 TWh, and Argentine [195] 127 TWh.

Data centers were initially located near the places in which data were used. The extensive deployment of fiber-optic cables has changed the landscape as it permits easy access to data that is actually located very far away. Then, data centers have been moved to locations with secure environments with lower costs, even if the data is used somewhere else. In particular, to decrease cooling costs, some centers are now placed in arctic locations, so they can use outside air. Also, some use renewable energies and promote themselves as green data centers. Some of the countries that exploit cool air and renewable energies include Canada, Iceland, Finland, Norway, Sweden, and Switzerland. The case of Iceland [112] is paradigmatic, as data is actually far away of most of their users. For others, in addition to energy, cooling may require large amounts of water. E.g., 125 million litters of water per year per data center (data from 2024 [157]). In average, Sweden uses 140 liters of water per person and day [162] (similar averages are given for other countries in Europe [60]). So, the consumption of a data center in a year is equivalent to the one of a town of 2446 people. In face of these energy problems, some AI-based tools [138] have been implemented to reduce consumption.

Side effects of computation and machines go well beyond energy consumption. It is well known that computer products require a variety of metals, including rare-earth metals which are difficult to find in the earth, and difficult to mine and extract. They are used in electronics and are key in the green energy transition, because they are essential for batteries, solar panels, wind turbines, and electric vehicles, but also used in computers, mobile devices, and smart phones. See e.g. the book by Pitron [133].

7.5 Labor-Intensive AI

Machine learning algorithms run on data, and it is the data that is the cornerstone of any data-driven model. For developing successful applications, data needs to be labeled. Nevertheless, such information is usually not available, and it is very time consuming. This is the task of data annotators. In its *simplest* form consists on assigning classes to records or cases. Nevertheless, for images, films and recordings, annotations can correspond to assigning them all kind of tags. For example, it can correspond to marking and tagging pedestrians in videos, and animals in photographs, etc. For this, annotators can use bounding boxes, polygons, etc.; but also mark keypoints in images. This is a labor-intensive work.

Data annotation tasks are often outsourced. As Muldoon et al. [112] explain, outsourcing offices are often competing globally, tasks are very easy to relocate, as at most only data is moved from one office to another. In fact, data may not even be in companies' facilities but stored in the cloud. This is a cause for low salaries and strict labor discipline. In these offices, monitoring of work is common [112], and workers must meet targets in both speed and quality. Those that do not meet them, may be fired.

Validation of data-driven models also require human support. This is particularly relevant for language models. The text produced by these models needs to be safe, and, as training data has been extracted from the internet, it may contain inappropriate sentences which can be reproduced with some probability in the output. Inappropriate text can range from sexually explicit and offensive content to issues related to geopolitics and inclusive language. Moreover, outputs of these models can also be biased, as the data used for the training were. To implement this type of validation, and also to provide additional data for improving the data-driven models, companies require a specific work force, which is also often outsourced.

Moderation of social networks has become another source of intensive work. This includes tagging and removing content that does not follow the policies of the platform. This work [151] can cause psychological harm, as workers need to see videos with terrible scenes for their tagging.

7.6 AI and Labor

We have mentioned in the previous section annotators and work monitoring. The use of digital tools for work monitoring is a general trend that extends well beyond AI-related work. Specific software have been developed for this purpose, and increasingly used in different economic sectors. Muldoon et al. [112] describe historical cases from the 18th century, showing that this monitoring is by no means new. They inform about a New York Times report that states that eight of the ten largest private employers in US track the productivity of individual workers. Multiple cases have been reported to the media, in which monitoring was combined with strict labor conditions causing both physically and psychological harm. See, for example, the report [4] by the French agency ANSES, about the workers on a digital food delivery platform. This report underlines that platforms suppressed human management, that there is a huge information asymmetry between the platform and the workers, and that there is a big difference between the work as described and the actual work. Information asymmetry refers to the fact that the companies have detailed information on all workers' activities. On the contrary, workers don't have information on how the algorithms assign rides. This fact affects workers salaries, and make them to compete among themselves to have acceptable incomes, and hinders the formation of unions. In relation to work monitoring, it is not so clear that it increases substantially the productivity ("little productivity gain, despite substantial costs for workers", Acemoglu and Johnson [2, p. 323]).

Distribution of salaries is usually skewed. In particular, there is a significant number of people with low salaries and only a few people with large salaries. For a distribution as this one, the difference between mean and median can illustrate this skewness. The mean salary corresponds to the addition of all salaries, and distributes this sum uniformly among all wage-earners. So, when we add to the population a single person with an extremely huge salary, the mean salary (*of all* the members of that population) improves. In contrast, to compute the median, we need to rank all

7.6 AI and Labor

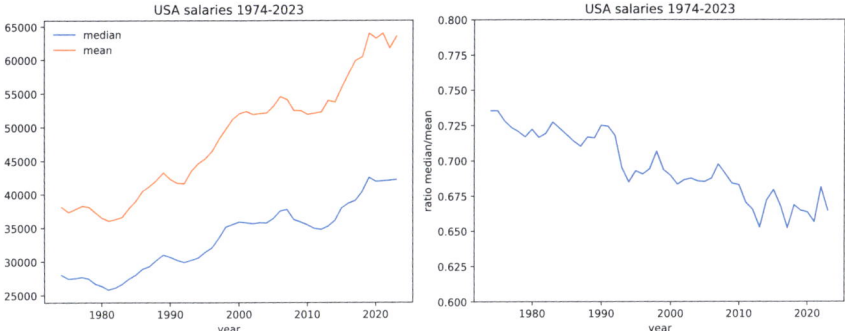

Fig. 7.1 Median and mean salaries in USA (left), and the ratio between median and mean (right). Data extracted from the Federal Reserve Economic Data (FRED), Federal Reserve Bank of St. Louis [70]

salaries and then we look for the salary that is in the center position in this ranking. In this case, adding a few people with high salaries do not impact the median significantly. Figure 7.1 (left) shows the median and mean salaries in US in the period 1974–2023, and Fig. 7.1 (right) shows the ratio between the median and the mean. The lower this ratio (when lower than one), the larger the difference between both. It can be seen that this ratio is in general decreasing, because, probably, of an increasing skewness.

In addition to that, there are strong discussions [2] on whether the salaries have increased or not in real terms, adjusted by inflation (and taking into account technological developments), and on the effect of education on salaries. This was already pointed out in 2014 by Brynjolfsson and McAfee [25]. They attributed part of the problem to the winner-take-all markets, and mention stars and superstars with very high incomes. Internet and digitalization reduce the cost of production. In addition, digital products are ready to be distributed. There is also ongoing discussion [82, 189] about whether education is still sufficient, and whether all in our society benefit from meritocracy or only a select few.

AI also affects fulfillment at work, with both positive and negative aspects. Among the latter, we have loss of autonomy. When decision making tasks are delegated to AI systems, the type of work employers do, or the type of workers needed can change dramatically. Tasks may not be as fulfilling as before, and workers may lose skills and become demotivated. For example, Eubanks [66] explains the case of replacing in-person social caseworkers by online applications and privatized call-centers. The problem of workers becoming supervisors is also well-known. Then, they are no longer able to understand the systems they supervise. This is known as the out-of-the-loop performance problem [92]

David Graeber, Professor of Anthropology, introduced in his work [77] the idea of pointless and unnecessary jobs. He calls them "bullshit jobs" following the study of Frankfurt [69] that distinguishes the first term from lie. While in a lie we are supposed to believe something that is supposed to be false, in the other term truth-values of statements are not central. In Graeber's definition, these jobs [77, p. 9] are "a form of paid employment that is so completely pointless, unnecessary, or pernicious that even the employee cannot justify its existence even though, as part of the conditions of employment, the employee feels obliged to pretend that this is not the case". He provides a categorization of these jobs in five varieties, and one of them for example is "box ticker". In his book, as well as in his other work on bureaucracy [78], Graeber highlights that past expectations about our present time envisioned shorter working hours than the ones we currently experience. In contrast, he argues that the amount of useless work has increased. One may wonder whether digitalization and AI are contributing to this trend. The deployment of large language models (LLMs) may have even amplified some pernicious trends. E.g., an increasing number of forms, reports, and bureaucratic tasks.

Note also that, in some contexts, a whole ecosystem of AI-based systems that fully affect processes and tasks emerges. For example, in the context of job applications and candidate selection: job applicants using LLMs to prepare CVs, former supervisors and department heads turning to LLMs to write recommendation letters, HR departments applying AI to shortlist candidates, AI chatbots conducting interviews, candidates recording presentations, and AI systems evaluating these recordings. In this respect, Ikea [164] in 2025 asked job seekers not to use AI to write applications. Similarly, in academia, there is a growing inflation of academic publications—some written by LLMs—while some reviewers, in turn, use LLMs to evaluate publications.

7.7 Synthetic Data, Creation, and Art

> Nicklausse:
> Âme poétique!
> Plaît-il?
>
> Spalanzani:
> Rien! la physique! ah monsieur! la physique!
>
> Jacques Offenbach, Les contes d'Hoffmann, Act II, Olympia, Scene 8.

We have discussed in Sect. 5.2.3 the creation of synthetic data. Data-driven models (e.g., deep learning models) are trained from real data and then used to generate artificial data that satisfies a set of requirements. While first methods were built to generate new records as for census data, it is well known that now we can produce all type of data.

In particular, language models produce artificial texts based on corpus of documents. We have outlined in Sect. 5.2.3 that the long term effects of using synthetic data for building data-driven models are not clear. Synthetic data is expected to have effects beyond the construction of data driven models.

7.7 Synthetic Data, Creation, and Art

An example is, what are the effects of the generalized adoption of large language models? They have been trained with corpus consisting on existing digital text, with a significant portion of them extracted from the internet. The more the LLMs are used, and the more the information posted in internet is generated from LLMs, new generations of LLMs will be trained with increasing proportion of synthetic text. It is unclear what will be the long term effects of such practice. It is not only about the quality of the text (performance using some kind of mathematically defined metric), but also the social impact of generalized synthetic text. This technology, as others did in the past, will for sure effect language evolution.

Generative models have been used for text generation, but also for image, video and music. They are built using existing text, images, videos, and music and, then, they produce new instances of them. Nevertheless, there are traces of these texts, images, videos, and music in their output. It is precisely their goal that the output has resemblance to the material used to build them. Then, questions arise. Are (human) creators properly recognized? Who are the owners of the new creations? There has been discussion about copyright infringement when collecting, storing and using works to build the ML systems. Some of these systems, which are based on works by artists, do not always pay [86] royalties to them, and even how to split the economic benefits of the models between original creators is not so clear. Ethical AI music generators is a term used to refer to those that try to address this problem. The same type of issues appear in images and pictures. An example [165] is the case ChatGPT producing images in the style of Studio Ghibli.

Social networks and digital platforms are based on algorithms that recommend what is the next post you are going to read, the next music you are going to listen, and the next video you are going to see. These recommendations are based on data-driven models built on data from other customers. For example, have similar customers actually listened such recommended music?, to the end? or have they skipped it? In most of the occasions, the platform goal is to supply endless streaming, and keep customers hooked. Chayka [29] and others discuss that these policies cause homogenization. When the goal is to maximize consumption (i.e., time using the platform), recommendations are good when the user passively accepts what comes next. The alternative, the user skips or cancels a recommendation (i.e., a song or video), or even leaves the platform (even for a few hours), is a failure. So, when algorithms decide, they decide for no surprises, no differences, minimize variety, and homogeneity. Frictionless and to maximize engagement, as AccountableTech [1] says, or flatness and reduction to simplicity, as Chayka [29] states.

Filter bubble, a term created by Pariser [122], is a consequence of these personalized decisions from algorithms. The filter bubble stands for the cultural, ideological, and political isolation caused by the algorithms. This mainly refers to texts and news. Users don't face disagreements, nor differences of significance, and they see what they like. Their virtual world is populated only with people with similar opinions. The same happens with non-textual and artistic content. Exposition to diversity is reduced. Chayka [29] discusses the effects of algorithmic policies in music streaming, which have been studied by several authors. Effects include the reduction of song length, lyrics requiring less attention, and rhythm more dominant than melody.

Then, synthetic music produced by generative AI models can be competitive, and can be produced and broadcasted on demand without the need of paying creators rights.

Overall, the use of AI has effects [112] on the opportunities of creators, and to creativity. These effects include the difficulty of having the work recognized and remunerated, the *need to create* works similar to those existing to be prioritized and recommended, and the reduction of paid works that while considered as with less artistic value helped them to make their living as such works are increasingly done with generative AI.

From a creative point of view, and in terms of supporting creation, these problems are very clear. Nevertheless, it is not so clear with respect to art itself. I mean, is art threatened by AI? or, is AI able to produce art? There are artists that stress that art is intentional, and needs to have political and social roles. Also, some argue that art is embodied. Then, it is unclear that some of these questions even make sense in the context of AI or within a generative AI system. AI and generative models are then just tools to be placed in the hands of artists and creators so that they can produce art. It is mainly only people that produce art or, maybe, that can produce our art. Generative AI and AI systems in general are just a new gadget, that can reshape art, as e.g. photography did before.

About the need of art in connection to social roles, it is worth to remind how the industrial revolutions, and the moral of the times impacted art. In the Victorian era, at the end of the 19th century in England, art was expected to contribute to the moral values of the period, while socialists (with different opinions, some in conflict with the Victorian moral) considered that art needed to visualize and strengthen socialist values. In contrast, Oscar Wilde (1854–1900), as well as others, as e.g. the poet Algernon Charles Swinburne (1837–1909) and the painter James McNeill Whistler (1834–1903), considered *art for the art's sake*. This arrived to England from France, for example, the poet Charles Baudelaire (1821–1867) had a similar opinion, that contrasted e.g. with the one of Victor Hugo (1802–1885), that considered the art should be associated to progress.

The need or not for social support, and public engagement in the works of artists has also a long history in art. Digital platforms are just another iteration of the same problem. In fact, Oscar Wilde already discussed the same problems. He stated in his text "The Soul of Man" [186] that in developing art, "public opinion is of no value whatsoever", and added "they are continually asking Art to be popular, to please their want of taste, to flatter their absurd vanity, to tell them what they have been told before, to show them what they ought to be tired of seeing, to amuse them when they feel heavy after eating too much, and to distract their thoughts when they are wearied of their own stupidity. Now Art should never try to be popular". In the same text, he adds "Art is Individualism, and Individualism is a disturbing and disintegrating force. Therein lies its immense value. For what it seeks to disturb is monotony of type, slavery of custom, tyranny of habit, and the reduction of man to the level of a machine". In relation to this struggle between art, novelty, and both public and official support, we can also recall that the first impressionist exhibition was held in 1874 in Paris, and was organized by artists whose works were rejected by an official exhibition (the Salon, the official art exhibition of the Académie des Beaux-Arts). The originality of their works in both techniques and topics made them unacceptable and they went for an alternative location. The contrast between the Salon and the first impressionist exhibition is large in both painting techniques and topics, and, nowadays, are these impressionists the ones that are remembered and valued. An exhibition in Paris, at the Musée d'Orsay [114] contrasted them well. So, the problems are not new, they only change in form, and maybe more acute as digital platforms have strong power, and the fear of missing out reinforces their usage.

In addition, we cannot discard that the impression that the room for creation is shrinking is an effect of discussants own age. Marc Augé (1935–2023), a French anthropologist, coined the phrase "non-place" in his book [11]. He referred to places in which people is anonymous, and no one takes them as their own spaces, and where people has just a consumer relationship. This book appeared in 1992, and in 2010 and 2012 Marco Lazzari [46, 98] published works showing that shopping malls were no longer such non-places. In his paper [98] states "Whilst for many adults shopping malls are (at least in Italy) still prejudicially regarded as non-places [11], where people come and pass through without interacting, they seem to be natively concerned with the identity of the digital native generation". Observe also the relevance of the shopping mall in Season 3 of the series Stranger Things. Similarly, while it is clear that streaming and automatic recommender systems in major online shops and digital platforms do not produce the same type of personalized recommendations as shops, there are digital constellations outside them, and in remote digital villages, that are mediators between creators and consumers. There are, thus, curators using the words of Chayka [29] that expand and change the cannon.

Exercise 7.2 Discuss the role of AI and generative AI in the arts. For example, the use of large language models for writing stories and poetry.

Exercise 7.3 Digitalization has transformed the way we interact with the world. One example is personal property—particularly in relation to music, films, and books (see the book by Perzanowski and Schultz [128]). Discuss these transformations.

7.8 The Future of AI Is Not Written

We start this section repeating the same sentence we used in Sect. 7.3. AI systems are part of a socio-technical context. As Roehl [139] states, "technology frames human possibilities for action but does not determine the action", and as Acemoglu and Johnson [2] write, "the broad-based prosperity of the past was not the result of any automatic, guaranteed gains of technological progress". The investment in technology by corporations and public administrations has effects on the type of technology that is being produced. Naturally, political decisions influence the way the society is built, and, in particular, how the benefits of current technology are going to be shared among citizens.

Acemoglu and Johnson [2] in their book provide different historical examples showing the struggles to achieve that the benefits of the technological innovations were distributed among the population, instead of being kept in the hands of few. E.g. advances in the agricultural technology in the middle ages did not improve living standards of most peasants, and the technological advances that lead to the industrial revolution meant very hard times for a significant part of the population. It took a lot of years and social fights to have the benefits distributed. They also explain the social costs of some visions (as Lesseps' with the construction first of the Suez Canal and then of the Panama Canal).

Artificial intelligence and machine learning can be used in different ways, and, not only that, they can also be developed following different directions. Automation of tasks, and the replacement of labor by software is one way. Nevertheless, providing tools to support people is another way. "Encouraging the use of machines and algorithms to complement human capabilities and empower people has, in the past, led to breakthrough innovations with high machine usefulness. In contrast, infatuation with machine intelligence encourages mass-scale data collection, the disempowerment of workers and citizens, and a scramble to automate work, even when this is no more than so-so automation—meaning that it has only small productivity benefits. Not coincidentally, automation and large-scale data collection enrich those who control digital technologies" [2, pp. 299–300].

So, both the development of AI techniques, and the actual implementation of AI and ML in the real world, in particular in social sciences, need to take into account the benefits but also the risks.

7.9 Bibliography

This chapter includes a variety of topics, and references have been included in the different sections.

In relation to the development of technology and that progress is not automatic, the book by Acemoglu and Johnson [2] is very interesting and well documented. The ecological costs of computation and AI are discussed in the books by Pitron [132, 133]. Social costs of building AI and ML systems are discussed by Muldoon, Grahan, and Cant [112]. Eubanks [66] discusses social costs of applying ML systems. The section on AI and art is influenced by the book by Oscar Wilde [186].

References

1. AccountableTech (2024) Democracy by design: social media's policy scores, report. https://accountabletech.org/research/democracy-by-design-social-medias-policy-scores/
2. Acemoglu D, Johnson S (2023) Power and progress: our thousand-year struggle over technology and prosperity. Basic Books UK
3. AI HLEG (2019) Ethics guidelines for trustworthy AI, European Commission. Prepared by the High-Level Expert Group on Artificial Intelligence (AI HLEG)
4. ANSES (2025) Travailleurs des plateformes numériques de livraison de repas, Report prepared by ANSES (Agence nationale de sécurité sanitaire de l'alimentation, de l'environnement et du travail), France, March 2025. https://www.anses.fr/fr/content/livreurs-de-repas-des-plateformes-numeriques
5. Antònia Font (2011) Me sobren paraules, from the CD Lamparetes. Joan Miquel Oliver, Lyrics
6. Aoshima K (2025) High-performance autonomous wheel loading-a computational approach, PhD dissertation, Umeå University
7. Asatiani A (2022) What can public sector organizations learn from private sector experiences of robotic process automation? In: Juell-Skielse G, Lindgren I, Åkesson M (eds) Service automation in the public sector, concepts, empirical examples and challenges. Springer, pp 219–227
8. Asatiani A, Copeland O, Penttinen E (2023) Deciding on the robotic process automation operating model: a checklist for RPA managers. Bus Horiz 66(1):109–121. https://doi.org/10.1016/j.bushor.2022.03.004
9. Ashok Kumar A, Pennebaker JW (2002) Social media conversations reveal large psychological shifts caused by COVID-19's onset across U.S. cities. J Personal Soc Psychol 82(2):239–251. https://doi.org/10.1037/0022-3514.82.2.239
10. ATI DEG (2017) Ethics advisory report for West Midlands Police, written by The Alan Turing Institute Data Ethics Group (ATI DEG). https://www.turing.ac.uk/news/using-analytics-policing-ethics-advisory-report-west-midlands-police
11. Augé M.(1992) Non-lieux, introduction à une anthropologie de la surmodernité, Le Seuil
12. Baker JE, Hobart LN, Mittelsteadt MG (2021) AI for judges, CSET policy brief
13. Bankins S, Hu X, Yuan Y (2024) Artificial intelligence, workers, and future of work skills. Curr Opin Psychol 58:101828
14. Barabas C, Bavitz C, Budish R, Dinakar K, Gasser, U, Hessekiel K, Ito J, Kortz M, Virza M, Zittrain J (2018) Letter to the members of the criminal justice reform committee of conference of the massachusetts legislature regarding the adoption of actuarial risk assessment tools in the criminal justice system, Medium 9 Feb 2018. https://medium.com/berkman-klein-center/a-letter-to-the-members-of-the-criminal-justice-reform-committee-of-conference-of-the-massachusetts-2911d65969df. Accessed 6 June 2025

15. Baxter G, Sommerville I (2011) Socio-technical systems: from design methods to systems engineering. Interact Comput 23(1):4–17. https://doi.org/10.1016/j.intcom.2010.07.003
16. BBC (2018) Facebook removes 8.7m child nudity images in three months, 24 Oct 2018. https://www.bbc.com/news/technology-45967301
17. Berk R (2012) Criminal justice forecasts of risk: a machine learning approach. Springer
18. Bezdek JC (1993) Fuzzy models-What are they, and why? IEEE Trans on Fuzzy Syst 1:1–1993
19. Birchall S (2023) How predictive analytics reduced homelessness by 40%. Gov Transf Mag. 7 Feb 2023
20. Björklund F (2024) A review on risk assessment in organised crime group members: the use of risk assessment tools and methodological challenges, Thesis (Criminology Master's Programm), Malmö Universitet
21. Boddington P (2023) AI ethics. Springer
22. Brand R (2002) Microdata protection through noise addition. In: Domingo-Ferrer J (ed) Inference control in statistical databases, LNCS 2316 97-116
23. Brown TB et al (2020) Language models are few-shot learners. arXiv: 2005.14165
24. Brucker AD, Petritsch H (2009) Extending access control models with break-glass. Proc SACMAT
25. Brynjolfsson E, McAfee A (2014) The second machine age. W. W Norton & Company
26. Caton S, Haas C (2024) Fairness in machine learning: a survey. ACM Comput Surv 56(7). Article 166
27. Cavoukian A (2011) Privacy by design. The 7 foundational principles. Implementation and mapping of fair information practices
28. Chan F, Mátyás L (eds) (2022) Econometrics with machine learning. Springer
29. Chayka K (2024) Filterworld: How algorithms flattened culture. Doubleday, Penguin Random House LLC
30. Chomsky N (1956) Three models for the description of language. IRE Trans Inf Theory 2(3):113–124. https://doi.org/10.1109/TIT.1956.1056813
31. Chomsky N (1959) On certain formal properties of grammars. Inf Control 2(2):137–167. https://doi.org/10.1016/S0019-9958(59)90362-6
32. Church A (1932) A set of postulates for the foundation of logic. Ann Math Ser 2 33(2):346–366. 10.2307/1968337
33. Church A (1936) An unsolvable problem of elementary number theory. Am J Math 58(2):345–363
34. Clayton V, Sanders M, Schoenwald E, Surkis L, Gibbons D (2020) Machine learning in children's services, Technical report What Works for Children's Social Care, Sept 2020
35. Collins LM (2018) Optimization of behavioral, biobehavioral, and biomedical interventions: the multiphase optimization strategy (MOST). Springer
36. Colon D (2023) Guerre de l'information: Les etats à la conquête de nos esprits, Tallandier
37. Copeland BJ (2024) The church-Turing thesis. In: Zalta EN, Nodelman U (eds) The Stanford encyclopedia of philosophy (Winter 2024 ed.). https://plato.stanford.edu/archives/win2024/entries/church-turing
38. Corny J, Rajkumar A, Martin O, Dode X, Lajonchère JP, Billuart O, Bêzie Y, Buronfosse A (2020) A machine learning-based clinical decision support system to identify prescriptions with a high risk of medication error. J Am Med Inf Assoc 27(11):1688–1694
39. Craik A, Han L, Sullivan L, Landsiedel J, Travers T, Spaull C, Howard P (2024) Revalidation: risk of recidivism tools an evaluation of the actuarial instruments developed to assess recidivism risk in England and Wales, Ministry of Justice. http://www.justice.gov.uk/publications/research-and-analysis/moj
40. Dalenius T, Reiss SP (1978) Data-swapping-a technique for disclosure control. In: Proceedings ASA section on survey research methods, pp 191–194
41. Dalenius T, Reiss SP (1982) Data-swapping: a technique for disclosure control. J Stat Plan Inference 6:73–85
42. Dean W, Naibo A (2025) Recursive functions. In: Zalta EN, Nodelman U (eds) The Stanford encyclopedia of philosophy (Summer 2025 ed.). https://plato.stanford.edu/archives/sum2025/entries/recursive-functions

43. Capitani D, di Vimercati C, Foresti S, Livraga G, Samarati P (2023) k-anonymity: from theory to applications. Trans Data Privacy 16(1):25–49
44. De Capitani di Vimercati S, Foresti S, Livraga G, Samarati P (2012) Data privacy: definitions and techniques. Int J Unc Fuzz Knowl Based Syst 20(6):793–817
45. Defays D, Nanopoulos P (1993) Panels of enterprises and confidentiality: the small aggregates method. In: Proceedings of the 1992 symposium on design and analysis of longitudinal surveys, statistics Canada, pp 195–204
46. De Fiori A, Quarantino MJ, Lazzari M (2010) L'uso degli strumenti di comunicazione telematica fra gli adolescenti. In: Lazzari M, Quarantino MJ (eds) Adolescenti tra piazze reali e piazze virtuali. Bergamo University Press, pp 171–203
47. Diehl T, Weeks BE, Gil de Zuñiga H (2016) Political persuasion on social media: tracing direct and indirect effects of news use and social interaction. New Media Soc 18:1875–1895
48. Dignum F (ed) (2021) Social simulation for a crisis: results and lessons from simulating the COVID-19 crisis. Springer
49. Dignum V (2019) Responsible artificial intelligence: How to develop and use AI in a responsible way. Springer
50. Domingo-Ferrer J, Torra V (2005) Ordinal, continuous and heterogeneous k-anonymity through microaggregation. Data Min Knowl Disc 11(2):195–212
51. Dubois D, Prade H (1988) Possibilistic and fuzzy logics. In: Smets P, Mamdani EH, Dubois D, Prade H (eds) Non-standard logics for automated reasoning. Academic Press, pp 287–315
52. Dujmović JJ (2018) Soft computing evaluation logic. John Wiley and IEEE Press
53. Dujmović J (2025) Graded logic: modeling human commonsense reasoning in decision-making and AI. Springer
54. Dujmović J, Tomasevich D (2021) COVID-19 vaccination priority Evaluation. Proc NAFIPS
55. Dujmović JJ, Torra V (2021) Properties and comparison of andness-characterized aggregators. Int J of Intel Syst 36(3):1366–1385
56. Dujmović JJ, Torra V (2021) Aggregation functions in decision engineering: ten necessary properties and parameter-directedness. Proc INFUS 2021:173–181
57. Dujmović JJ, Torra V (2021) Logic aggregators and their implementation. Proc MDAI 2023. LNAI 13890:3–42
58. Dwork C (2006) Differential privacy. Proc ICALP 2006. LNCS 4052:1–12
59. Dwork C (2008) Differential privacy: a survey of results. Proc TAMC 2008. LNCS 4978:1–19
60. EEA (2018) Water use in Europe — Quantity and quality face big challenges. https://www.eea.europa.eu/signals-archived/signals-2018-content-list/articles/water-use-in-europe-2014
61. Eller E (2025) Regeringen stopper kontroversielle test af grønlandske forældre, DR 17 January 2025. https://www.dr.dk/nyheder/politik/regeringen-stopper-kontroversielle-test-af-groenlandske-foraeldre
62. Elliot A (ed) (2022) The Routledge social science handbook of AI. Routledge, Taylor and Francis Group
63. Emery FE, Trist EL (1960) Socio-technical systems. In: Churchman CW, Verhulst M (eds) Management science models and techniques, vol 2. Pergamon. Oxford, UK, pp 83–97
64. Ensolution, Project titled: Effective preventative care supported by Artificial Intelligence. https://www.vetlandaposten.se/2024-01-29/sa-ska-ai-hitta-vetlandaborna-som-behover-vard-och-hjalp. https://www.esn-eu.org/practices/effective-preventative-care-supported-artificial-intelligence-ai
65. EU (2024) AI Act. Regulation (EU) 2024/1689 of the European Parliament and of the Council of 13 June 2024 laying down harmonised rules on artificial intelligence and amending Regulations (EC) No 300/2008, (EU) No 167/2013, (EU) No 168/2013, (EU) 2018/858, (EU) 2018/1139 and (EU) 2019/2144 and Directives 2014/90/EU, (EU) 2016/797 and (EU) 2020/1828 (Artificial Intelligence Act)
66. Eubanks V (2018) Automating inequality: How high-tech tools profile, police, and punish the poor. St. Martin's Press
67. Europol (2024) AI and policing: the benefits and challenges of artificial intelligence for law enforcement. Europol Innovation Lab report. 10.2813/0321023

68. Falconer E, El-Hay T, Alevras D, Docherty JP, Ynover C, Kalton A, Goldschmidt Y, Rosen-Zvi M (2017) Integrated multisystem analysis in a mental health and criminal justice ecosystem. Health Justice 5:4
69. Frankfurt H (1986) On bullshit Raritan 6(2):81–100
70. FRED (2025) Federal Reserve Economic Data, Federal reserve bank of St. Louis. Mean salaries in US from https://fred.stlouisfed.org/series/MAPAINUSA672N and Median salaries in US from https://fred.stlouisfed.org/series/MEPAINUSA672N
71. Fienberg SE (2014) What is statistics? Ann. Rev. Stat. Appl. 1:1–9
72. Fienberg SE, McIntyre J (2004) Data swapping: variations on a theme by Dalenius and Reiss. Proc PSD 2004. LNCS 3050:14–29
73. Gilboa I (2009) Theory of decision under uncertainty. Cambridge University Press
74. Gödel K (1934) On undecidable propositions of formal mathematical systems. Princeton lectures. Reprinted in Gödel (1986) [75]:338–371
75. Gödel K (1986) Collected works. Feferman S, Dawson JW, Jr Kleene SC, Moore GH, Solovay RM, van Heijenoort J (eds) I: Publications 1929–1936. Oxford University Press, Oxford
76. Good IJ (1966) Speculations concerning the first ultraintelligent machine. Adv Comput 6:31–88
77. Graeber D (2018) Bullshit jobs: a theory, Simon and Schuster paperbacks
78. Graeber D (2015) The utopia of rules: on technology, stupidity, and the secret joys of bureaucracy. Melville House
79. Green S, Sjöström K, Wangel A-M (2023) Nurses' perceptions of telephone triage in child and adolescent psychiatric services-an enhanced critical incident technique study. Issues Ment Health Nurs 44(10):974–983
80. Grosof NB, Horrocks I, Volz R, Cecker S (2003) Description logic programs: combining logic programs with description logic. In: Proceeding of 12th international conference world wide web WWW2003, pp 48–57
81. Guay M (2025) I Tested 9 AI-powered scheduling assistants. My favorite is the one with the least AI. The New York Times, April 11. https://www.nytimes.com/wirecutter/reviews/best-ai-scheduling-apps/
82. Guilluy C (2019) Twilight of the elites: prosperity, the periphery, and the future of France. Yale University Press. (English translation of "Le crépuscule de la France d'en haut", 2016)
83. Gurses S, Troncoso C, Diaz C (2015) Engineering privacy by design reloaded. In: Proceedings Amsterdam privacy conference 2015
84. Hand DJ (2020) Dark data. Princeton University Press
85. Hastie T, Tibshirani R, Friedman J (2009) The elements of statistical learning. Springer
86. Herremans D (2025) Royalties in the age of AI: paying artists for AI-generated songs. WIPO Mag. https://www.wipo.int/web/wipo-magazine/articles/royalties-in-the-age-of-ai-paying-artists-for-ai-generated-songs-73739
87. Hivert A-F (2025) Le long combat des Groenlandais contre le placement abusif de leurs enfants, Le Monde 11 April 2025. https://www.lemonde.fr/m-le-mag/article/2025/04/11/le-long-combat-des-groenlandais-contre-le-placement-abusif-de-leurs-enfants_6594034_4500055.html
88. Hoepman J-H (2014) Privacy design strategies. In: Proceedings of IFIP SEC 2014, pp 446–459
89. IEEE Computational Intelligence Society. https://cis.ieee.org/. Accessed 20 Nov 2024
90. Jongeneel MJ, Oliva A, Nordfeldth F, Duarte R, Fisinger S, Sandee H, Lacoursière C, Saccon A (2024) Evaluating the sim-to-real gap for contact-rich robotic manipulation tasks using suction cups. 2024. hal-04673156
91. Juell-Skielse G, Lindgren I, Åkesson M (2022) Towards service automation in public organizations. In: Juell-Skielse G, Lindgren I, Åkesson M (eds) Service automation in the public sector. Springer, pp 3–9
92. Kaber DB, Endsley MR (1997) Out-of-the-loop performance problems and the use of intermediate levels of automation for improved control system functioning and safety. Process Saf Prog 16(3):126–131

93. Katz J, Lindell Y (2021) Introduction to modern cryptography, 3rd ed. Routledge, Taylor and Francis Group
94. Klir GJ, Yuan B (1995) Fuzzy sets and fuzzy logic: theory and applications. Prentice Hall, UK
95. Kurzweil R (2005) The singularity is near. Viking
96. Landau AY, Ferrarello S, Blanchard A, Cato K, Atkins N, Salazar S, Patton DU, Topaz M (2022) Developing machine learning-based models to help identify child abuse and neglect: key ethical challenges and recommended solutions. J Am Medical Inform Assoc 29(3):576–580. https://doi.org/10.1093/jamia/ocab286
97. Lara-Montero A (2024) The transformation potential of AI on social services. European Public Mosaic, 23 May 2024
98. Lazzari M (2012) The role of social networking services to shape the double virtual citizenship of young immigrants in Italy. In: Proceedings of the IADIS international conference on ICT, society and human beings 2012, Lisbon, Portugal, 21–23 July 2012
99. Leitgöb H, Prandner D, Wolbring T (2023) Editorial: big data and machine learning in sociology. Front Sociol 8:1173155
100. Lichte M (2023) Using data and AI for good. European Social Network, 28 June 2023. https://www.esn-eu.org/news/using-data-and-ai-good. Accessed 19 Mar 2025
101. Lieberman A, Schroeder J (2020) Two social lives: how differences between online and offline interaction influence social outcomes. Curr Opin Psychol 31:16–21
102. Lin L, Hu PJ-H, Liu Sheng OR (2006) A decision support system for lower back pain diagnosis: uncertainty management and clinical evaluations. Decis Support Syst 42(2):1152–1169
103. Loi M, Spielkamp M (2021) Towards accountability in the use of artificial intelligence for public administrations. Algorithm watch. AIES'21 ACM. 10.1145/3461702.3462631
104. Lu-Myers Y, Myers CG, Patil SV (2025) Nous avons conçu des machines intelligentes, puis demandé aux médecins d'être encore plus intelligents, Le Monde, 3 June 2025. https://www.lemonde.fr/sciences/article/2025/06/03/nous-avons-concu-des-machines-intelligentes-puis-demande-aux-medecins-d-etre-encore-plus-intelligents_6610355_1650684.html
105. Martinson H (1959) Dikter. Albert Bonniers Förlag
106. Mas M, Mesiar R, Monserrat M, Torrens J (2005) Aggregation operators with annihilator. Int J Gen Syst 34(1):17–38
107. Mascheroni G (2020) Datafied childhoods: contextualising datafication in everyday life. Current Soc Rev 68(6):798–813
108. Matzen T, Kukurin C, van de Wetering J, Ariëns S, Bosma W, Knijnenberg A, Stamouli A, Ypma YJF (2022) Objectifying evidence evaluation for gunshot residue comparisons using machine learning on criminal case data. Forensic Sci Int 335:111293. https://doi.org/10.1016/j.forsciint.2022.111293
109. Mendez JA (2024) Making fairness actionable. Licenciate thesis, Umeå University
110. MIGRI (2023) The Finnish Immigration service introduces automatic post-decision monitoring of student residence permits, press release 28.9.2023. https://migri.fi/en/-/the-finnish-immigration-service-introduces-automatic-post-decision-monitoring-of-student-residence-permits. Accessed 9 June 2025
111. MIGRI (2025) Finnish Immigration Service introduces automated post-decision monitoring of residence permits for employed persons, press release 20.1.2025. https://migri.fi/en/-/finnish-immigration-service-introduces-automated-post-decision-monitoring-of-residence-permits-for-employed-persons. Accessed 9 June 2025
112. Muldoon J, Graham M, Cant C (2024) Feeding the machine: the hidden human labour powering AI, Canongate
113. Murray D (2024) Police use of retrospective facial recognition technology: a step change in surveillance capability necessitating an evolution of the human rights law framework. Mod Law Rev 87(4):833–863. https://doi.org/10.1111/1468-2230.12862
114. Musée d'Orsay (2024) Exhibition "Paris 1874: Inventing Impressionism", Musée d'Orsay, Paris, March 26th to July 14th, 2024. https://www.musee-orsay.fr/en/whats-on/exhibitions/paris-1874-inventing-impressionism

115. Novelli C, Taddeo M, Floridi L (2024) Accountability in artificial intelligence: what it is and how it works. AI Soc 39:1871–1882. https://doi.org/10.1007/s00146-023-01635-y
116. Nyholm S (2020) Humans and robots: ethics, agency, and anthropomorphism. Rowman and Littlefield
117. Ohlenburg T (2020) AI in social protection-exploring opportunities and mitigating risks. Deutsche Gesellschaft für Internationale Zusammenarbeit (GIZ) GmbH
118. Oliver MA, Joana E (1992) Edicions 62
119. Oshana M (2001) International encyclopedia of the social & behavioral sciences. Elsevier
120. Oztas B, Cetinkaya D, Adedoyin F, Budka M, Aksu G, Dogan H (2024) Transaction monitoring in anti-money laundering: a qualitative analysis and points of view from industry. Futur Gener Comput Syst 159:161–171. https://doi.org/10.1016/j.future.2024.05.027
121. Pardo-Guerra JP (2019) Automating finance: infrastructures, engineers, and the making of electronic markets. Cambridge University Press
122. Pariser E (2011) The filter bubble: what the internet is hiding from you. Penguin Press
123. Patil SV, Myers CG, Lu-Myers Y (2025) Calibrating AI reliance–a physician's superhuman dilemma. JAMA Health Forum 6(3):e250106. https://doi.org/10.1001/jamahealthforum.2025.0106
124. Pearl J (2009) Causality: models, reasoning, and inference. Cambridge University Press (2009)
125. Pearl J, Mackenzie D (2018) The book of why. Penguin Random House
126. Perron BE, Hiltz BS, Khang EM, Savas SA (2025) AI-enhanced social work: developing and evaluating retrieval-augmented generation (RAG) support systems. J Soc Work Educ 61(1):3–13. https://doi.org/10.1080/10437797.2024.2411172
127. Persson M, Wallo A (2022) Automation and public service values in human resource management. In: Juell-Skielse G, Lindgren I, Åkesson M (eds) Service automation in the public sector. Springer, pp 91–108
128. Perzanowski A, Schultz J (2016) The end of ownership: personal property in the digital economy. The MIT Press
129. Pesantez Narvaez JE (2021) Risk analytics in econometrics. PhD Dissertation, Universitat de Barcelona
130. Peters H (2015) Game theory: a multi-leveled approach, 2nd ed. Springer
131. Petritsch H (2014) Break-glass: handling exceptional situations in access control. Springer
132. Pitron G (2021) L'enfer numérique: Voyage au bout d'un like. Éditions les liens qui libèrent
133. Pitron G (2019) La guerre des métaux rares. Éditions les liens qui libèrent
134. Ranerup A, Henriksen HZ (2019) Value positions viewed through the lens of automated decision-making: the case of social services. Gov Inf Q 36(4):101377. https://doi.org/10.1016/j.giq.2019.05.004
135. Rao A (2017) A strategist's guide to artificial intelligence. Strategy + Business 87. (Summer, 2017)
136. Ribeiro MT, Singh S, Guestrin C (2016) Why should i trust you? Explaining the predictions of any classifier. Proc KDD
137. Rigano C (2019) Using artificial intelligence to address criminal justice needs. NIJ J 280. https://www.nij.gov/journals/280/Pages/using-artificialintelligence-to-address-criminal-justice-needs.aspx
138. RISE (2025) How AI can make data centres energy efficient. https://www.ri.se/en/how-ai-can-make-data-centres-energy-efficient. Accessed 22 May 2025
139. Roehl UBU (2022) Understanding automated decision-making in the public sector: a classification of automated, administrative decision making. In: Juell-Skielse G, Lindgren I, Åkesson M (eds) Service automation in the public sector. Springer, pp 35–88
140. Russell SJ, Norvig P (2021) Artificial Intelligence: A Modern Approach, 4th ed., Prentice Hall (Global edition)
141. SAE (2021) Taxonomy and definitions for terms related to driving automation systems for on-road motor vehicles, Issued 2013-01, Revision 2021-04
142. Sagarra JM (1947) Obra poètica. Editorial Selecta

143. Said A, Torra V (2019) Data science: an introduction. In: Said A, Torra V (eds) Data science in practice. Springer, pp 1–6
144. Sales T (2007) El que tenim i el que ens espera, Butlletí de l'ACIA 40. Tardor 2007
145. Samarati P (2001) Protecting respondents' identities in microdata release. IEEE Trans Knowl Data Eng 13(6):1010–1027
146. Sandvik KB (2023) Humanitarian extractivism: the digital transformation of aid. Manchester University Press
147. Scaruffi P (2016) Intelligence is not artificial. Omnipublishing
148. Schoonvelde M, Schumacher G, Bakker BN (2019) Friends with text as data benefits: assessing and extending the use of automated text analysis in political science and political. Psychology 7(1):124–143. https://doi.org/10.5964/jspp.v7i1.964
149. Searle J (1980) Minds, brains and programs. Behav Brain Sci 3(3):417–457
150. Shagrir O (2002) Effective computation by humans and machines. Mind Mach 12:221–240. https://doi.org/10.1023/A:1015694932257
151. Shaw J (2022) Content moderators pay a psychological toll to keep social media clean. We should be helping them. BBC Science Focus. Published 2 Nov 2022. https://www.sciencefocus.com/news/content-moderators-pay-a-psychological-toll-to-keep-social-media-clean-we-should-be-helping-them
152. Shehabi A, Smith SJ, Hubbard A, Newkirk A, Lei N, Siddik MAB, Holecek B, Koomey J, Masanet E, Sartor D (2024) 2024 United States data center energy usage report. Lawrence Berkeley National Laboratory, Berkeley, California. LBNL-2001637
153. Shoham Y, Leyton-Brown K (2012) Multiagent systems: algorithmic, game-theoretic, and logical foundations. Cambridge University Press
154. Sikos LF (2023) Cybersecurity knowledge graphs. Knowl Inf Syst 65:3511–3531. https://doi.org/10.1007/s10115-023-01860-3
155. Simmler M, Canova G (2025) Facial recognition technology in law enforcement: regulating data analysis of another kind. Comput Law Secur Rev 56:106092. https://doi.org/10.1016/j.clsr.2024.106092
156. Simon HA (1995) Artificial intelligence: an empirical science. Artif Intell 77(1):95–127
157. Solomon S (2024) Sustainable by design: next-generation datacenters consume zero water for cooling. https://www.microsoft.com/en-us/microsoft-cloud/blog/2024/12/09/sustainable-by-design-next-generation-datacenters-consume-zero-water-for-cooling/. Accessed 21 May 2025
158. Soma R, Bratteteig T, Saplacan D, Schimmer R, Campano E, Verne GB (2022) Strengthening human autonomy. In the era of autonomous technology. Scand. J. Inf. Syst. 34(2) Article 5. https://aisel.aisnet.org/sjis/vol34/iss2/5
159. Soma R, Søyseth VD, Søyland M, Schulz TW (2018) Facilitating robots at home: a framework for understanding robot facilitation. Proc ACHI
160. Sorensen R (2023) Vagueness. In: Zalta EN, Nodelman U (eds) The Stanford encyclopedia of philosophy (Winter 2023 ed.). https://plato.stanford.edu/archives/win2023/entries/vagueness/. Accessed 28 Apr 2025
161. Su Y, Liu H-W (2017) Discrete aggregation operators with annihilator. Fuzzy Sets Syst 308:72–84
162. SvensktVatten (2025) Dricksvattenfakta. https://www.svensktvatten.se/om-oss/verksamhet-och-strategi/fakta-om-vatten/dricksvattenfakta/#:~:text=dygn%20i%20Sverige.-,F%C3%B6rdelning%20dricksvatten,vatten%20per%20person%20och%20dygn. Accessed 22 May 2025
163. Svensson L (2019) "Tekniken är den enkla biten" Om att implementera digital automatisering i handläggningen av försörjningsstöd, Lund University, Report. https://portal.research.lu.se/ws/files/72102327/RRSW_2019_12.pdf
164. SVT (2025) Ikea har tröttnat–vill inte ha ansökningar skrivna med AI: "Ingen personlighet" (27 April 2025). https://www.svt.se/nyheter/lokalt/vast/ikea-har-trottnat-vill-inte-ha-ansokningar-skrivna-med-ai-ingen-personlighet

165. Szadkowski M, Clairouin O (2025) Pourquoi les images de ChatGPT imitant le Studio Ghibli font polémique, Le Monde, 31 March 2025. https://www.lemonde.fr/pixels/article/2025/03/31/pourquoi-les-images-de-chatgpt-imitant-le-studio-ghibli-font-polemique_6589005_4408996.html
166. Tabar M, Park H, Winkler S, Lee D, Barman-Adhikari A, Yadav A (2020) Identifying homeless youth at-risk of substance use disorder: data-driven insights for policymakers. Proc KDD
167. Tafvelin S, Hjelte J, Schimmer R, Forsgren M, Torra V, Stenling A (2023) Introducing robots and AI in human service organizations: what are the implications for employees and service users? In: Lindgren S (ed. Handbook of critical studies of artificial intelligence. Edward Elgar Publishing, Chapter 63, pp 726–736. 10.4337/9781803928562.00074
168. Taylor C (1985) Human agency and language: philosophical papers. Cambridge University Press
169. Tisseron S (2025) La psychologie du XXIe siècle sera celle des interactions entre l'humain et la machine. L'éducation doit y préparer la jeunesse. Interview at Le Monde, 26 April 2025. https://www.lemonde.fr/m-perso/article/2025/04/26/serge-tisseron-psychiatre-et-psychanalyste-des-qu-une-ia-dit-je-vous-apprecie-c-est-le-moment-de-prendre-ses-jambes-a-son-cou_6600263_4497916.html
170. Toll D (2024) Process automation in Swedish municipalities: stakeholders, challenges, and public values. Linköping University, PhD dissertation
171. Torra V (1996) Weighted OWA operators for synthesis of information. In: Proceedings of the 5th IEEE international conference on fuzzy systems, pp 966–971
172. Torra V (1997) The weighted OWA operator. Int J of Intel Syst 12:153–166
173. Torra V (2022) Andness directedness for t-Norms and t-Conorms. Mathematics 10:1598
174. Torra V (2021) Andness directedness for operators of the OWA and WOWA families. Fuzzy Sets Syst 414:28–37
175. Torra V (2022) Guide to data privacy: models, technologies, solutions. Springer
176. Torra V, Narukawa Y (2007) Modeling decisions: information fusion and aggregation operators. Springer
177. Torra V, Narukawa Y (2007) Modelització de decisions: fusió d'informació i operadors d'agregació. UAB Press
178. Torra V, Narukawa Y, Sugeno M (eds) (2013) Non-additive measures: theory and applications. Springer
179. Turing AM (1936) On computable numbers, with an application to the Entscheidungsproblem, Proc Lond Math Soc 2(42):230–265. 10.1112/plms/s2-42.1.230. (published 1937)
180. Turing A (1950) Computing machinery and intelligence. Mind 59(236):433–460
181. Trist EL, Bamforth KW (1951) Some social and psychological consequences of the longwall method of coal-getting: an examination of the psychological situation and defences of a work group in relation to the social structure and technological content of the work system. Hum Relat 4(1):3–38. https://doi.org/10.1177/001872675100400101
182. van den Berg G, Kunaschk M, Lang J, Stephan G, Uhlendorff A (2023) Predicting re-employment: machine learning versus assessments by unemployed workers and by their caseworkers, Working Paper Series 2023:22, IFAU-Institute for Evaluation of Labour Market and Education Policy
183. Vernon D (2014) Artificial cognitive systems-a primer. MIT Press
184. Vinge V (1993) The coming technological singularity: how to survive in the post-human era. https://ntrs.nasa.gov/citations/19940022856. Accessed 16 May 2025
185. von Neumann J, Morgenstern O (1944) Theory of games and economic behavior. Princeton University Press
186. Wilde O (1900) The soul of man. Arthur L, Humphreys, London
187. Winter SJ (2023) Computing ethics: ethical AI is not about AI. Commun ACM 66:2. (Feb 2023)
188. Wireklint SC (2023) Emergency department triage in Sweden occurrence, validity, reliability and registered nurses' experiences. Linnaeus University Dissertations No 477/2023
189. Wooldridge A (2021) The aristocracy of talent. Penguin Random House

190. Wooldridge M (2006) An introduction to multiagent systems. John Wiley and Sons
191. Wykman C (2023) Artificial intelligence in social work: a PRISMA scoping review on its applications. Bachelor's Thesis in Social Work, Marie Cederschiöld University
192. Xu R, Sun Y, Ren M, Guo S, Pan R, Lin H, Sun L, Han X (2024) AI for social science and social science of AI: a survey. Inf Process Manag 61:103665
193. Zadeh LA (1981) Test-score semantics for natural languages and meaning representation via PRUF. Technical Note 247, SRI International, Menlo Park, California. (Also in Empirical Semantics (Rieger BB ed). Brockmeyer, Bochum, 1982, , pp 281–349)
194. https://www.collinsdictionary.com/dictionary/english/automation. Accessed 19 Nov 2024
195. https://www.enerdata.net/estore/energy-market/argentina/
196. https://www.energimyndigheten.se/en/energysystem/energy-consumption/
197. https://www.merriam-webster.com/dictionary/automation. Accessed 19 Nov 2024

Index

A

Access control, 113–115, 123, 124, 152
  break-glass, 115
  discretionary, 115
  mandatory, 115
  role-based, 115
Accessibility, 141
Action, 19
  effects, 19
Activation function, 87, 88, 92
Actuator, 14, 15
Agent
  non-rational, 69
  rational, 69
AGI, *see* artificial general intelligence
AI for good, 149
Allais paradox, 69, 70
Andness, 62–65, 67, 68
  directedness, 63, 67
Anonymization, 123, 129, 132, 134
Approximate reasoning, 14, 35
Architecture, 93
Artificial general intelligence, 13
Artificial Intelligence (AI), 149
  acting humanly, 12
  acting rationally, 12
  AI Act, 13, 152
  definition, 7, 11, 13
  distributed, 14
  narrow, 13
  parallel, 14
  strong, 13
  thinking humanly, 12
  thinking rationally, 12
  weak, 13
ASCII/UTF-8, 116
Assessment, 47, 57, 141
  criteria, 48, 50
  overall, 48, 53, 67
  partial, 48
Assisted
  AI systems, 10
Attacks
  membership inference, 126, 127
Augmented
  AI systems, 11
Authentication, 113, 114, 136
Authorization, 113–115, 123, 136
Automation, 1, 3, 9, 142, 143, 162
  process, 142
Autonomous, 1, 9, 11
  AI systems, 11, 151
  cars, 9, 151
Autonomy, 9, 13, 151, 152

B

Barcelona, 20, 25, 37, 41, 49
Bayesian networks, 41
Bias, 5, 77, 78, 102, 107, 144–146, 152, 156
  bias-variance trade-off, 105

C

Camera, 142
Carmichael function, 117, 119–121
Causal inference, 109
Causal modeling, 109

Causation, 109
ChatGPT, 153, 154, 159
Choquet expected utility, 70
Choquet integral, 66, 70
Classification, 74, 93, 94
Clause, 30, 32
   Horn, 30, 32
Closed World Assumption (CWA), 36
Clustering, 110, 130, 134
Completeness, 35
Computer vision, 14
Control systems, 1, 3
Correlation, 109, 134
Cost, 22, 23, 25
COVID-19, 14, 50, 55, 56, 66
Crime policing, 145
Cryptography
   public-key, 116

D
Dark data, 99, 101, 147
Dark web, 145
Data
   analysis, 9, 101, 124, 140, 141, 145
   extraction, 140, 145
   visualization, 140
Data cleaning, 99
Datafication, 1
Data governance, 152
Data integrity, 113, 121, 136
Data minimization, 136
Data preprocessing, 99
Data transformation, 99
Decidable, 31, 32
Decision Support Systems (DDS), 47, 141
Decision theory, 52
Decision trees, 14, 77, 94, 107, 108
Deep learning, 77, 87, 93, 98, 108, 136, 158
Deep web, 146
Differential privacy, 131
Digitalization, 1, 2, 142, 149, 150, 157
Digital platforms, 159–161
Dimensionality reduction, 110
Disclosure
   attribute, 125
   identity, 125
Distributed AI, 14
Document sanitization, 133

E
Ellsberg paradox, 69, 70
Ethical AI music generators, 159

Example
   mortgage repayments, 147
   stock exchange, 147
   unemployment, 147
Explainability, 108, 151, 152

F
Facial recognition, 145
Facilitation, 11
Factorization, 120–122
Fairness, 107, 152
Feature, 6, 74
   selection, 107
Fuzzy
   integrals, 66
   interval, 52
Fuzzy logics, *see* logics, fuzzy
Fuzzy measure, 70
Fuzzy sets, 14, 39, 40, 43, 45, 52

G
Gadgets, 141
Games, 8, 13, 25, 27, 136
   chess, 25, 26
   go, 25, 26
   imitation game, 12, 150
Game theory, 70
GDPR, 123
Generative AI, 160
Generative model, 153, 159
Goal, 19
Graphical models, 41

H
Hash functions, 121, 122
Hearing impaired devices, 141
Height (search tree), 22
Horn clause, *see* clause, horn
Human resource management, 143

I
Imitation game, 12, 150
Industry 4.0, 2
Industry 5.0, 3
Instance, 100
   generative models, 159
Interpretable models, 108

K
K-anonymity, 130
Knowledge acquisition, 33

Knowledge elicitation, 35, 69
Knowledge graphs, 45
Knowledge representation, 8, 13, 14, 26, 27, 30, 33, 37, 47

L

Language models, 2, 46, 98
Logic programming, 27
Logics, 13, 14, 17, 27, 30, 33, 35, 54, 66, 67
   description, 32
   first-order, 32, 38
   fuzzy, 38–40, 45
   modal, 38
   propositional, 31, 32, 38
   temporal, 38
Logic Scoring of Preference (LSP), 50, 70
Loss function, 80–86, 94, 100, 101
Luddites, 143
Lyrics, 159

M

Machine learning, 1–8, 13, 14, 34, 47, 73, 123, 127, 136, 139–142, 145, 146, 149, 152, 155, 162
   reinforcement, 110
   supervised, 110
Martinson, Harry, 1
Mean
   arithmetic, 54, 57, 58, 61–63
   geometric, 63, 64
   harmonic, 63–65
   power, 63
   weighted, 61–63, 66
Mean Squared Error (MSE), 6, 81, 82, 94, 100, 103
Membership functions, 52
Missing data, 99, 147
Missing values, 99
Model
   data-driven, 5, 47, 74, 77–79, 82, 100, 107, 135, 136, 146, 152, 156, 158, 159
   definition, 4
Modeling, 33, 40
Modular multiplicative inverse, 118–121
Modus ponens, 31
Modus tollens, 31
Monotonicity, 59, 60
Multiagent systems, 14, 15, 46
Multiphase Optimization Strategy (MOST), 143
Music, 159
   synthetic, 160

N

Natural language, 11, 14, 15, 140
Neural networks, 77, 87, 93, 98, 99, 101, 108, 136
NoSQL, 75

O

Ontology, 14, 45
Ordered Weighted Aggregation operator, *see* OWA
Order statistics, 63
Orness, 62–64, 67
   directedness, 67
Over-fitting, 104
OWA, 63, 68

P

Pareto front, 58–61
Paris, 20, 25, 40, 47, 160
Planning, 15, 17, 25, 46
Political science, 140
Prediction, *see* predictive model
Predictive analytics, *see* predictive model
Predictive model, 73, 74, 93, 140, 141
Predictive policing, 145
Privacy, 109, 123, 152
Privacy by design, 136
Privacy from re-identification, 127
Privacy model, 113, 127, 130, 132, 134
Probability, 8, 14, 36, 37, 40, 41, 98, 102, 122, 127, 128, 147, 156
Problem solving, 8, 13, 14, 17
Psychology, 140, 142

Q

Quantum computers, 122

R

Rational
   acting, 12
   agents, 151
   behavior, 12
   decisions, 12, 69
   preferences, 12, 69
   thinking, 12
Reasoning under uncertainty, 14, 35
Recommender system, 2, 140, 141, 159, 161
Regression, 7, 74, 83, 100, 103
   linear, 6, 7, 78, 79
   linear, Huber, 79
   linear, Ransac, 79

quadratic, 78, 81
robust, 7, 77–79, 106
Retrieval-Augmented Generation (RAG), 99, 143
Robot
  medicine-dispensing, 141
Robotic process automation, 4, 143
Robotics, 14
Robotic wheelchairs, 142
Robust regression, *see* regression, robust
RSA cryptosystem, 117, 118, 122
RSA-250, 121

S
Sagarra, Josep M., 113
Scheduling, 17
Search, 8, 13, 14, 17, 26, 30
Search tree, 22
Secure communication, 113, 116, 123, 136
Security, 152
Security by design, 136
Sensor, 2–4, 14, 15, 142
SHA-256, 121, 122
Smart building, 3, 4
Smart walkers, 141
Socialists, 160
Social media, 140, 142, 145, 154
Social networks, 2, 75, 133, 140, 154, 156, 159
Social sciences, 139, 141, 143
Social services, 2, 4, 125, 126, 132, 140, 142, 144, 145, 153
Social simulations, 46
Social welfare programs, 47, 74
Social work, 144
Social workers, 2, 141
Society of Automotive Engineers (SAE), 9
Sociology, 140
Socio-technical systems, 13, 152, 153, 161
Song, 159
  length, 159
Speech recognition, 14
State, 19

Statistics, 5, 6, 8, 140
Sudoku, 8, 17, 18, 22, 26–29
  instructions, 18
Sugeno integral, 66, 70
Surveillance, 145
Synthetic data, 135

T
Thermostat, 3
Time series, 147
Tokyo, 41
Trustworthy AI, 149, 152
Truth table, 44
Turing
  test, 12, 150
Turing, Alan, 12, 150

U
Under-fitting, 104
Utility theory, 69

V
Variable, 4, 6, 41–43, 45, 74, 75, 77, 82, 86, 94, 96, 97, 107, 109, 123–125, 130, 131, 140, 153
  categorical, 74, 93, 96, 140
  numerical, 74, 93, 96
Video, 135, 140, 145, 155, 156, 159
Virtual reality, 136

W
Weighted OWA, *see* WOWA
Work design, 142, 152
Work experience, 142
Workflow, 142
Workload, 140
Work meaningfulness, 143
Work monitoring, 156
Workplace, 142
WOWA, 68

MIX
Papier aus verantwortungsvollen Quellen
Paper from responsible sources
FSC® C105338

If you have any concerns about our products,
you can contact us on
ProductSafety@springernature.com

In case Publisher is established outside the EU,
the EU authorized representative is:
**Springer Nature Customer Service Center GmbH
Europaplatz 3, 69115 Heidelberg, Germany**

Printed by Libri Plureos GmbH
in Hamburg, Germany